ADVANCE PRAISE FOR

Legislating Indian Country

"This is a very important and timely book which should be required reading for anyone with a serious interest in law, regulation, and genocide in Indian country. Laurence Armand French has masterfully explained why American Indians have been subjugated in almost all legal matters and how this has had a devastating effect on their health, well-being, and long term survival. The book describes and analyzes the importance of understanding the long term historical relationship between American Indians and the federal government. The material is rich in detail and political analysis and the writing is exceptionally clear."

Jeffrey Ian Ross,
Co-Editor, Native Americans and the Criminal Justice System

"This book is a potent reminder of the long and destructive shadow cast by colonialism as it relates to American Indians. Laurence Armand French provides abundant examples of how federal Indian law and policy, even in the modern era, is still infected with the stain of racism, cultural genocide, avarice, and just plain ignorance. Indian tribes and individuals have actively pushed back against these colonial impulses and challenged the nation to act upon its commitment to governance by the rule of law. French's account reveals that as a nation, we still have a long way to go in striking the proper balance in managing relations with Indian tribes."

N. Bruce Duthu, Professor of Law, Vermont Law School

Legislating Indian Country

PETER LANG
New York • Washington, D.C./Baltimore • Bern
Frankfurt am Main • Berlin • Brussels • Vienna • Oxford

Laurence Armand French

Legislating Indian Country

Significant Milestones in Transforming Tribalism

PETER LANG
New York • Washington, D.C./Baltimore • Bern
Frankfurt am Main • Berlin • Brussels • Vienna • Oxford

Library of Congress Cataloging-in-Publication Data
French, Laurence.
Legislating Indian country: significant milestones in transforming tribalism /
Laurence Armand French.
p. cm.
Includes bibliographical references and index.
1. Indians of North America—Government relations. 2. Indians of North America—
Social conditions. 3. Indians of North America—Relocation. 4. United States—Ethnic relations.
5. United States—Race relations. 6. United States—History. I. Title.
E93.F74   323.1197—dc22   2006102419
ISBN 978-0-8204-8844-8

Bibliographic information published by **Die Deutsche Bibliothek**.
Die Deutsche Bibliothek lists this publication in the "Deutsche
Nationalbibliografie"; detailed bibliographic data is available
on the Internet at http://dnb.ddb.de/.

Cover design by Clear Point Designs

© 2007 Peter Lang Publishing, Inc., New York
29 Broadway, 18th floor, New York, NY 10006
www.peterlang.com

All rights reserved.
Reprint or reproduction, even partially, in all forms such as microfilm,
xerography, microfiche, microcard, and offset strictly prohibited.

Contents

Foreword by S. Alan Ray ix

Chapter One. Introduction 1
   Colonial/Pre-Republic Influences 1
      Native American Demographics:
         Decimated by Disease, Genocide, and Slavery 1
      Native American Aboriginal Cooperative Worldview:
         The Harmony Ethos 3
      The Navajo Beauty Way 6
      Cherokee Blood Vengeance 9
      The Four Virtues of Harmony among Sioux Warrior Societies 11
      The Savage Indian Stereotype: White Justification for Genocide ... 14
   The Protestant Ethic, Manifest Destiny, and the Belief
      in Predestined White Supremacy 16
      The Acadian Expulsion: The Blueprint for Ethnic Cleansing 18
      Indian Relations during the Revolutionary War 20
   Outline of the Book 22

Chapter Two. The Early Republic Era: Defining Indian Country 25
   The Washington Doctrine: A Modified British Model 25
   Thomas Jefferson's Assimilation Model
      and the Road to Ethnic Cleansing 33
      The Louisiana Purchase and the Creation of Indian Territory:
         The Prelude to Removal 33
      The Cherokee Transformation:
         The Separate but Similar Assimilation Model 38
      Enforcing the Jacksonian Policy of U.S. Ethnic Cleansing: Removal of
         the Civilized Tribes 40
      Chief Justice Marshall's Rulings regarding Indian Sovereignty 40
      The Trail of Tears 49

**Chapter Three. Manifesting America's Destiny
   through Indian Wars and Cultural Genocide** 53
   Establishing Anglo-American Ethnocentrism
      as the Foundation of U.S. Indian Policy 53

The Post–Civil War Era of Punitive Indian Policy:
   Increased Physical and Cultural Genocide 56
Indian Education and the Mechanisms of Cultural Genocide 60
Jurisprudence and Cultural Genocide: Outlawing Traditionalism 65
   The Crow Dog Case and the Major Crimes Act 69
   Allotment: The Era of Forced Acculturation 73
   The Individual Indian Money Fund Scandal 80

Chapter Four. Indian Reorganization: Preserving Indian Country 83
   Introduction: The Pueblo Land Scandal as a Catalyst
      for Government Reform in Indian Country 83
   Report on Allotment by the Indian Policy Review Commission 83
   New Deal Indian Policies:
      Establishing Contemporary Tribal Standards 88
   The Merriam Report: Promoting Education
      as a Tool for Forced Assimilation 88
   The Johnson–O'Malley Act 91
   John Collier's Legacy: The Indian Reorganization Act 92
   The American Indian Policy Commission on the IRA 101

Chapter Five. Termination and Relocation:
The Last Major Effort at Cultural Genocide 103
   Prelude to the Eisenhower Indian Policy 103
      The Eisenhower Attempt at Purging Indian Country 106
      House Concurrent Resolution 108 and Public Law 280 107
      Relocation of Indians to Urban Ghettos 112
   The Backlash to Termination and Relocation 114
      The Advent of Tribal Activism 114
      The Indian Civil Rights Act of 1965 117
      Report on Indian Education 124
   The Nixon Initiative toward Reversing the Eisenhower Legacy 125

Chapter Six. Indian Self-Determination and the New Federalism 129
   Establishing the American Indian Policy Review Commission 129
   Indian Self-Determination and Education Act 132
   Self-Determination, Indian Education, and Religious Freedom 138
      Indian Education 138

Religious Freedom 143
New Federalism, Self-Determination, and Indian Health 147
    Indian Health Status and the Indian Health Service 147
    New Federalism and Indian Child Welfare................................... 151
Indian Gaming 154
    The Stormy Process of Legitimizing
        Contemporary Indian Gaming... 158
    Indian Gaming Controversies 162
    The Effects of Gaming in Indian Country................................... 167
    "Gimmie Five": Investigation of Tribal Lobbying Matters 168
Epilogue 172

Notes... 175
Index 185

Foreword

S. Alan Ray[1]

Once there was no Indian country. The land Europeans named North America was inhabited by millions of people, speaking more than 300 languages, who created cultures of sophistication and subtlety. Through their arts and medicine, performance of justice, and responsibility to land-based spiritual practices, the indigenous peoples of North America thrived and fought, failed and succeeded according to their own lights. There was no "Indian country." There were no "Indians."

Today, more than five hundred years later, a different order of things prevails. Since its inception the United States has endeavored to colonize the aboriginal peoples within its borders. Its methods have been alternately brutal and sublime, and sometimes both at once. When the Frenchman Alexis de Tocqueville observed the condition of several of the Eastern tribes in 1831, he remarked:

> The Spaniards were unable to exterminate the Indian race by those unparalleled atrocities which brand them with indelible shame, nor did they even succeed in wholly depriving it of its rights; but the Americans of the United States have accomplished this twofold purpose with singular felicity; tranquilly, legally, philanthropically, without shedding blood, and without violating a single great principle of morality in the eyes of the world. It is impossible to destroy men with more respect for the laws of humanity.[2]

Tocqueville exaggerates for effect: by 1831, Indian blood had been shed. But his central insight is correct. Today we can see that the justificatory power of the 19th-century federal government rationalized or elided the effects of military force deployed in the service of avarice. The brutality of white settlers' land-lust was masked by the decorum of law, but organized by it, too, resulting simultaneously in vast new tracts for natural resource

---

[1] S. Alan Ray (Cherokee) is senior vice provost and affiliate associate professor of political science, philosophy, and justice studies at the University of New Hampshire, where his research and teaching focus on federal Indian law and its impact on Native American cultures.

[2] Alexis de Tocqueville, *Democracy in America*, trans. Henry Reeve, rev. ed., vol.1 (New York: Colonial Press, 1899), 360.

exploitation and, later, homesteading, and new geopolitical domains where indigenous populations could be controlled and, in aspiration, transformed. First in Indian Territory (present-day Oklahoma) and later on hundreds of Indian reservations, the injunction of Colonel Richard Pratt, founder of the 1879 Carlisle Indian School, took hold: "Kill the Indian, and save the man." "Indian country" became a legal descriptor of specific geographical sites where, in addition to tribal law, the United States and its agents (secular and religious) could legally and routinely intervene in the lives of Native Americans to fulfill the federal government's self-imposed "trust responsibility" to tribal members.

Rather than decline with the legendary closing of the American frontier, the definition and regulation of Indians and Indian country by Congress in the 20th and 21st centuries have accelerated. By 1978, federal statutes and regulations contained more than 33 definitions of "Indian." Extra-tribal authorities and influences—federal and state actors but also private interests and their lobbyists—increasingly contest tribal control over the resources, safety and even identity of Native Americans. As a result, tribes hold increasingly fragile sway over matters deemed "internal" to them, such as determining their citizenship criteria and policing on-reservation crimes committed by other Indians, while the federal government or (by federal delegation) state authorities exercise lawful control over all other, "external" affairs. Frequent and strenuous claims to tribal sovereignty express the legitimate fear that that the governmentally imposed distinction, always tenuous, between that which is properly within tribal control and that which may be regulated or even denied by the federal sovereign is blurring, and may one day vanish, as the political winds blow in the direction of Congress and away from tribal nations.

What explains this ever-increasing regulation of Indian country? Why is tribal sovereignty both acknowledged and contested by Congress and the federal courts (leading to what Justice Thomas has described as the Supreme Court's "schizophrenic" Indian law jurisprudence)? Why are the citizens of tribal nations still faced with stereotypes of the "vanishing Red Man" and the irrelevance of their lives to so-called mainstream America and its legal and political systems? As scholars of many disciplines have shown, the answer is complex and lies in the metaphysical, legal, economic, and even religious underpinnings of white American society. This society has, from its inception, assigned racial stigma and inferiority to persons of non-European ancestry and encouraged Native Americans to follow suit and adopt those prejudices in their own self-construction (which is to say, self-deconstruction). Stubbornly, heroically, tribes have refused to follow a script which calls for their obsolescence and assimilation.

Recent Native American activism and coalition-building have led to unprecedented political gains. Since the 1970s, Congress, the executive branch, and even the courts have at times encouraged tribal self-determination, and affirmed the principle of inherent tribal sovereignty in a number of important contexts, even as they recognize the ultimate authority of Congress to "legislate Indian country."

Nonetheless, as the present volume makes clear, race continues to matter in federal Indian law and policy. Flashpoints like tribal gaming reveal that old notions of the "essential" aborigine and the behaviors thought appropriate to the "Noble Savage" are very much alive, and while they may include a kitschy souvenir stand, they do not include running successful multimillion-dollar businesses. Yet each time the courts and Congress act to diminish tribal sovereignty—that first principle of the nation-state—indigenous peoples organize to resist a racist praxis that would eliminate the political preconditions of their cultural self-determination.

By examining the history of federal Indian law and policy through the lens of genocide, *Legislating Indian Country* reminds us that the work of sovereignty cannot be divorced from the critique of race. If indigenous communities are to flourish in the 21st century, they must first look inward, to identify the effects of racism and other world-defining and negating features of colonialism on and within their living traditions, including their systems of governance and justice. But more is necessary: to thrive, tribes must look outward, to the arena of politics, both domestic and international, and continue to assert, define and defend visions of sovereignty that are worthy of them as distinguished post-colonial nations.

Chapter One
Introduction

Any viable analysis of U.S. Indian policy needs to revisit the basic geopolitical foundations of American society and its emerging epistemological ideals. These ideals forged a biased democracy based on elitism and moral privilege—one that promoted discriminatory policy against non-Christians and people of color. Clearly the group that bore the brunt of this prejudicial ideal was the American Indians. The dual Christian ideals of white supremacy and cultural ethnocentrism were expressed in America's unique concept of *Manifest Destiny*. The roots of white supremacy and cultural ethnocentrism extend back to the colonial era.

Colonial/Pre-Republic Influences

Native American Demographics:
Decimated by Disease, Genocide, and Slavery
The pre-Columbian natives in North and South America and the Caribbean represented a diversity of cultures and societies from hunting and gathering tribes to horticultural groups and even sophisticated city-states such as those developed by the Aztec, Inca, and Mayan empires of Mexico and Central and South America. The population of pre-Columbian America is estimated to have been between fifteen million and eighty million at the time of white contact. The noted Smithsonian anthropologist James Mooney put the U.S. pre-Columbian aboriginal population at 1,152,950.[1] However, Douglas H. Ubelaker felt that this was a low estimate in that Mooney most likely did not factor in deaths brought about by epidemics of European and African diseases such as smallpox, measles, and plague.[2] More recent research puts the pre-Columbian U.S. American Indian population at more than five million. By 1800, the American Indian population is estimated to have been only six hundred thousand. Ironically, while the American Indian population was greatly reduced by disease, slaughter, slavery, wars, and cultural genocide (removal, concentration camps, militarized boarding schools, etc.), some fifteen million African slaves were brought to the Americas between the 16th and 19th centuries. Nearly half of the African slaves (seven million) were brought to the Americas during the 1700s. Although some North American

Indian tribes kept captured enemies as individual slaves prior to white contact, this paled in comparison with the enslavement of the Tlaxcalan Indians by the Aztec Indian empire of central Mexico. Hence, while Indian slavery already existed in the Americas prior to European conquests and the arrival of African slaves, the colonial powers expanded this practice considerably among the tribes north of central Mexico. Indian and black slavery played a significant role in both the colonial trade and the extermination of most of the southeastern tribes. The combination of disease, physical genocide, and slavery reduced the numerous southeastern tribes to five durable groups that became known as "the Five Civilized Tribes"—the Cherokee, Choctaw, Chickasaw, Creek, and Seminole. Indian slavery emerged as a deliberate process of exploitation used mostly by the British as a lever for generating inter-tribal hostilities. Enslaved Indians were often forced to fight against other European colonial powers, notably the French and Spanish. Gary Nash, in his book *Red, White and Black*, notes that the Indian slave trade was a feature of all British colonies and was especially crucial to the development of Charleston, South Carolina. He cites the 1708 Charleston census, which listed a population of 5,300 whites and 4,300 slaves, of whom 1,400 were American Indians.[3]

The Indian slave trade involved all the horrors associated with the worst images of this institution, including beatings, killings, and tribal and family separation. And the British were not alone in this practice. The Spanish had Indian slaves in their western American colonies, where they were widely used to build and maintain the Catholic missions. American Indian slavery was an integral part of the colonial economy. This practice also resulted in the emergence of *black Indians*—a situation brought about by the miscegenation of black and Indian slaves. Many of these individuals sought refuge in the Florida Everglades, comprising a significant proportion of the Seminole Indian tribe. William Loren Katz, in his book *Black Indians*, posits that a new race of mixed Indians and blacks emerged during the colonial era originating from escaped slaves who forged new interracial alliances for their joint survival. He notes that this came about because Africans and Native Americans shared a common economic worldview based on cooperation against the Eurocentric concept of economic competition. More questionable is Katz's contention that eighty million Native Americans populated pre-Columbian America in the late 15th century, with only ten million surviving the combined impact of disease, genocide, and slavery a century later.[4]

Today there are more than 500 federally recognized Native groups comprising *Indian Country* in the forty-eight contiguous states and Alaska. There are another 244 non–federally recognized Indian tribes in the United States. Special Indian laws pertain only to federally recognized tribes—the officially designated Indian Country. Currently, the three largest American Indian groups in the United States are the Navajo, Cherokee, and Sioux. The Cherokee and Sioux consist of a number of separate tribes, and the Navajo and Sioux also have bands and tribes residing in Canada.[5]

Native American Aboriginal Cooperative Worldview: The Harmony Ethos
Intergroup wars and intragroup conflicts abounded throughout aboriginal times, as they always have among human groups. Yet, despite the complexities of clan obligations and tribal taboos of certain native groups, they achieved viable lifestyles and cultures without the benefit of the major beast of burden and transportation throughout the world at that time—the horse. Accordingly, no wheeled vehicles were evident at this time. Consequently, many of these societies stagnated in a semi–Stone Age existence. This was the case among the tribes that lived in what is now the United States and Canada. While most of these societies subscribed to a harmonious worldview, conflict and competition were part of their cycle of maintaining both intra- and intergroup balance. These were societies where tradition was passed on orally, with only major events graphically documented with pictographs. Indeed, it is estimated that there were some 350 different languages spoken by native groups in what is now the United States and Canada, including Eskimos and Aleuts, and another 1,500 languages spoken in Mexico and Central and South America. Tribal groups usually formed larger allegiances based upon their linguistic group. Yet, no tribal group is known to have had a written language or methods for the mass dissemination of written literature during aboriginal times.

During these times the clan provided the basic group structure. Clan folkways provided the basic control mechanism and psychocultural identity for the group sharing a common language and geographical region. Indeed, linguistic grouping and clan membership predate the contemporary *tribal* classification format. Unfortunately, European colonists generally viewed Native Americans' aboriginal Stone Age existence and illiteracy as indicators of biological and racial inferiority. This view prevailed despite the fact that the great Aztec pyramid of Cholula in the Mexican state of Puebla is the largest ancient pyramid monument constructed in the world, being nearly a third larger that the Great Pyramid of Giza in Egypt. Indeed, most ancient Mesoamerican civilizations (Aztec, Inca, Mayan) built substantial pyramids that were engineering feats as sophisticated as any in Europe, doing so with Stone Age tools.[6] Indigenous slave labor was involved in these endeavors, illustrating the large-scale use of slave labor during aboriginal times. The Aztec regularly raided their neighbors, the Tlaxcalan Indians, in order to obtain slave labor and sacrificial victims. This aboriginal relationship led the Tlaxcalans to aid the Spanish in their conquest of the Aztec empire. The Tlaxcala were subsequently rewarded when Spain made their traditional lands an autonomous tribal community, eventually resulting in the Mexican state of Tlaxcala, which is sandwiched between the states of Mexico and Puebla.

Native American groups north of central Mexico and extending through Canada were not as developed as their southern Mesoamerican counterparts. In the southeastern United States, archeological evidence traces these tribes to hunter societies during the isolated Paleo-Indian era (10000–8500 BC). More archaeological evidence dating to the Woodland Phase (700 BC to AD 600) indicates band-level horticultural settlements among the Eastern Woodland tribes, while hunting and gathering activities still predominated in the mountainous regions. Archaeological evidence indicates that the eastern Indian groups made the transition from hunting and gathering to horticultural settlements during the Late Archaic Phase (3000–1000 BC).[7]

In a similar fashion, Preston Holder describes the aboriginal lifestyle of the Plains Indians in his book *The Hoe and the Horse on the Plains*.[8] Here, Holder defines the Plains area as those states from North Dakota to the Gulf Coast region of Texas, with the Rocky Mountains marking the western border and the 96th and 100th meridians establishing the eastern border. The pre-Columbian Indian groups in this region lived a more primitive existence mainly as nomadic hunting and gathering societies with some marginal horticultural traits until European influence. This influence was also indicated by eastern tribes being forced west by the impact of Europeans, notably the British colonists. The horticultural tribes mainly lived beside the waterways, residing in small temporary settlements made up of families and clans living in large structures suitable for accommodating eight to ten families. These settlements were scattered along the rivers and separated by substantial space between villages. Home villages would house the group's clan ceremonial centers. The introduction of the horse, along with the greater threat this mobility represented to both the European intruders and the displaced eastern tribes, resulted in the consolidation of these scattered settlements into larger, more stable fortified villages for the purpose of mutual protection. This process began in the southwest in the 16th century and encompassed the entire region by the middle of the 18th century. Even then, certain groups remained nomadic, greatly expanding their hunting territory via the use of the horse.

Holder notes that this interaction process resulted in rapid cultural adaptation not only among Indian groups but among whites as well. This merging of cultures was most prevalent among the French trappers:

> The French developed a system which utilized lower-class members who had much to gain and little to lose in changing cultures. Working as individuals, these men formed the avant-garde of French colonial ambitions. Taking the native peoples as their model and becoming somewhat more than half native themselves, they sketched in the lines of communication and supply which were later expanded in an organized fashion. . . . In changing culture these men may well have found more status among the indigenous people than they had in their own society.[9]

Despite competition among clans within a linguistic group and conflict between tribes, a balance was maintained on the basis of the Harmony Ethos—values derived from the natural relationship existing between Mother Earth and Father Sky. The particular values fostered by the Harmony Ethos had their roots in a group's creation myths, which were then passed on orally from generation to generation. Twelve basic tenets comprise the essence of the Harmony Ethos:

1. The avoidance of overt hostilities regarding interpersonal matters and an emphasis on nonaggression in intrafamilial/clan/tribal interactions.
2. The use of a neutral third person, or intermediary, for resolving personal altercations within the tribal community (avoidance of direct confrontations).
3. A high value placed on independence (personal freedom to act as long as these actions conform to tribal folkways and do not violate sacred taboos).

4. A resentment of authority (leaders command respect as against demanding subordination by forced authority).
5. A general hesitancy to command others.
6. Caution in interactions with others, especially strangers.
7. A reluctance to refuse favors and an emphasis on generosity within the clan and tribe (the basis for *giveaways*).
8. A reluctance to voice individual opinions publicly (the person's identity is seen as being part of a larger collective clan persona).
9. Avoidance of eye and body contact when interacting with others, especially with those outside the family/clan structure.
10. Emphasis placed on group cooperation and not on individual competition.
11. Deference to elders: "old equals good equals honor."
12. Challenging life in the raw (exploring life firsthand for the sake of the experience—*counting coup*).[10]

The Navajo Beauty Way

The Navajo (*Táá Diné*), the largest tribe in the United States of the Athapaskan linguistic group, have a unique Harmony Ethos in their *Beauty Way of Life* social philosophy. The Navajo post the definition provided by Herbert J. Benally on their web page:

> The strength of Táá Diné philosophy of a harmonious life is a holistic view of life that strives for beauty, peace, joy and harmony in daily living. Inherent to this philosophy is the balancing of all sacred knowledge of the Four Cardinal Directions. Understanding and practicing the essence of the principles placed in each of the Four Directions will give us a strong foundation to make wise decisions for ourselves, our families and our communities. When we recognize and activate the Divine Power-Within, we experience the Beauty Way of Life, *Hózh´q*. Through this realization, we live with respect and reverence for all of creation. It is up to each of us to inspire our youth to cherish and perpetuate beauty, peace, and joy as a Way of Life.[11]

The Navajo creation myths and ceremonies and rituals are well guarded, like those of their Pueblo neighbors. What is generally understood about the Navajo origin legend is that Father Sky is called *Bekotsidi* and Mother Earth is named *Estsanatlehi*. Bekotsidi, the powerful Sun God, started out as a mortal Diné, as one of the people, while Estsanatlehi, The Woman Who Changes, represents Earth itself. Estsanatlehi is reborn each spring with the planting of the crops, notably corn, and ages until harvest time, becoming an old woman during the winter. Accordingly, the Navajo believe that Mother Earth changes with the seasons. She is represented on Earth by turquoise and is the wife of Bekotsidi. Mother Earth also has a sister, *Yolkai Estsan*, according to Diné myth. Yolkai Estsan is a lesser deity and is represented by white shells (*heishi*)—the symbol for water. Bekotsidi and Estsanatlehi have two sons named *Nayenezgani* (Slayer of Alien Gods) and *Tobadzistsini* (Child of Water). Their role in Navajo society is to destroy alien gods, assist warriors in battle, and aid those afflicted by witchcraft or who are otherwise ill. The twin sons play a significant role in Navajo healing ceremonies, especially those involving the *Kethawans*, sand altars, and masked shamans (see below). Lesser gods, called *Yei*, complement the Diné creation myth personas.

Navajo ceremonies are unique, and elements of these ceremonies continue today, notably the corn pollen blessing, tobacco rituals (reeds filled with feathers and a local herbal mix), sacrificial sticks, sand altars, and masked shamans. *Kethawans* consist of sacrificial sticks and tobacco (a medium for communicating with Father Sky) set in a sacred basket for use in special ceremonies. *Kethawans* are considered sacred rituals. Sand, or dry, paintings (sand altars) are used in all the major Diné rituals. In these ceremonies, sand is brought into the medicine lodge (the *Hogan*, the traditional six-sided Navajo dwelling, is used for lesser rites) and spread out to a depth of about three inches. Five pigments—white, red, yellow, black, and gray—are used in the ceremony. Once completed, the painting is blessed with corn pollen and used in specific ceremonies, most notably the sand altar for healing. Traditional shamans reproduce the sand paintings from memory, and the sand altars are dismantled following the ceremony. Masks are also used in Navajo ceremonies, much like those used by the Hopi (*Kachinas*) and the aboriginal Iroquois and Cherokees.

In their origin myth, the Navajo believe that they passed through three previous worlds. The first world was dark and consisted of four corners with a black, white, blue, and yellow cloud overhead, respectively. Here, the black cloud represented Female Being, or Earth proper, while the white cloud represented Male Being, which together created the first Diné. When the first world became crowded, the myth posits, everyone climbed to the second world, represented by the blue cloud. However, other humans already resided on the blue cloud, resulting in conflict between the original settlers and the newly arrived Diné. In order to escape this conflict, the Diné climbed into the third world, on the yellow cloud. But this world had no sun, so they then climbed into the present world, emerging via a lake surrounded by four sacred mountains. These four mountains continue to define the Navajo Nation, with Mount Blanca (*Sisnaajini*) establishing the eastern boundary and represented by the color white. Mount Taylor (*Tdoodzil*) establishes the southern boundary and is represented by the color blue (turquoise). The San Francisco Peak (*Dook'soosliid*) represents the western boundary and is represented by the color yellow (abalone and coral), while Mount Hesperus (*Dibénitsaa*) denotes the northern boundary and is represented by the color black (jet). The Navajo offer chants to these mountains in rituals known as *Dressing the Mountain*. Corn pollen is the medium for communication with Father Sky during these rituals.[12]

Aboriginal Navajo society was organized by clans. The four original clans were the Towering House Clan (*Kinyaaáani*), One Walks-Around Clan (*Honaghaahnii*), Bitter Water Clan (*Todichiinii*), and the Mud Clan (*Hashilishnii*). As members of a matrilineal clan society, Navajo married outside their clan, identifying themselves by their maternal clan (born to) and outside clan affiliation (born for). Traditional Navajo continue this practice. Another traditional Beauty Way practice was the use of respected elders to resolve disputes via the peacemaker (*Naatánii*). Peacemakers helped preserve ongoing relationships within the immediate family and extended clan relatives. The desired outcome of the peacemaking was a consensus and the restoration of harmony within the clan. The labels of "victims" and "offenders" were avoided in this process.

> The Navajo Nation initiated a contemporary version of this model in 1982 with the reintroduction of the Navajo Peacemaker Court. The desired outcome of the Peacemaker Court is the restoration of balance among individuals, families, and the larger community. The Peacemaker Court exists alongside the formal Navajo adult and juvenile district court systems. It is currently used to resolve minor disputes such as domestic problems, problems between neighbors, substance abuse issues, minor property damage, some sexual misconduct issues, and business matters of $1,500 or less—a far cry from its aboriginal mandate allowing it to address all levels of conflict, including homicide. As in the past, there is no formal legal representation in the Peacemaker Court. A major departure is that under the current system a district judge needs to appoint the peacemaker and provide oversight to ensure that all parties cooperate in the process. Peacemakers are selected on a case-by-case basis and need to be recognized as respected members of the community. French compared the current Peacemaker Court with its aboriginal counterpart:

> Clearly, the Navajo Peacemaker Court is not as cut-and-dried as one would expect. Its symbiotic entanglement with the Anglo-American-driven district courts obviates a truly stigma-free adjudication process. Interviews with traditional elders, those selected to serve as Peacemakers, indicate ... that the current process is a far cry from the aboriginal process that occurred in a legal vacuum involving only the relevant clans. . . . In aboriginal times, the Navajo (Diné) were a homogeneous society with a single belief system. This is a far cry from the numerous Christian-based religions and the Native American Church, which compete with the traditional Beauty Way spirituality. Obviously, trying to be everything for everyone has greatly compromised the original Peacemaker process. Moreover, during aboriginal times, harmony restoration was a process without a record. It dealt with the here-and-now and was forgotten once harmony was restored. In its current application a record exists, even if it does not lend itself to case law.[13]

While the Navajo represent a uniquely peaceful adaptation of the aboriginal Harmony Ethos, the Cherokee illustrate pre-Columbian harmony via blood vengeance.

Cherokee Blood Vengeance

The Cherokee, the largest southeastern tribe at the time of white contact, were a horticultural culture much like their Muskhogean neighbors. Interestingly, the Cherokee are members of the Iroquoian linguistic family, although their separation and migration from the northeast are not noted in their oral history. Their permanent villages were spread over an area currently encompassing western North Carolina, north Georgia, east Tennessee, northeast Alabama, and portions of South Carolina. The Cherokee aboriginal creation myth viewed Mother Earth as a great floating rock island suspended by four cords attaching it to Father Sky. The cords kept Mother Earth above the water below. The Cherokee myth credits insects and animals with first discovering Mother Earth. Before the creation of Mother Earth, all living things, including humans, were thought to have existed in a sky vault (*Galunlati*). Crowded conditions forced living things to seek out a new home, and when Water Beetle discovered mud below the water on Galunlati it was brought to the surface and attached at the four corners by cords to the sky vault. Initially the mud was too wet to use, and Great Buzzard kept flying down from Galunlati to monitor conditions on Mother Earth. Once, while flying his reconnaissance to Mother Earth, his wings got tired and hit the surface, with the downswing creating valleys and the mountains being created by his wings' upswing. Once conditions were dry enough on Mother

Earth, all living things left Galunlati and resettled on her surface. Great Buzzard then got the Sun to track daily over Mother Earth from east to west. The Sun, which is believed to be female, is called *Nunda that dwells in the day*, while the moon, which is male, is called *Nunda that dwells at night*.[14]

A major tenet of the Cherokee creation myth is the need to cooperate with all living things to produce harmony. The myth established the roles of insects, plants, animals, and minerals on Mother Earth. The aboriginal Cherokee believed in *little people* who reside in the forest and assist Cherokees in need. Two of the little people were transformed into poisonous snakes—the copperhead and rattlesnake—hence giving reptiles special status among the Cherokee. Indeed, all animals are respected with special prayers performed when they are killed for food, skins, and tools. Intragroup cooperation and harmony were promoted within and between the horticultural villages. Here, the seven clans provided the most prominent social structure and regulatory unit. The Cherokee, like the Navajo, were matrilineal, and this system placed considerable importance on women in family, village, and clan structures. The seven clans are the Wolf (*Ani-Wadi*), Deer (*Ani-Kawi*), Bird (*Ani-Tsiskwa*), Paint (*Ani-Wadi*), Long Hair or Blue (*Ani-Sahani*), Wild Potato or Wild Savannah (*Ani-Gatage*), and the Holly or Twisters (*Ani-Gilahi*) clans. Of the dozens of villages scattered over this vast territory, seven are Mother Villages, each the headquarters of a clan.

Moreover, each clan was represented in the village via the Town House, a seven-sided structure where all village decisions were made. Interestingly, both adult men and women had the vote during aboriginal times. As this was a matrilocal society, men moved into their wives' domiciles, and single and married individuals sat and voted in their clan's section of the Town House. The two sanctioned institutions governing the aboriginal Cherokees were the village council and the clan, with the latter being the more powerful influence. The council did not legislate or adjudicate; its role was to seek consensus and compromise in order to maintain harmony within the village. Each village council consisted of a white chief, who regulated domestic affairs during the agricultural season, and a red chief (priest warrior) who presided during the winter or war season. While these village officials were male, a female leader, *war woman* or *pretty woman*, provided counsel to the chiefs.

Blood vengeance was the traditional vehicle used in resolving serious transgressions, the most serious being the violation of marriage taboos and homicide. The clans played the major role in these matters. Violation of taboos was a clan matter and not necessarily a village or personal issue. Aboriginal Cherokee justice was based on clan blood vengeance. Sometimes the compromise included capital punishment. Here, the honorable method of dying was being killed in an intra-clan game of stickball. Otherwise, the condemned offender was hunted down by the avenging clan and killed. However, if the offender could escape to a neutral village undetected until the weeklong new year purification ritual, this transgression, and all other transgressions, were forgiven. Hence, the statute of limitations for all offences in aboriginal Cherokee society did not exceed one year. The new year purification ritual represented an annual rebirth for the Cherokees, allowing them to focus anew on the upcoming spring planting and the rituals and ceremonies associated with their horticultural lifestyle.[15]

The Four Virtues of Harmony among Sioux Warrior Societies
The aboriginal Sioux comprised the second-largest linguistic group in what is now the United States and Canada, second only to the Algonquians. The Siouan groups were once members of the Knoll people, mound builders who resided in the Ohio Valley as woodland natives. Of these groups, the northern woodland Sioux groups migrated onto the Great Plains hundreds of years prior to white contact and the introduction of the horse. The Sioux, at the time of white contact, roamed a region of the Great Plains from the Missouri River to the Black Hills.

The Plains Sioux were nomadic warrior-oriented societies relying on hunting and raiding for their subsistence. The bands were divided into three linguistic subgroups, the Dakota, Nakota, and Lacota Sioux. These bands met periodically as a group during the summer gathering of the Teton Seven Counsels Fires. It was at these gatherings that the Sun Dance ritual was performed. The number four was significant among the Sioux. Like the Navajo they placed importance on the four directions, with east being the holiest. The aboriginal Siouan belief system divided the universe into four elements supporting Mother Earth, the sky, the Sun, the Moon, and the stars. Also they recognized four parts of time (day, night, month, and year), four phases of life (infancy, childhood, maturity, and old age), four classes of animals (crawling, flying, two-legged, and four-legged), and four Sioux virtues (bravery, fortitude, generosity, and wisdom).

In their creation myth, *Wakan Tanka* represents the *Great Mystery* surrounding our understanding of essence and being. Wakan Tanka has four titles among the Sioux: Chief God, Great Spirit, Creator, and Executive. Sioux myth addresses the good and evil forces in life. Accordingly, *Iya*, personified by tornadoes, is the chief of all evil. There is also *Iktomi*, the son of Rock, who plays the role of trickster. The evil family of spirits include *Waziya*, the father; his wife, *Wakonaka*, the witch; and their daughter, *Anog-Lte*, the double-faced woman. *Sicun* represents the power of good along with four other gods: *Inyan*, the Rock, representing authority; *Skan*, the Sky, the source of force and power; *Manka*, Earth, the protector; and *Wi*, the Sun, which denotes bravery. The four associate gods are *Hanwi*, the Moon, an associate of the Sun; *Tate*, the Wind, also an associate of the Sun; *Woope*, the Beautiful One, an associate of Earth; and *Wakinyan*, the Winged One, an associate of Rock.

According to the Sioux creation myth, in the beginning, before any other thing or time, there was Inyan, and his spirit was Wakan Tanka. Also present was *Hanhepi*, the spirit of darkness. Inyan's power was in his blood, which is blue like water. Being lonely, Inyan used his powers to create a companion, Manka, also known as Mother Earth. In making Manka, Inyan ruptured himself, spilling his blood and his power upon Manka, where it became water that transformed into *Mahpiyato*—the Sky spirit. Inyan, without water, lost his power and became hard, forming the rocks and mountains on his creation, Mother Earth. This is how earth, water, and sky came into being according to the Sioux creation myth.

Mahpiyato, the Sky, then created *Anpetu* (day) to keep time, adding Wi (the Sun) for warmth and light. Mahpiyato then gave Wi a wife, Hanwi, the Moon. The first people were the *Pte*, who initially lived in the underworld. The chief of the Pte was *Wazi*. He and his wife, *Wankanda*, had a beautiful daughter, *Ite*, who married Tate (the Wind god). This liaison produced quadruplets, the Four Winds: North, West, East, and South. At this time the Pte lived below the earth and not on the surface, but they were tricked by Iktomi, the Trickster, into venturing to the surface. Once the people migrated to the surface, Wazi and Wankanda brought them to the Great Plains and taught them to hunt and survive on Manka. Once they were established in the ways of Mother Earth, Woope (the Beautiful One) appeared to the Pte as the White Buffalo Maiden, explaining to the people (the Lacota Sioux) their powers and relationship with the gods. The White Buffalo Maiden introduced the sacred pipe (*Ikce*) to the Lacota, presenting it to *Tokahe*, the first Lacota medicine man. The pipe is symbolic of the universe, with the red pipestone bowl representing Mother Earth and human blood, while the colored beads on the stem represent the four directions: red for west, blue for north, green for east, and yellow for south. The shells, leather, and feathers adorning the stem represent those things of the water, the land, and the sky. The smoke is the medium of spiritual communication with Wakan Tanka (the Great Spirit and Creator).

The Siouan moral code is "good outweighs evil." Good signifies intragroup harmony and cooperation where the virtues of bravery, fortitude, generosity, and wisdom are practiced:

- *Bravery:* This is the most important Siouan virtue for both men and women. It involves self-sacrifice. Counting coup, dog soldiering (standing alone in the presence of the enemy), and the Sun Dance illustrate this virtue.
- *Fortitude:* This virtue specifies how to be brave and how to behave. This includes a complex set of rules governing public behavior along with sanctions and taboos. These tenets follow those of the Harmony Ethos.
- *Generosity:* The giveaway is the vehicle for generosity. Sioux accumulated material wealth so that it could be distributed within the group in a ritual that brought high status and recognition to the benefactor. Inheritance was unheard of among the aboriginal bands, with any surviving personal property being buried, or burned, along with the deceased. The giveaway was an institutional form of Sioux generosity whereby the more people gave, the greater was their prestige within the band and tribe. During aboriginal times, this process guaranteed the welfare of the sick, crippled, and feeble—those otherwise likely to be abandoned by a mobile society.
- *Wisdom:* This virtue is acquired through experiencing life itself. Life experiences, augmented by spirituality, were the components of this elusive virtue. Wisdom came with age and experience. Among the requirements were successful participation in the major Siouan rituals and success as a warrior for men, and childbearing, industry, and fidelity for females. Those Sioux recognized as having wisdom held the society's highest status—that of Elder.[16]

The religious ceremonies aid in fulfilling the power and status relationships within Plains Sioux society. Prestige and self-sacrifice are core components of the seven sacred ceremonies. The pipe and sweat ceremonies, along with the Vision Quest and Sun Dance, have been adopted by many contemporary Native American groups, providing the foundations of the pan-Indian movement established in the 1960s.[17] Seven is another important number among the Sioux, much as it is among the Cherokee. There was the annual summer Seven Council Fires gathering, as well as seven sacred ceremonies: Purification, Vision Seeking, Sun Dance, Ball Throwing, Making a Buffalo Woman, Making as Brothers, and Owning a Ghost. Of these, the Sun Dance is the most significant ritual, one that continues to the present. The Sun Dance is the major vehicle for a warrior to gain power and discipline from Wakan Tanka and to be successful in life's battles. Four Sun Dances are required for full warrior status. This standard continues to be maintained.

The Savage Indian Stereotype: White Justification for Genocide

Georg Simmel, the noted German social philosopher of the early 20th century, posited a significant group dynamic—that of the psychological divisions existing between competing and/or conflicting groups in their effort to maintain their sociocultural boundaries and identity. His basic tenet is that *out-group hostility increases in-group cohesion*. Hence, the greater the perceived outside threat, the more cohesive the threatened group becomes. In these instances, internal disputes are suspended, as are class and subcultural differences during the crisis, allowing for a more cohesive in-group coalition. Simmel also stated that the hostility toward out-groups greatly intensifies when there is reciprocal antagonism between the two conflicting groups. A consequence of this phenomenon is that strong societal values such as justice and humanity, while they are maintained for the respective in-group(s), are denied members of the perceived out-group(s).[18] It is under these circumstances that torture, massacres, and other forms of physical genocide occur. Moreover, these forms of brutality are projected onto the out-group members whether they actually engage in these behaviors, so that reciprocal violence is justified against out-group members. This was certainly the case in the conflicts between European colonizers and Native Americans, a practice that not only continued in the new U.S. Republic but actually intensified.

Despite the fact that some aboriginal groups used the heads of their enemies to denote a confirmed kill or that postmortem mutilation and, in some cases, torture and human sacrifices were practiced, these behaviors were limited in scope and used mainly to balance the death rate between warring parties. Aboriginal blood vengeance followed the dictates of the Harmony Ethos, avoiding excessive killings or brutality. Nonetheless, examples of these social practices were used by the Christian Europeans to paint Native Americans as savages.

The irony here is that torture was a common practice in Europe during the long tenure of the Christian judicial practice of *trial by ordeal*. Trial by ordeal and arbitrary justice doled out by royal and Church authority were widely practiced until two parallel interventions occurred in 1215—Pope Innocent III ended trials by priests during the Fourth Lateran Council and King John of England was forced to sign the *Magna Carta*. The ending of these forms of subjective justice led to the rise of the judicial process known as inquisition investigation in continental Europe and trial by jury in England. Even then, the arbitrary use of royal authority was not adequately checked until 1679, with the introduction of the Habeas Corpus Act, which stipulated that an individual had the right to know why he or she was being detained or incarcerated. The death penalty was a common sanction for a host of crimes throughout Europe and America well into the 20th century. During the Renaissance, public floggings, torture, hangings, and burning at the stake were common religion-based sanctions, despite the inroads initially made in the early 13th century. Clearly, Christian Europeans were equally guilty of savage practices, practices that they took with them to the New World.[19]

The early European settlers were first introduced to the aboriginal practice of scalping, which was used by warriors to collect war trophies. According to a section of the 1906 *Annual Report of the Smithsonian Institution*, two Spanish and French explorers were the first to document the scalping practice of North American Indians. These early explorers were Francisco de Garay in 1520 and Jaques Cartier in 1535. Ostensibly, the widespread use of scalping was influenced by European settlers, who introduced the steel knife, firearms, and the horse, three ingredients that greatly increased the kill factor in intergroup conflicts in the New World. Moreover, European settlers warring against both white and Indian enemies encouraged the scalping practice among their native allies by offering scalp premiums, a practice initiated by the British. Georg Friederici, in the Smithsonian article, attributed to the Huron Iroquois the origination of scalping in what became the Canadian

New England colonial realm, stating that they probably learned this custom from the Cherokee. He also noted that scalping at this time was common in Florida and among the Indians of the Yucatan regions of Mexico.[20]

The Smithsonian article noted that the first to offer scalp premiums for the heads of native enemies were the Puritans of New England, who began this practice in 1637. As a result, the heads of Pequots as well as allied Indians were brought in large numbers for the monetary award of thirty to fifty shillings each. The French Canadians followed suit, offering scalp premiums for Indian enemies. Soon the scalp award was offered for white enemies as well, with the British paying for French scalps and vice versa. The Puritans made a heroine of Hannah Dustin, "who with her own hands is said to have taken and brought in the scalps of 2 Indian men, 2 women, and 6 children, the colony paid 50 (shillings), beside which she received many expressions of thanks and numerous gifts, including a substantial one from Governor Nicholson."[21] Hannah Dustin has statues in her honor in both Penacook, New Hampshire, and Haverhill, Massachusetts. In 2006, the Haverhill city council proposed making Hannah Dustin the community's ambassador and major tourist attraction. The Abenaki tribe, whose members Dustin killed, opposed the idea.

Scalping quickly spread to the other colonies and eventually throughout the country, with both the United States and Mexico offering scalp rewards until the 19th century. During the settling of the West following the War with Mexico and the U.S. Civil War, Indian scalp premiums were used to expedite the extermination of Apache Indians who refused to be placed in military-run concentration camps such as San Carlos in what is now the state of Arizona. Many of these Indians fled into northern Mexico to escape U.S. military pursuits, resulting in the Mexican states of Sonora and Chihuahua offering up to $100 for adult male scalps, $50 for female scalps, and $25 for Indian children. These awards rose to $250 for adult Indian males by the 1880s when the Apache War ended in the southwestern United States. Unfortunately, many Mexican *mestizos*—those of mixed Spanish/Indian blood—were slaughtered by unscrupulous white bounty hunters during this period.

The Protestant Ethic, Manifest Destiny, and the Belief in Predestined White Supremacy

While the Harmony Ethos provided the cooperative social foundation for aboriginal groups, the United States, from its colonial beginning, subscribed to the Protestant Ethic. The relationship between the Protestant Ethic and capitalist competition was best articulated by the German social philosopher Max Weber in his works in the early 20th century. His book *The Protestant Ethic and the Spirit of Capitalism* continues to be a mainstay for the study of American socioeconomics and politics. According to Weber, competitive capitalism arose from the Protestant concept of predestination. This new worldview emerged out of Calvinism, which is based upon the concept that certain individuals are predestined as superior to other humans by God and that these individuals would be readily recognized by their possession of certain virtues, including asceticism, elevated social status, and private wealth. These elements of social status and private wealth sowed the seeds for capitalism. Once the sacred element of asceticism was diminished, this paved the way for a secular mode of capitalism along with material wealth, social privilege, and conspicuous consumption. Fierce competition soon became the primary vehicle for these desired attributes.[22]

In assessing American capitalism, Weber noted that it maintained a moral ethos as well, one that provided justification for expansionism. This moral ethos, the proclaimed Covenant of Divine Providence, became the foundation of Manifest Destiny.

A major element of U.S. educational indoctrination of children in the public school curriculum is that the early colonial settlers came to the New World to escape religious intolerance. While that may have been the case, what is omitted is the fact that these religious cults were not popular in Great Britain due to their own intolerance. Moreover, the emerging United States had its auspicious beginning as a business contractor for the British government. The Massachusetts Bay Colony was a chartered business corporation with legal authority to exercise law and order among its inhabitants. Such business charters were sanctioned by governmental authority managed by a colonial governor, deputy governor, and a board of eighteen stockholders known as freemen. The freemen constituted the General Court, with the authority to create laws—in essence, a legislature. Today, many of the New England states continue to call their legislative bodies General Courts.

If anything was lacking in the Massachusetts Bay Colony, it was religious freedom. Clearly, the Puritan leaders held an elitist and conservative view of Protestantism. Accordingly, only church members were enfranchised in the New England colonies, with church membership strictly restricted so that only a small elite held power. Church membership required an endorsement from a minister so as to maintain a strict and limited social stratum even among free whites within the colony. Indentured whites and people of color (blacks and Indians) suffered even more within this social milieu. Kai Erikson addressed this theocratic process in his work *Wayward Puritans*: "God had chosen an elite to represent Him on Earth and to join Him in Heaven. People who belonged to this elite learned of their appointment through the agency of a deep conversion experience, giving them a special responsibility and special competence to control the destinies of others."[23]

Intolerance soon became the norm as these religious cults became more isolated from their home base in Britain. They were able to carry out the conservative, restrictive, and elitist plan that Cromwell initially established in England. Cromwell's Puritan movement ended with his death in England but continued in the New England colonies. The original Puritans eventually split into two factions, the Scottish Presbyterian moderates and the more conservative Congregational Independents. The New England Puritans transformed into the Congregationalists, forming the official State Church, a status that was maintained even following Independence. Indeed, the New England Puritan theocracy was a harsh and bloody era of persecutions, intolerance, executions, exterminations, and ethnic cleansing. Even white challenges to the Puritan theocracy were met with brutal force. This is illustrated by the Quaker persecutions of 1656–1665, where anti-Quaker laws sanctioned the death penalty for anyone professing to be a Quaker within the Puritan colonies. This same theocracy advocated the extermination of the indigenous Indian populations. This was so effective that with the exception of a spill-over of Canadian Algonquian tribes along the northeastern borders of the United States (New York and Maine), the Native American population was virtually exterminated in the New England colonies.

The Acadian Expulsion: The Blueprint for Ethnic Cleansing

Manifest Destiny, the concept of God-given predestined supremacy over others, had its roots in Colonial America first in the extermination of Indian groups and exclusion of whites of other denominational affiliations.

This process was expanded to coveted lands in the Canadian Maritime Islands, notably Nova Scotia, populated by the indigenous Míkmaq Indians and French settlers. The Míkmaq, decimated by the diseases introduced via European contact, had a population of only several thousand at this time, a mere 10 percent of their aboriginal population. Nonetheless, the French settlers (*engagés*) of Acadia, who were mainly men, adapted well to the Míkmaq culture, marrying Indian women and assimilating into their traditional fishing and horticultural villages. This liaison produced generations of Métis, who came to represent a good portion of the French targeted for expulsion.

The Acadian French, white settlers in Maritime Canada, differed from most other white colonial settlers in that they integrated into the Míkmaq culture, forging a harmonious community of mixed Indian/white people known as Métis—a significant subcultural distinction in Canadian society that continues to the present. In this scheme, the British colonial governors of Nova Scotia and Massachusetts authorized, in the fall of 1755, the forceful removal of the Acadian French, citing their friendliness with the local Indians as a pretext for this exercise in ethnic cleansing. John Mack Faragher, in his book on this topic, *A Great and Noble Scheme*, cites an article in the September 4, 1755, *Pennsylvania Gazette*:

> We are now upon a great and noble Scheme of sending the neutral French out of this Province, who have always been secret enemies, and have encouraged our Savages to cut our Throats. If we effect their Expulsion, it will be one of the greatest Things that ever the English did in America; for by all Accounts, that Part of the Country they possess, is as good Land as any in the World: In case therefore we could get some good English Farmers in their Room, this Province would abound with all Kinds of Provisions.[24]

Consequently, some seven thousand French-speaking, Catholic Acadians were forcefully removed from the rich lands along the shores of the Bay of Fundy so that English colonists could occupy them. This action also gave the British and Americans an excuse to attempt to displace and disperse the Míkmaq Indians.

Acadia was the name the French gave to the region comprising Nova Scotia, New Brunswick, Prince Edward Island, Quebec's Gaspé Peninsula, and portions of northern Maine bordering on the Gaspé and New Brunswick. This entire region, except Prince Edward Island and the Cape Breton section of Nova Scotia, was claimed by Great Britain following the Treaty of Utrecht of 1713. The plan to forcefully remove the French, Métis, and

Míkmaq Indians from this region was orchestrated by William Shirley, governor of Massachusetts Bay in New England, and Charles Lawrence, governor of the Canadian Maritimes headquartered in Halifax, Nova Scotia. Both Shirley and Lawrence ignored the pleas of Major General Paul Mascarene (a French Huguenot refugee), who was British military commander of the region prior to expulsion. Mascarene noted that the Acadian French, Métis, and Míkmaq populations remained neutral and were not involved in any of the French and Indian raids on the British colonies in America. But a stronger voice overshadowed that of Mascarene—that of Cotton Mather, the Puritan leader of the New England colonies. Mather wanted all American Indians eliminated from the region, as well as the Acadian Métis, who represented his other major prejudice—French Catholics.

The ulterior motive for the Acadian expulsion is clouded by the fact that the French *engagés*, Métis, and Míkmaq all clearly stated their neutrality during the ongoing French and British conflicts, refusing to take either side and never participating in any of the raids cited as justification by governors Shirley and Lawrence for their removal. The purpose of the Acadian expulsion was twofold: one intention was to rid the region of "Indian-loving Frenchmen," while the other was to displace the Míkmaq from their aboriginal home so that Yankee families from Massachusetts, Rhode Island, and Connecticut could relocate and take over this fertile region. Massachusetts, at this time, included what is now the state of Maine and eastern portions of New Hampshire.

The ethnic cleansing exercise lasted from 1755 until the conclusion of the Seven Year War in 1763. It cost thousands of French, Métis, and Míkmaq lives and displaced over ten thousand residents, sending many as slaves or prisoners-of-war to southern colonies. Some were deported to France, while others escaped to other French communities, including Louisiana. Henry Wadsworth Longfellow depicted this tragedy in his tale *Evangeline*. Most significant, the Acadian expulsion set the stage for the new U.S. Republic's forceful removal of Indian tribes from coveted landholdings.[25]

Indian Relations during the Revolutionary War

Anders Stephanson, author of *Manifest Destiny*, credits John O'Sullivan with coining the term "Manifest Destiny." O'Sullivan, a strong supporter of U.S. expansionism in the 1840s, came up with the term to describe the concept of divine providence used by the United States as justification for its dominance and supremacy over the American continent. The concept of a white moral imperative to territorial expansionism at any cost existed from the colonial era, but greater emphasis was given to this endeavor once the new Republic was formed. Stephanson, like Weber before him, links the American concept of divine providence to the idea of Protestant destinarianism.[26]

Although the idea of Protestant supremacy had its roots in Britain, the New England colonists were more conservative in their pursuit of divine purpose. Stephanson notes that the Puritan separatists of New England felt that Old England was still corrupt in that it had not totally broken with the satanic ways of popery and Catholicism. The New England Puritans felt that their divine purpose could flourish only in this new, uncorrupted land—hence the extreme animosities directed toward both American Indians and French Catholics, especially when these two populations were allies. This sentiment was articulated by Jonathan Edwards, the leading Protestant theologian of the American Colonies during the Great Awakening of the 1730s and 1740s, who equated French Quebec with the Whore of Babylon.[27]

Indian/white alliances were common during the colonial era as the major colonial powers in the Americas—Britain, France, Spain—jockeyed for territory. This was especially the case during the Revolutionary War. Colin Calloway, in his book *The American Revolution in Indian Country*, states that the role of American Indians in this conflict was minimized by U.S. historians mainly because many tribes sided with the British. Often labeled as enemies of the Republic, these tribes were fighting for their own freedom—something universally denied them following the establishment of the new white Republic—the United States of America. Calloway curtly states: "The Indians' 'War of Independence' was well under way before 1775, was waged on many fronts—economic, cultural, political, and military—and continued long after 1783."[28]

All of Indian Country east of the Mississippi River was engulfed in the ravages of the Revolutionary War, forcing Indian refugees into western French-held territory and south into Spanish-held territory. No one treated Native Americans as badly as did the Americans. In the end, American Indians were excluded from the Republic. It soon became clear that the American revolutionaries wanted to replace the British, French, and Spanish as a colonial power so that they alone could dominate the continent. The emerging new Republic was committed to expansionism from the start, with a vision of a new society—one based on white supremacy and free from Native Americans. This vision soon became national policy. Our book looks at how this policy transformed Indian Country.

Outline of the Book

The remainder of this book is divided into five chapters, each dealing with a unique epoch of U.S. Indian policy. Clearly, policies were often driven by presidential mandates and judicial reviews, but Congressional authority was, and continues to be, required for subsequent implementation. Chapter Two (on the early Republic era) examines how the United States' definition of Native Americans as a subspecies of human beings justified their harsh treatment and eradication from desired lands in the eastern states comprising the emerging United States. Much of the initial Indian policy was defined under the administration of President Jefferson. His plan for territorial expansion and U.S. dominance of North America was clearly stated when he articulated the four obstacles to this plan: (1) the British in Canada, (2) the Spanish in the southeast and Mexico, (3) the French in New Orleans, and (4) *the Indian problem*. The major transformation during this period was the forceful removal of tribes to designated Indian territories—a practice that extended until the late 1800s. Chapter Three (on the post–Civil War Reconstruction era) addresses the further destruction of tribalism through Indian wars, the establishment of military-run concentration camps for uncooperative tribes, notably those of the Plains and the southwest, and the opening up of established Indian territories to non-Indian settlers. These first two chapters cover policies initiated during the post-colonial period and continuing to the end of the 19th century. It is important to note that physical genocide and ethnic cleansing were major components of U.S. policies during these times.

The subsequent chapters indicate a shift in policy from physical to cultural genocide. Chapter Four (on the Indian Reorganization) covers legislation that set the stage for federally controlled tribal administration within Indian Country, creating the foundation for contemporary tribalism. This epoch began with federal citizenship for Native Americans in 1924 and efforts to bring social, educational, and health services to federally recognized tribes (the Indian Reorganization Act). Here, tribes were forced to adopt U.S.-style governments, with tribal chiefs (presidents or governors) and representatives elected for specific periods. Police, courts, and economic elements of Indian Country were strictly regulated under this form of tribalism.

Chapter Five (on the harsh backlash against tribalism) examines the attempt during the 1950s to dissolve tribes, forcing them instead into capitalist-based corporations with tribal members assigned stockholder status (termination and relocation). Part of this plan for reducing federal treaty responsibilities included transferring judicial oversight to state and local agencies (Public Law 280). A dire failure, these plans were suspended in the mid-1970s with the Menominee Restoration Act, but they were not reversed for other tribes already affected. The failure of these attempts at reducing federal treaty responsibilities relating to Indian tribes led to the current situation. Chapter Six (on self-determination and New Federalism) addresses a middle ground between the strict federal oversight posited by Indian reorganization and the harsh policies of termination and relocation. Indian self-determination has opened the door to greater tribal autonomy in their internal affairs, especially in the areas of education, economic development, and law enforcement. Indeed, the combination of Indian self-determination and New Federalism provided the opportunity for Indian gaming as well as a reevaluation of federal exploitation with the mismanagement of the Individual Indian Monetary fund—the two major controversies facing Indian tribalism today.

Chapter Two
The Early Republic Era
Defining Indian Country

One of the first actions of the new Republic of the United States of America was to redefine what constituted an American Indian. Clearly, this definition was necessary if any legal protection was to be afforded this ethnic group. It was necessary to separate them from pests that could be hunted down at will and destroyed without legal recourse. Consequently, this legal definition established the boundaries of acceptability for American Indians within the new Republic. Those who fell outside these legal/political boundaries had few protections against the dominant Anglo society.

Unfortunately, the U.S. Republic chose to restrict the legal status of American Indians in its society much as it did for African slaves. Furthermore, the basic legal/political category for American Indians was determined to be their *tribal* status, an artificially constructed entity that relied on Anglo documentation via tribal rolls. This process consolidated American Indians into political units that did not necessarily exist prior to U.S. independence, raising questions as to who was a federally recognized American Indian. It is these statutory definitions, subjected to judicial review, that have regulated U.S. Indian policy from the late 18th century to the present. Henceforth, this policy referred to "Indian Country" and its recognized membership.

The Washington Doctrine: A Modified British Model

The *Reference Library of Native North American* notes that the acquisition of Indian lands during the colonial era was dictated by European international laws established in the sixteenth century. Here it was felt that indigenous peoples in conquered lands were entitled to sovereignty and property rights. These rights were expanded to all tribes, even those that did not convert to Christianity. Under these rules, conflict with aboriginal groups was justified only when the local tribes refused Europeans the right to trade and to preach Christianity. Another element of this Christian capitalist colonial pact was the "doctrine of discovery," which gave exclusive rights of negotiation with tribes to the European nation that first claimed the territory. This not only established a superior/subordinate relationship between European powers and native tribes; it provided the impetus for conflict among the European colonial powers themselves, including conflict between the European colonizer and its colony's residents, as illustrated by the Revolutionary War. Greed, in the form of a desire to acquire wealth from land acquisition, was one of the major contributing factors to the U.S. Revolutionary War. This conflict between the authority of the king of England and the colonists soon evolved into challenges between the newly established U.S. federal government and those states coveting Indian lands protected by federal law. While the first president of the Republic, George Washington, attempted to establish federal authority over Indian matters, the inadequacies of the Articles of Confederation made most of his efforts advisory at best.

Unfortunately, the treaties ending the Revolutionary War did not articulate the role of Native Americans now residing with the boundaries of the new Republic. Nonetheless, President Washington held considerable insights into the delicacies of Indian relations, especially relating to the westward expansion of the United States. While he alluded to a *peace policy*, it was clear to Washington that unscrupulous white settlers and opportunists could easily initiate conflict in Indian Country—a phenomenon that plagued U.S.–Indian relations from the outset. Unfortunately, President Washington also set the stage for federal paternalism and exploitation of Indians by assigning to them less-than-human status, equating them with wolves and other predatory animals. Ironically, despite attributing full responsibility for their actions during the Revolutionary War as equal partners with the British, Washington then reduces their capacity for reasoning by likening them to animals. Clearly, George Washington's policy statement on "Indian and Land Policy" is one of the first documents indicating the direction the United States would take toward American Indians (Letter of September 7, 1783, to Congress via James Duane):

> My sentiments with respect to the proper line of Conduct to be observed toward these peoples [American Indians] coincides precisely with those delivered by Genl. Schuyler, so far as he has gone in his Letter of 29th. July to Congress, and for the reasons he has there assigned; a repetition of them therefore by me would be unnecessary. But independent of the arguments made use of by him the following considerations have no small weight in my Mind.
>
> To suffer a wide extended Country to be over run with Land Jobbers, Speculators, and Monopolisers or even with scatter'd settlers, is, in my opinion, inconsistent with that wisdom and policy which our true interests dictates, or that an enlightened People ought to adopt and, besides, is pregnant of disputes with the Savages, and among ourselves, the evils of which are easier, to be conceived than described; and

for what? But to aggrandize a few avaricious Men to the prejudice of many, and the embarrassment of Government. For the People engaged in these pursuits without contributing in the smallest degree to the support of Government, or considering themselves as amenable to its Laws, will involve it by their unrestrained conduct, in inextricable perplexities, and more than probable in a great deal of Bloodshed.

My ideas therefore of the line of Conduct proper to be observed not only towards the Indians, but for the government of the Citizens of America, in their Settlement of the Western Country (which is intimately connected therewith) are simply these.

First and as a preliminary, that all Prisoners of whatever age or Sex, among the Indians shall be delivered up.

That all Indians should be informed, that after a Contest of eight years for the Sovereignty of this Country G; Britain has ceded all the Lands of the United States within the limits discribed by the arte of the Provisional Treaty.

That as they (the Indians) maugre all the advice and admonition which could be given them at the commencement; and during the prosecution of the War could not be restrained from acts of Hostility, but where determined to join their Arms to those of G Britain and to share their fortune; so, consequently, with a less generous People than Americans they would be made to share the same fate; and be compelld to retire along with them beyond the Lakes. But as we prefer Peace to a state of Warfare, as we consider them as a deluded People; as we perswade ourselves that they are convinced, from experience, of their error in taking up the Hatchet against us, and that their true Interest and safety must now depend upon our friendship. As the Country, is large enough to contain us all; and as we are disposed to be kind to them and to partake of their Trade, we will from these considerations and from motives of Compn., draw a veil over what is past and establish a boundary line between them and us beyond which we will endeavor to restrain our People from Hunting or Settling, and within which they shall not come, but for the purpose of Trading, Treating, or other business unexceptionable in its nature.

In establishing this line, in the first instance, care should be taken neither to yield nor to grasp at too much. But to endeavor to impress the Indians with an idea of the generosity of our disposition to accommodate them, and with the necessity we are under, of providing for our Warriors, our Young People who are growing up, and strangers who are coming from other Countries to live among us. And if they should make a point of it, or appear dissatisfied at the line we may find it necessary to establish, compensation should be made them for their claims within it.

It is needless for me to express more explicitly because the tendency of my observns. evinces it is my opinion that if the Legislature of the State of New York should insist upon expelling the Six Nations from all the Country they Inhabited previous to the War, within their Territory (as General Schuyler seems to be apprehensive of) that it will end in another Indian War. I have every reason to believe from my enquiries, and the information I have received, that they will not suffer their Country (if it was our policy to take it before we could settle it) to be wrested from them without another struggle. That they would compromise for a part of it I have very little doubt, and that it would be the cheapest way of coming at it, I have no doubt at all. The same observations, I am perswaded, will hold good with respect to Virginia, or any other state which has powerful Tribes of Indians on their Frontiers; and the reason of my mentioning New York is because General Schuyler has expressed his opinion of the temper of its Legislature; and because I have been more in the way of learning the Sentiments of the Six Nations, than of any other Tribes of Indians on this Subject.

The limits being sufficiently extensive (in the New Ctry.) to comply with all the engagements of Government and to admit such emigrations as may be supposed to happen within a given time not only from the several States of the Union but from foreign Countries, and moreover of such magnitude as to form a distinct and proper Government; a Proclamation in my opinion, should issue, making it a Felony for any person to Survey or Settle beyond the Line; and the Officers Commanding the Frontier Garrison should have pointed and peremptory orders to see that the Proclamation is carried into effect.

Measures of this sort would not only obtain Peace from the Indians, but would, in my opinion, be the surest means of preserving it. It would dispose of the Land to the best advantage; People the Country progressively, and check Land Jobbing and Monopolizing (which is now going forward with great avidity) while the door would be open, and the terms known for every one to obtain what is reasonable and proper for himself upon legal and constitutional ground.

Every advantage that could be expected or even wished for would result from such a mode of preceedure our Settlements would be compact, Government well established, and our Barrier formidable, not only for ourselves but against our Neighbours, and the Indians as has been observed in Genl Schuylers Letter will ever retreat as our Settlements advance upon them and they will be as ready to sell, as we are to buy; That it is the cheapest as well as the least distressing way of dealing with them, none who are acquainted with the Nature of Indian warfare, and has ever been at the trouble of estimating the expense of one, and comparing it with the cost of purchasing their Lands, will hesitate to acknowledge.

Unless some such measures as I have here taken the liberty to suggesting are speedily adopted one of two capital evils, in my opinion, will inevitably result, and is near at hand; either that the settling, or rather overspreading the Western Country will take place, by a parcel of Banditti, who will bid defiance to all Authority while they are skimming and disposing the Cream of the Country at the expence of many suffering Officers and Soldiers who have fought and bled to obtain it, and are now waiting the decision of Congress to point them to the promised reward of their past dangers and toils, or a renewal of Hostilities with the Indians, brought about more than probably, by this very means.

How far agents for Indian Affrs. are indispensably necessary I shall not take upon to decide; but if any should be appointed, their powers, in my opinion should be circumscribed, accurately defined, and themselves rigidly punished for every infraction of them. A recurrence to the conduct of these People under the British Administration of Indian Affairs will manifest the propriety of this caution, as it will there be found, that self Interest was the principle by which their Agents were actuated; and to promote this by accumulating Lands and passing large quantities of Goods thro their hands, the Indians were made to speak any language they pleased by their representation; were pacific or hostile as their purposes were most likely to be promoted by the one or the other. No purchase under any pretence whatever should be made by any other authority than that of the Sovereign power, or the Legislature of the State in which such Lands may happen to be. Nor should the Agents be permitted directly or indirectly to trade; but to have a fixed, and ample Salary allowed them as full compensation for their trouble.

Whether in practice the measure may answer as well as it appears in theory to me, I will not undertake to say; but I think, if the Indian Trade was carried on, on Government Acct., and with no greater advance than what would be necessary to defray the expence and risk, and bring in a small profit, that it would supply the Indians upon much better terms than they usually are; engross their Trade, and fix them strongly in our Interest; and would be a much better mode of treating them than that of giving presents; where a few only are benefitted by them. I confess there is a difficulty in getting a Man, or set of Men, in whose Abilities and integrity there can be a perfect reliance; without which, the scheme is liable to such abuse as to defeat the salutary ends which are proposed from it. At any rate, no person should be suffered to Trade with the Indians without first obtaining a license, and giving security to conform to such rules and regulations as shall be prescribed; as was the case before the War.

In giving my Sentiments in the Month of May last (at the request of a Committee of Congress) on a Peace Establishmt. I took the liberty of suggesting the propriety, which in my opinion there appeared, of paying particular attention to the French and other Settlers at Detroit and other parts within the limits of the Western Country; the perusal of a late Pamphlet entitled "Observations on the Commerce of the American States with Europe and the West Indies" impresses the necessity of it more forcibly than ever on my Mind. The author of that Piece strongly recommends a liberal change in the Government of Canada, and tho' he is too sanguine in his expectations of the benefits arising from it, there can be no doubt of the good policy of the measure. It behooves us to therefore to counteract them, by anticipation. These People have a disposition towards us susceptible of favorable Impressions; but as no Arts will be left unattempted by the British to withdraw them from our Interest, the prest. moment should be employed by us to fix them in it, or we may loose them forever; and with them, the advantages, or disadvantages consequent of the choice they may make. From the best information and Maps of that Country, it would appear that from the Mouth of the Great Miami River which. empties into the Ohio to its confluence with the Mad River, thence by a Line to the Miami Fort and Village on the other Miami River wch. empties into Lake Erie, and Thence by a Line to include the Settlement of Detroit would with Lake Erie to the No. ward Penas. to the Eastwd. and the Ohio to the Soward form a Governmt. sufficiently extensive to fulfill all the public engagements, and to receive moreover a large population of Emigrants, and to confine The Settlement of the New States within these bounds would, in my opinion, be infinitely better even supposing no disputes were to happen with the Indians and that it was not necessary to guard against those other evils which have been enumerated than to suffer the same number of People to roam over a Country of at least 500,000 Square Miles contributing nothing to the support, but much perhaps to the Embarrassment of the Federal Government.

Was it not for the purpose of comprehending the Settlement of Detroit within the Jurisdn. of the New Government a more compact and better shaped district for a State would be for the line to proceed from the Miami Fort and Village along the River of that name to Lake Erie leaving In that case the Settlement of Detroit, and all the Territory No. of the Rivers Miami and St. Josephs between the lakes Erie, St. Clair, Huron, and Michigan to form, hereafter, another State equally large compact and water bounded.

At first view, it may seem a little extraneous, when I am called upon to give an opinion upon the terms of Peace proper to be made with the Indians, that I should go into the formation of New States; but the Settlemt. of the Western Country and making a Peace with the Indians are so analogous that there can be no definitions of the other without involving considerations of the other. For I repeat it, again, and I am clear in my opinion, that policy and economy point very strongly to the expediency of being upon good terms with the Indians, and the propriety of purchasing their Lands in preference to attempting to drive them by force of arms out of their Country; which we have already experienced is like driving the Wild Beasts of the Forest which will return as soon as the pursuit is at an end and fall perhaps on those that are left there; when the gradual extension of our Settlements will as certainly cause the Savage as the Wolf to retire; both being beasts of prey tho' they differ in shape. In a word there is nothing to be obtained by an Indian War but the Soil they live on and this can be had by purchase at less expense, and without that bloodshed, and those distresses which helpless Women and Children are made partakers of in all kinds of disputes with them.

If there is any thing in these thoughts (which I have fully and freely communicated) worthy attention I shall be happy and Sir Yr. etc.

P.S. A formal Address, and memorial from the Oneida Indians when I was on the Mohawk River, setting forth their Grievances and distresses and praying relief, induced me to order a pound of Powder and 3 lbs. Of Lead to be issued to each Man, from the Military Magazines in the care of Colo. Willet; this, I presume, was unknown to Genl. Schuyler at the time he recommended the like measure in his Letter to Congress.[2]

In referring to American Indians as simple-minded savages and expressing fear of continued bloodshed among Indians and white settlers, President Washington set the stage for the "trickery by treaty" Indian policy. Also clear from the beginning of the Republic were its expansionist designs, marking its intention of challenging fellow colonial nations in the New World, notably Britain, Spain, and France. Two weeks after President Washington's letter to

James Duane, the Continental Congress issued a proclamation addressing the steady encroachment of white settlers on Indian lands that prohibited unauthorized settlements. In October of that same year (1783), James Duane, the de facto head of Indian affairs in the new Republic, and his select committee provided a formal report to the Continental Congress articulating the president's blueprint for dealing with American Indians in still contested territories in the north and west:

> Resolved, That a committee be appointed with instructions to prepare and report an ordinance for regulating the Indian trade, with a clause therein strictly prohibiting all civil and military officers, and particularly all commissioners and agents for Indian affairs, from trading with the Indians, or purchasing, or being directly or indirectly concerned in purchasing lands from Indians, except only by the express license and authority of the United States in Congress assembled.[3]

Thus, the exclusive authority of the U.S. Congress to regulate Indian Country, on the advice of President George Washington, was formally established on October 15, 1783. Treaties, ordinances, and reports soon followed, including the Treaty with the Six Nations on October 22, 1784; the Treaty of Fort McIntosh on January 21, 1785; the Treaty of Hopewell with the Cherokees on November 28, 1785; the Ordinance for the Regulation of Indian Affairs of August 7, 1786; and the Northwest Ordinance of July 13, 1787. From the outset, states questioned the sole role of Congress in dealing with Indian Country. Loopholes were found to exist within the Articles of Confederation relevant to federal versus state authority relevant to Indian affairs. North Carolina and Georgia were guilty of violating federal protection of Indian County that lay within the claimed boundaries of these two southern states. A report of a committee of the Continental Congress dated August 3, 1787, attempted to reiterate federal authority in the matter of Indian policy:

> (Regarding the actions of North Carolina and Georgia.) This construction appears to the committee not only to be productive of confusion, disputes and embarrassments in managing affairs with the Independent tribes within the limits of the States, but by no means the true one. The clause referred to is, "Congress shall have the sole and exclusive right and power of regulating the trade and managing all affairs with the Indians, not members of any of the States; provided that the Legislative right of any State within its own limits be not infringed or violated." In forming this clause, the parties to the federal compact, must have had some definite objects in view, the objects that come into view principally, in forming treaties or managing Affairs with

the Indians, had been long understood and pretty well ascertained in this country. The committee conceives that it has been long the opinion of the country, supported by Justice and humanity, that the Indians have just claims to all lands occupied by and not fairly purchased from them; and that in managing affairs with them, the principal objects have been those of making war and peace, purchasing certain tracts of their lands, fixing the boundaries between them and our people, and preventing the latter settling on lands left in possession of the former. . . . The laws of the State can have no effect upon a tribe of Indians or their lands within the limits of the state so long as that tribe is independent, and not a member of the state, yet the laws of the state may be executed upon debtors, criminals, and other proper objects of those laws in all parts of it, and therefore the union may make stipulations with any such tribe, secure it in the enjoyment of all or part of its lands, without infringing upon the legislative right in question . . . for the Indian tribes are justly considered the common friends or enemies of the United States, and no particular state can have an exclusive interest in the management of Affairs with any of the tribes, except in some uncommon cases.[4]

In trying to assert its exclusive jurisdictional authority over Indian Country, the First Congress under the new Constitution established the War Department on August 7, 1789, making it responsible for Indian affairs until the establishment of the Interior Department in 1849. Congress then legislated federal laws outlining U.S. relations within Indian Country. These became known as the Trade and Intercourse Acts—the first being enacted in July 1790. This was also the year the first U.S. federal census was initiated, under the direction of Secretary of State Thomas Jefferson. U.S. Marshals began their count in August 1790, and it was not concluded until March 1792. The function of the census was to apportion seats in the U.S. House of Representatives and to assess federal taxes. Distinctions were made according to social and political status: free white men aged 16 or older, free white men under age 16, free white women, number of slaves, and all other persons regardless of race or gender. Slaves counted as three-fifths of a human being for the purpose of apportioning seats in the U.S. House of Representatives, while American Indians were largely excluded by the clause "not taxed," which meant those not fully assimilated into the white, Euro-American society. The ratification of the 14th Amendment to the U.S. Constitution ended the fractional count of African Americans, but it was not until 1940 that American Indians were removed from the "not taxed" status and counted as full members of U.S. society for federal purposes.[5] Clearly, American Indians were at a disadvantage in terms of legal status in the United States during the 18th and 19th centuries, unprotected by any judicial due process offered other Americans with the exception of black slaves until emancipation. This legal disadvantage certainly clouded President Jefferson's "assimilation" model that replaced the accommodation policies of President Washington.

Thomas Jefferson's Assimilation Model and the Road to Ethnic Cleansing

The Louisiana Purchase and the Creation of Indian Territory: The Prelude to Removal

While President Washington continued to lend his strong support for federal Congressional authority over Indian affairs and Indian Country, this momentum was halted with the Jefferson presidency and the Louisiana Purchase of 1803. Jefferson's Indian policy differed markedly from Washington's in that he sowed the seeds of assimilation of Indian societies as long as they mimicked white U.S. society. This change in policy also gave false hope to the major tribes of the southeast, which were being constantly harassed by white settlers. Jefferson had the difficult job of balancing the impact of new white immigrants to the new Republic and the need to deal humanely with the indigenous Indian population. His awareness of these difficulties was expressed in his November 24, 1801, correspondence to the governor of Virginia, James Monroe:

> The idea seems to be to provide for these people by a purchase of lands; and it is asked whether such a purchase can be made of the United States in their western territory? A very great extent of country, north of the Ohio, has been laid off into townships, and is now at market, according to the provisions of the acts of Congress, with which you are acquainted. There is nothing which would restrain the State of Virginia either in the purchase or the application of these lands; but a purchase by the acre, might perhaps be a more expensive provision than the House of Representatives contemplated. Questions would also arise whether the establishment of such a colony within our limits, and to the State of Virginia itself, or to the other States—especially those who would be in its vicinity?
>
> Could we procure lands beyond this limits of the United States to form a receptacle for these people? On our northern boundary, the country not occupied by British subjects, is the property of Indian nations, whose title would be to be extinguished, with the consent of Great Britain; and the new settlers would be British subjects. It is hardly to be believed that either Great Britain or the Indian proprietors have so disinterested a regard for us, as to be willing to relieve us, by receiving such a colony themselves; and as much to be doubted whether that race of men could long exist in so rigorous a climate. On our western and southern frontiers, Spain holds an immense country, the occupancy of which, however, is in the Indian natives, except a

few insulated spots possessed by Spanish subjects. It is very questionable, indeed, whether the Indians would sell? Whether Spain would be willing to receive those people? And nearly certain that she would not alienate the sovereignty. The same question to ourselves would recur here also, as did in the first case: should we be willing to have such a colony in contact with us? However our present interests may restrain us within our own limits, it is impossible not to look forward to distant times, when our rapid multiplication will expand itself beyond those limits, and cover the whole northern, if not the southern continent, with a people speaking the same language, governed in similar forms, and by similar laws; nor can we contemplate with satisfaction either blot or mixture on that surface. Spain, France, and Portugal hold possessions on the southern continent, as to which I am not well enough informed to say how far they might meet our views.[6]

Clearly, President Jefferson's 1801 letter articulated the United States' expansionistic desires, but it also laid the foundation for the Monroe Doctrine, which continues to dominate the American continent today.

Jefferson was also bound by previous treaties that recognized Indian tribes' right of occupancy of their traditional lands. His assimilation plan was twofold: one, to reduce the size of traditional tribal lands and, two, to have the tribes adopt the Euro-American lifestyle so as to dilute their "savage" image. Tribes felt that they would be able to remain on their traditional lands if they adopted the white Euro-American lifestyle. The five major tribes to subscribe to the Euro-American social and political lifestyle were the Cherokee, Choctaw, Chickasaw, Creek, and Seminole. They became known as the "Five Civilized Tribes." Assimilation was a failed concept from the outset owing to a number of factors—mainly the fact that American Indians did not hold equal status before the U.S. legal system. President Jefferson also sent a mixed message when he noted that the major problem with settling the United States' massive new acquisition, the Louisiana Purchase, was the *Indian problem.* Many feel that Jefferson's perspective on Indian matters was articulated in his February 27, 1803, letter to William Henry Harrison (ninth U.S. president), then governor of Indian Territory:

Dear Sir, While at Monticello in August last I received your favor of August 8th, and meant to have acknowledged it on my return to the seat of government at the close of the ensuing month, but on my return I found that you were expected to be on here in person, and this expectation continued till winter. I have since received your favor of December 30th.

...You will receive herewith an answer to your letter as President of the Convention; from the Secretary of War you receive from time to time information and instructions as to our Indian affairs. These communications being for the public records, are restrained always to particular objects and occasions; but this letter being unofficial and private, I may with safety give you a more extensive view of our policy respecting the Indians, that you may the better comprehend the parts dealt out to you in detail through the official channel, and observing the system of which they make a part, conduct yourself in unison with it in cases where you are obliged to act without instruction. Our system is to live in perpetual peace with the Indians, to cultivate an affectionate attachment from them, by everything just and liberal which we can do for them within the bounds of reason, and by giving them effectual protection against wrongs from our own people. The decrease of game rendering their subsistence by hunting insufficient, we wish to draw them to agriculture, to spinning and weaving. The latter branches they take up with great readiness, because they fall to women, who gain by quitting the labors of the field for these which are exercised within doors. When they withdraw themselves to the culture of a small piece of land, they will perceive how useless to them are their extensive forests, and will be willing to pare them off from time to time in exchange for necessaries for their farms and families. To promote this disposition to exchange lands, which they have to spare and we want, we shall push our trade uses, and be glad to see the good and influential individuals among them run in debt, because we observe that when these debts get beyond what the individual can pay, they become willing to lop them off by a cession of lands. At our trading houses, too, we mean to sell so low as merely to repay us cost and charges, so as neither to lessen nor enlarge our capital. This is what private traders cannot do, for they must gain; they will consequently retire from the competition, and we shall thus get clear of this pest without giving offence or umbrage to the Indians. In this way our settlements will gradually circumscribe and approach the Indians, and they will in time either incorporate with us as citizens of the United States, or remove beyond the Mississippi. The former is certainly the termination of their history most happy for themselves; but, in the whole course of this, it is essential to cultivate their love. As to their fear, we presume that our strength and their weakness is now visible that they must see we have only to shut our hand to crush them, and that all our liberalities to them proceed from motives of pure humanity only. Should any tribe be foolhardy enough to take up the hatchet at any time, the seizing the whole country of that tribe, and driving them across the Mississippi, as the only condition of peace, would be an example to others, and a furtherance of our final consolidation.

 Combined with these views, and to be prepared against the occupation of Louisiana, by a powerful and enterprising people, it is important that, setting less value on interior extension of purchases from the Indians, we bend our whole views to the purchase and settlement of the country on the Mississippi, from its mouth to its northern regions, that we may be able to present as strong a front on our western as on our eastern border, and plan on the Mississippi itself the means of its own defence. We now own from 31 to the Yazoo, and we hope this summer to purchase what belongs to the Choctaws from the Yazoo up to their boundary, supposed to be about opposite the mouth of Acanza. We wish at the same time to begin in your quarter, for there is at present a favorable opening. The Cahokias extinct, we are entitled to their country by our paramount sovereignty. The Piorias, we understand, have all been driven off from their country, and we might claim it in the same way; but as we understand there is one chief remaining, who would, as the survivor of the tribe, sell the right, it is better to give him such terms as will make him easy for life, and take a conveyance from him. The Kaskaskias being reduced to a few families, I presume we may purchase their whole country for what would place every individual of them at his ease, and be a small price to us, say by laying off for each family, whenever they would choose it, as much rich land as they could cultivate, adjacent to each other, enclosing the whole in a single fence, and giving them such an annuity in money or goods forever as would place them in happiness; and we might take them also under the protection of the United States. Thus possessed of the rights of these tribes, we should proceed to the settling their boundaries with the Poutewatamies and Kickapoos; claiming all doubtful territory, but paying them a price for the relinquishment of their concurrent claim, and even prevailing on them, if possible, to cede, for a price, such of their own unquestioned territory as would give us a convenient northern boundary. Before broaching this, and while we are bargaining with the Kaskaskies, the minds of the Poutewatamies and Kickapoos should be soothed and conciliated by liberalities and sincere assurances of friendship. Perhaps by sending a well-qualified character to stay some time in Decoigne's village, as if on other business, and to sound him and introduce the subject by degrees to his mind and that of the other heads of families, inculcating in the way of conversation, all those considerations which prove the advantages they would receive by a cession on these terms, the object might be more easily and effectually obtained than by abruptly proposing it to them at a formal treaty. Of the means, however, of obtaining what we wish, you will be the best judge; and I have given you this view of the system which we suppose will best promote the interest of the Indians and ourselves, and finally consolidate our whole country to one nation only; that you may be enable the better to adapt your means to the object for this purpose we have given you a general commission for treating. The crisis is pressing; what ever can now be obtained must be obtained quickly. The occupation of New Orleans, hourly expected, by the French, is already felt like a light breeze by the Indians. You know the sentiments they entertain of that nation; under the hope of their protection they will immediately stiffen against cessions of lands to us. We had better, therefore, do at once what can be done.

I must repeat that this letter is to be considered as private and friendly, and is not to control any particular instructions which you may receive through official channel. You will also perceive how sacredly it must be kept within your own breast, and especially how improper to be understood by the Indians. For their interests and their tranquility it is best they should see only the present age of their history. I pray you to accept assurances of my esteem and high consideration.[7]

Jefferson's plan for expansion and the deal to acquire the Louisiana Purchase from France went back to 1801, early in his first term as president. Louisiana returned to French control in 1800 under the conditions of the

Treaty of San Ildefonso when Napoleon Bonaparte took control of Louisiana from the Spanish. These terms were kept secret, and Spain continued to regulate the territory until November 1803—three weeks before it was ceded to the United States. This acquisition signaled the United States' expansionistic desires and open competition with the European colonial powers. It set the stage for the special moral entitlement the United States felt it, alone among nations, had—*Manifest Destiny*. The Louisiana Purchase included what is now the state of Louisiana as well as a swath of land extending from the Canadian border west of the Mississippi River and east of the Missouri River. It doubled the size of the United States and set the stage for the War with Mexico, the U.S. Civil War, and the bloody Indian wars of the 19th century. Anders Stephanson, in his work *Manifest Destiny*, notes that the combined doctrines of Manifest Destiny and the Monroe Doctrine, while based on Jeffersonian philosophy, were actually articulated by the sixth U.S. President, John Quincy Adams, a staunch New England Puritan. Stephanson attributes the following quotation to Adams in an 1811 letter to his father:

> The whole continent of North America appears to be destined by Divine Providence to be peopled by one nation, speaking one language, professing one general system or religious and political principles, and accustomed to one general tenor of social usages and customs.[8]

Adams links the destiny of the United States to the Old Testament's divine providence. From his perspective, Providence had provided the North American continent for the United States to conquer, occupy, and convert. Here, the "finger of God" directed the Puritans to America for its domination.

Bernard Sheehan, in his book *Seeds of Extinction: Jeffersonian Philanthropy and the American Indian*, notes that the Louisiana Purchase saved those advocating a philanthropic approach toward American Indians by providing a territory west of the Mississippi River in which to dump the unwanted eastern tribes. Sheehan contends that the primary reason for Jefferson's insistence on getting the Louisiana Purchase was to resolve the Indian problem. In the first five years, the removal idea was designed for those tribes that did not subscribe to the Euro-American social/legal model, allowing the "civilized" tribes to continue to transform their societies, with the implication that by doing so they would be allowed to retain their aboriginal lands.[9]

The Cherokee Transformation: The Separate but Similar Assimilation Model
Clearly, the Cherokee Indians, the largest southeastern tribe, best represent the Jeffersonian assimilative model. After the 1791 Treaty of Houston, the Cherokees were part of the scheme to transform eastern Indians into herdsmen and farmers along the European model. This lifestyle was to replace the Cherokees' aboriginal blood vengeance and warring practices. The Cherokee already had a long horticultural tradition, permanent villages, and a strong matrilineal and matrilocal clan system of social control and justice. There was also a marked split within Cherokee society, with strong resistance among traditionalists who wanted to maintain the old ways. Many tribal leaders were also suspicious of treaties that diminished their tribal landholdings. Nonetheless, the Cherokee tribe did establish a Euro-American-style society, terming it "the Cherokee Nation." The irony is that while the blood vengeance concept of justice was alien to the British common law that dominated U.S. laws, the Cherokee also had to give up other traditions that were actually more liberal than the Euro-American model of justice allowed. They had to disenfranchise adult women, who had long held equal voting status to their male counterparts and also were expected to acquire black slaves in order to adhere to the U.S. model of civilization. Another concession was the opening up of their society to Christian missionaries. After all, the United States was based on special divine providence—Manifest Destiny. The first agents of civilization among the Cherokee were the Moravian Society of United Brethren and the Presbyterians, later followed by the Methodists. They ran schools that indoctrinated Indian children into the Eurocentric Christian civilization, including the teaching of English.

A tribal police force known as the Light Horse Guard was established in 1808. Subsequently, in 1810, the National Council, comprising male village leaders, replaced maternal clans as the ultimate tribal authority. In 1817, a national bicameral legislature replaced the National Council. The new legislature mimicked that of the United States, with an upper house (Standing Committee) and a lower house (now called the National Council). As in the U.S. Senate at the time, Standing Committee members were selected from the National Council, while the council members were elected from the tribe's districts for two-year terms, as in the U.S. House of Representatives. Each of the eight districts had its own district judge and marshal. Four circuit judges comprised the appellate court system. In 1823, the Cherokee Nation established a Supreme Court, and, in 1827, a National Constitution was adopted and ratified, with New Echota established as the nation's capital. The preamble reflected the dominant U.S. influence on the Cherokee Nation:

> We, the representatives of the people of the Cherokee Nation in convention assembled, in order to establish justice, ensure tranquility, promote our common welfare, and secure to ourselves and our prosperity the blessing of liberty; acknowledging with humility and gratitude the goodness of the sovereign Ruler of the Universe, in offering was an opportunity so favorable to the design, and imploring His aid and direction in its accomplishment, do ordain and establish this Constitution for the Government of the Cherokee Nation.[10]

By 1825, the Cherokee were successful farmers, herdsmen, and merchants, and the Cherokee Nation's economy was operating in the black. Moreover, Cherokee plantations used black slaves, much like the other "civilized" tribes did. Indeed, the supporters of Jefferson's philanthropic scheme saw the transformation of the Cherokees into a Western-style society as a remarkable feat. The Cherokee were able to adopt a separate, yet parallel, cultural lifestyle similar to that of their white counterparts in the South. In an attempt to preserve their own cultural identity, the Cherokees created their own syllabary in 1821 so that their language could be transcribed in print. By 1828, their newspaper, *The Cherokee Phoenix*, was being distributed throughout the Cherokee Nation, and all official documents were written in both English and the Cherokee language. Indeed, it is estimated that by 1830 the Cherokee Nation had a 50 percent literacy rate in the Cherokee language.

Unfortunately, the seeds of destruction were being sown as the Cherokee Nation emerged. In ratifying the U.S. Constitution, the southern states disregarded the existence of the Cherokee Nation, incorporating it into their respective borders. Georgia, South Carolina, and Virginia did so in 1788; North Carolina in 1789. Kentucky, Alabama, and Tennessee soon followed suit. In the 1802 Georgia Compact, President Jefferson promised the state of Georgia that he would remove all Indian tribes from the state in exchange for clear U.S. title to all western lands formerly claimed by Georgia.

Enforcing the Jacksonian Policy of U.S. Ethnic Cleansing: Removal of the Civilized Tribes

Chief Justice Marshall's Rulings regarding Indian Sovereignty

Chief Justice John Marshall, the fourth head of the U.S. Supreme Court, attempted to articulate the role of tribes within American society, beginning with *Johnson v. McIntosh* in 1823. Here the high court reinforced the authority of the federal government as the major arbitrator with Indian groups, overthrowing the purchase of tribal lands by private individuals in 1773 and 1775 prior to the establishment of the Trade and Intercourse Acts by the U.S. Congress. In his decision, Marshall referred to the European colonial tenet that guaranteed Indian tribes collective occupancy of their traditional lands even when the colonial ownership changed:

> That at and before the commencement of the war in 1756, and during its whole continuance, and at the time of the treaty of February 10th, 1763, the Indian tribes or nations, inhabiting the country north and northwest of the Ohio, and east of the Mississippi, as far east as the river falling into the Ohio called the Great Miami, were called and known by the name of the Western Confederacy of Indians, and were the allies of France in the war, but not her subjects, never having been in any manner conquered by her, and held the country in absolute sovereignty as independent nations, both as to the right of jurisdiction and sovereignty, and the right of soil, except a few military posts, and a small territory around each, which they had ceded to France, and she held under them, and among which were the aforesaid posts of Kaskaskias and Vincennes; and that these Indians, after the treaty, became the allies of Great Britain, living under her protection as they had before lived under that of France, but were free and independent, owning no allegiance to any foreign power whatever, and holding their lands in absolute property; the territories of the respective tribes being separated from each other, and distinguished by certain natural marks and boundaries to the Indians well known; and each tribe claiming and exercising separate and absolute ownership, in and over its own territory, both as to the right of sovereignty and jurisdiction, and the right of soil.
>
> That among the tribes of Indians, thus holding and inhabiting the territory north and northwest of the Ohio, east of the Mississippi, and west of the Great Miami, within the limits of Virginia, as described in the letters patent of May 23d, 1609, were certain independent tribes or nations, called the Illinois or Kaskaskias, and Piankeshaw or Wabash Indians; the first of which consisted of three several tribes united into one called the Kaskaskias, the Pewarias, and the Cahoquias; that the Illinois owned, held, and inhabited, as their absolute and separate property, a large tract of country within the last mentioned limits, and situated on the Mississippi, Illinois, and Kaskaskias rivers, and on the Ohio below the mouth of the Wabash; and the Piankeshaws, another large track of country within the same limits,

and as their absolute and separate property, on the Wabash and Ohio rivers; and that these Indians remained in the sole and absolute ownership and possession of the country in question, until the sales made by them in the manner herein after set forth. . . .

That from time immemorial, and always up to the present time, all the Indian tribes, or nations of North America, and especially the Illinois and Piankeshaws, and other tribes holding, possessing, and inhabiting the said countries north and northeast of the Ohio, east of the Mississippi, and west of the Great Miami, held their respective lands and territories each in common, the individuals of each tribe or nation holding the lands and territories of such tribe in common with each other, and there being among them no separate property in the soil; and that their sole method of selling, granting, and conveying their lands, whether to governments or individuals, always has been, from time immemorial, and now is, for certain chiefs of the tribe selling, to represent the whole tribe; to receive for it the consideration, whether in money or commodities, or both; and, finally, to divide such consideration among the individuals of the tribe; and that the authority of the chiefs, so acting for the whole tribe, is attested by the presence and assent of the individuals composing the tribe, or some of them, and by the receipt by the individuals composing the tribe, or their respective shares of the price and in no other manner.[11]

Justice Marshall, in this decision, established the legal right of Indian tribes to occupy their traditional lands, thus establishing the concept of *aboriginal title* or *Indian title*. This ruling ostensibly protected these collectively held lands from being taken by individuals, corporations, or political entities other than the U.S. government, and only then through purchase or conquest.

Matters deteriorated rapidly under the administration of Andrew Jackson, the seventh president of the United States, serving from 1829–1837. Ethnic cleansing became a reality under the Jackson administration. A noted Indian fighter, Jackson is credited with forcing Spain to cede Florida following his illegal intrusion into Spanish Florida in pursuit of Seminole Indians while he was military commander of the U.S. Southern Army. Jackson's anti-Indian sentiments were well known, fostering strong support for the forceful removal of the major southern tribes, notably the Five Civilized Tribes west of the Mississippi River, into Indian Territory, a tragedy known as the "Trail of Tears." Toward this end, President Jackson was successful in getting the Indian Removal Act passed by a bitterly divided Congress:

An Act to provide for an exchange of lands with the Indians residing in any of the states or territories, and for their removal west of the river Mississippi.

Be it enacted . . . That it shall and may be lawful for the President of the United States to cause so much of any territory belonging to the United States, west of the river Mississippi, not included in any state or organized territory, and to which the Indian title has been extinguished, as he may judge necessary, to be divided into a suitable number of districts, for the reception of such tribes or nations of Indians as may choose to exchange the lands where they now reside, and remove there; and to cause each of said districts to be so described by natural or artificial marks, as to be easily distinguished from each other.

Section 2. And be it further enacted, That it shall and may be lawful for the President to exchange any or all of such districts, so to be laid off and described, with any tribe or nation of Indians now residing within the limits of any of the states or territories, and with which the United States have existing treaties, for the whole or any part or portion of the territory claimed and occupied by such tribe or nation, within the bounds of any one or more of the states or territories where the land claimed and occupied by the Indians, is owned by the United States, or the United States are bound to the state within which it lies to extinguish the Indian claim thereto.

Section 3. And be it further enacted, That in the making of any such exchange or exchanges, it shall and may be lawful for the President solemnly to assure the tribe or nation with which the exchange is made, that the United States will forever secure and guaranty to them, and their heirs or successors, the country so exchanged with them; and if they prefer it, that the United States will cause a patent or grant to be made and executed to them for the same: Provided always, That such lands shall revert to the United States, if the Indians become extinct or abandon the same.

Section 4. And be it further enacted, That if, upon any of the lands now occupied by the Indians, and to be exchanged for, there should be such improvements as add value to the land claimed by any individual or individuals of such tribes or nations, it shall and may lawful for the President to cause such value to be ascertained by appraisement or otherwise, and to cause such ascertained value to be paid to the person or persons rightfully claiming such improvements. And upon the payment of such valuation, the improvements so valued and paid for, shall pass to the United States, and possession shall not afterwards be permitted to any of the same tribe.

Section 5. And be it further enacted, That upon making any of such exchange as is contemplated by this Act, it shall and may be lawful for the President to cause such aid and assistance to be furnished to the emigrants as may be necessary and proper to enable them to remove to, and settle in, the country for which they may have exchanged; and also, to give them such aid and assistance as may be necessary for their support and subsistence for the first year after their removal.

Section 6. And be it further enacted, That it shall and may be lawful for the President to cause such tribe or nation to be protected, at their new residence, against all interruption or disturbance from any other tribe or nation of Indians, or from any other person or persons whatever.

Section 7. And be it further enacted, That it shall and may be lawful for the President to have the same superintendence and care over any tribe or nation in the country to which they may remove, as contemplated by this Act, that he is now authorized to have over them at their present places or residence: Provided, That noting in this act contained shall be construed as authorizing or directing the violation of any existing treaty between the United States and any of the Indian tribes.

Section 8. And be it further enacted, That for the purpose of giving effect to the provisions of this Act, the sum of five hundred thousand dollars is hereby appropriated, to be paid out of any money in the treasury, not otherwise appropriated.[12]

This law encouraged Georgia to lay claim to parts of the Cherokee Nation lying within its boundaries. Ironically, while Jefferson's concerns were with Virginia's westward expansion, he also set the stage for Georgia to challenge the federal concept of exclusive jurisdiction over Indian Country, leading to two more U.S. Supreme Court decisions handed down by Chief Justice John Marshall. As soon as Jackson became president, Georgia attempted to extinguish Indian title within its state boundaries, essentially invalidating the laws of the Cherokee Nation. These changes coincided with the finding of gold in Indian Country, which was followed by a massive invasion of whites into the Cherokee Nation. This led to the 1831 case *Cherokee Nation v. the State of Georgia*. Chief Justice Marshall delivered the opinion of the Court:

> This bill is brought by the Cherokee nation, praying an injunction to restrain the state of Georgia from the execution of certain laws of that state, which, as is alleged, go directly to annihilate the Cherokees as a political society, and to seize, for the use of Georgia, the lands of the nation which have been assured to them by the United States in solemn treaties repeatedly made and still in force.
>
> If courts were permitted to indulge their sympathies, a case better calculated to excite them can scarcely be imagined. A people once numerous, powerful, and truly independent, found by our ancestors in the quiet and uncontrolled possession of an ample domain, gradually sinking beneath our superior policy, our arts and our arms, have yielded their lands by successive treaties, each of which contains a solemn guarantee of the residue, until they retain no more of their formerly extensive territory than is deemed necessary to their comfortable subsistence. To preserve this remnant, the present application is made.
>
> Before we can look into the merits of the case, a preliminary inquiry presents itself. Has this Court jurisdiction of the cause?
>
> The third article of the Constitution describes the extent of the judicial power. The second section closes an enumeration of the cases to which it is extended, with "controversies" "between a state or the citizens thereof, and foreign states, citizens, or subjects." A subsequence clause of the same section gives the Supreme Court original jurisdiction in all cases in which a state shall be a party. The party defendant may then unquestionably be sued in this Court. May the plaintiff sue in it? Is the Cherokee Nation a foreign state in the sense in which that term is used in the Constitution?

The counsel for the plaintiffs have maintained the affirmative of this proposition with great earnestness and ability. So much of the argument as was intended to prove the character of the Cherokees as a state, as a distinct political society, separated from others, capable of managing its own affairs and governing itself, has, in the opinion of a majority of the judges, been completely successful. They have been uniformly treated as a state from the settlement of our country. The numerous treaties made with them by the United States recognize them as a people capable of maintaining the relations of peace and war, of being responsible in their political character for any violation of their engagements, or for any aggression committed on the citizens of the United States by any individual of their community. Laws have been enacted in the spirit of these treaties. The acts of our government plainly recognize the Cherokee Nation as a state, and the Courts are bound by those acts.

A question of much more difficulty remains. Do the Cherokee constitute a foreign state in the sense of the Constitution?

The counsel have shown conclusively that they are not a state of the Union, and have insisted that individually they are aliens, not owing allegiance to the United States. An aggregate of aliens composing a state must, they say, be a foreign state. Each individual being foreign, the whole must be foreign.

This argument is imposing, but we must examine it more closely before we yield to it. The condition of the Indians in relation to the United States is perhaps unlike that of any other two people in existence. In the general, nations not owing a common allegiance are foreign to each other. The term foreign nation is, with strict propriety, applicable by either to the other. But the relation of the Indians to the United States is marked by peculiar and cardinal distinctions which exist no where else.

The Indian territory is admitted to compose a part of the United States. In all our maps, geographical treaties, histories, and laws, it is so considered. In all our intercourse with foreign nations, in our commercial regulations, in any attempt at intercourse between Indians and foreign nations, they are considered as within the jurisdictional limits of the United States, subject to many of those restraints which are imposed upon our own citizens. They acknowledge themselves in treaties to be under the protection of the United States; they admit that the United States shall have the sole and exclusive right of regulating the trade with them, and managing all their affairs as they think proper; and the Cherokees in particular were allowed by the Treaty of Hopewell, which preceded the Constitution, "to send a deputy of their choice, whenever they think fit, to Congress." Treaties were made with some tribes by the state of New York, under a then unsettled construction of the confederation, by which they ceded all their lands to that state, taking back a limited grant for themselves, in which they admit their dependence.

Though the Indians are acknowledged to have an unquestionable, and, heretofore, unquestioned right to the lands they occupy, until that right shall be extinguished by a voluntary cession to our government; yet it may well be doubted whether those tribes which reside within the acknowledged boundaries of the United States can, with strict accuracy, be denominated foreign nations. They may, more correctly be denominated domestic dependent nations. They occupy a territory to which we assert a title independent of their will, which must take effect in point of possession when their right of possession ceases. Meanwhile, they are in a state of pupilage. Their relation to the United States resembles that of a ward to his guardian.

They look to our government for protection; rely upon its kindness and its power; appeal to it for relief to their wants; and address the President as their Great Father. They and their country are considered by foreign nations, as well as by ourselves, as being so completely under the sovereignty and dominion of the United States, that any attempt to acquire their lands, or to form a political connection with them, would be considered by all as an invasion of our territory, and an act of hostility. . . .

The Court has bestowed its best attention on this question, and, after mature deliberation, the majority is of opinion that an Indian tribe or nation within the United States is not a foreign state in the sense of the Constitution, and cannot maintain an action in the Courts of the United States.

A serious additional objection exists to the jurisdiction of the Court. Is the matter of the bill the proper subject for judicial inquiry and decision? It seeks to restrain a state from the forcible exercise of legislative power over a neighbouring people asserting their independence; their fight to which the state denies. On several of the matters alleged in the bill, for example on the laws making it criminal to exercise the usual powers of self-government in their own country by the Cherokee Nation, this Court cannot interpose; at least in the form in which those matters are presented. That part of the bill which respects the land occupied by the Indians, and prays the aid of the Court to protect their possession, may be more doubtful. The mere question of right might perhaps be decided by this Court in a proper case with proper parties. But the Court is asked to do more than decide on the title. The bill requires us to control the legislature of Georgia, and to restrain the exertion of its physical force. The propriety of such an interposition by the Court may be well questioned. It savors too much of the exercise of political power to be within the proper province of the judicial department. But this opinion on the point respecting parties makes it unnecessary to decide this question. If it be true that the Cherokee Nation have rights, this is not the tribunal in which those rights are to be asserted. If it be true that wrongs have been inflicted, and that still greater are to be apprehended, this is not the tribunal which can redress the past or prevent the future.

The Motion for an injunction is denied.[13]

The U.S. Supreme Court heard yet another challenge the following session, this one involving the arrest of white missionaries serving the Cherokee Nation. The case involved Samuel A. Worcester, a missionary who refused to abide by the Georgia law forbidding whites to reside in the Cherokee Nation without first taking an oath of allegiance to the State of Georgia and obtaining an official permit. This case became *Worcester v. Georgia*, with Chief Justice Marshall delivering the opinion:

This cause, in every point of view in which it can be placed, is of the deepest interest.

The defendant is a state, a member of the Union, which has exercised the powers of government over a people who deny its jurisdiction, and are under the protection of the United States.

The plaintiff is a citizen of the state of Vermont, condemned to hard labor for four years in the penitentiary of Georgia; under color of an act which he alleges to be repugnant to the Constitution and laws of the United States, the rights, if they have any, the political existence of a once numerous and powerful people, the personal liberty of a citizen, are all involved in the subject now to be considered. . . .

The Indian nations had always been considered as distinct, independent political communities, retaining their original natural rights, as the undisputed possessors of the soil, from time immemorial, with the single exception of that imposed by irresistible power, which excluded them from intercourse with any other European potentate than the first discoverer of the coast of the particular region claimed; and this was a restriction which those European potentates imposed on themselves, as well as on the Indians. The very term "nation," so generally applied to them, means "a people distinct from others." The Constitution, by declaring treaties already made, as well as those to be made, to be the supreme law of the land, has adopted and sanctioned the previous treaties with the Indian nations, and consequently admits their rank among those powers who are capable of making treaties. The words "treaty" and "nation" are words of our own language, selected in our diplomatic and legislative proceedings, by ourselves, having each a definite and well understood meaning. We have applied them to Indians, as we have applied them to the other nations of the earth. They are applied to all in the same sense.

Georgia, herself, has furnished conclusive evidence that her former opinions on this subject concurred with those entertained by her sister states, and by the government of the United States. Various acts of her legislature have been cited in the argument, including the contract of cession made in the year 1802, all tending to prove her acquiescence in the universal conviction that the Indian nations possessed a full right to the lands they occupied, until that right should be extinguished by the United States, with their consent: that their territory was separated from that of any state within whose chartered limits they might reside, by a boundary line, established by treaties: that, within their boundary, they possessed rights with which no state could interfere; and that the whole power of regulating the intercourse with them was vested in the United States. A review of these acts, on the part of Georgia, would occupy too much time, and is the less necessary, because they have been accurately detailed in the argument at the bar. Her new series of laws, manifesting her abandonment of these opinions, appears to have commenced in December, 1828.

In opposition to this original right, possessed by the undisputed occupants of every country; to this recognition of that right, which is evidenced by our history, in every change through which we have passed; is placed the charters granted by the monarch of a distant and distinct region, parceling out a territory in possession of others whom he could not remove and did not attempt to remove, and the cession made of his claims by the treaty of peace.

The actual state of things at the time, and all history since, explain these charters; and the King of Great Britain, at the treaty of peace, could cede only what belonged to his crown. These newly asserted titles can derive no aid from the articles so often repeated in Indian treaties; extending to them, first, the protection of Great Britain, and afterwards that of the United States. These articles are associated with others, recognizing their title to self-government. The very fact of repeated treaties with them recognizes it; and the settled doctrine of the law of nations is, that a weaker power does not surrender its independence—its right to self-government, by associating with a stronger, and taking its protection. A weak state, in order to provide for its safety, may place itself under the protection of one more powerful, without stripping itself of the right of government, and ceasing to be a state. . . .

The Cherokee nation, then, is a distinct community occupying its own territory, with boundaries accurately described, in which the laws of Georgia can have no force, and which the citizens of Georgia have no right to enter, but with the assent of the Cherokees themselves, or in conformity with treaties, and with the acts of Congress. The whole intercourse between the United States and this nation, is, by our Constitution and laws, vested in the government of the United States.

The act of the state of Georgia, under which the plaintiff in error was prosecuted, is consequently void, and the judgment a nullity. Can this Court revise and reverse it?

If the objection to the system of legislation, lately adopted by the legislature of Georgia, in relation to the Cherokee nation, was confined to its extra-territory operation, the objection, through complete, so far as respected mere right, would give this Court no power over the subject. But it goes much further. If the review which has been taken be correct, and we think it is, the acts of Georgia are repugnant to the Constitution, laws, and treaties of the United States.

They interfere forcibly with the relations established between the United States and the Cherokee nation, the regulation of which, according to the settled principles of our Constitution, are committed exclusively to the government of the Union.

They are in direct hostility with treaties, repeated in a succession of years, which mark out the boundary that separates the Cherokee country from Georgia; guaranty to them all the land within their boundary; solemnly pledge the faith of the United States to restrain their citizens from trespassing on it; and recognize the pre-existing power of the nation to govern itself.

They are in equal hostility with the acts of Congress for regulating this intercourse, and giving effect to the treaties.

The forcible seizure and abduction of the plaintiff in error, who was residing in the nation with its permission, and by authority of the President of the United States, is also a violation of the acts which authorize the chief magistrate to exercise this authority. . . .

It is the opinion of this Court that the judgment of the Superior Court for the country of Gwinnett, in the state of Georgia, condemning Samuel A. Worcester to hard labor in the penitentiary of the state of Georgia, for four years, was pronounced by that Court under colour of a law which is void, as being repugnant to the Constitution, treaties, and laws of the United States, and ought, therefore, to be reversed and annulled.[14]

These two U.S. Supreme Court decisions constitute the foundation for federally recognized tribes. Chief Justice Marshall, in the 1831 *Cherokee Nation v. Georgia* decision, established that Indian tribes were "domestic dependent nations"—essentially protected wards of the U.S. government—providing the format for the structure and organization of Indian Country today. The 1832 *Worcester v. Georgia* decision further articulated what constitutes Indian Country by noting that tribes were distinct political entities with territorial boundaries and land held in common, protected by the federal government. This decision consolidated the federal government's authority over Indian Country, superseding that of the states, with the exception of those states that had prior recognition and protective treaties with their tribes, notably New York and Maine. Following removal, North Carolina established such a relationship with the Qualla Band of Cherokees, those who escaped the Trail of Tears. Today, federal authority extends to all recognized tribes. Clearly, the *Worcester* decision established the U.S. Congress as the ultimate authority with respect to recognized Indian tribes, those residing in U.S.-approved reservations. Ironically, this decision also legitimized the 1830 Removal Act.

Unfortunately, the pressure for ethnic cleansing and U.S. expansionism resulted in a sorry history of Indian removal and wars extending into the 1890s. Part of this process involved the Executive Branch and Congress certifying unwilling tribes to be "savages" and therefore not entitled to the judicial protections provided by the U.S. Constitution. Removal as a policy of expansionism in the United States drew on the expulsion of Acadian French and Métis from the Canadian Maritimes 75 years earlier and became the model for many 20th-century purges and ethnic cleansings. Hitler justified the genocide of Jews, gypsies, and the mentally deficient by denying them citizen status and the legal protection afforded other members of society. Ethnic cleansing and genocide from the 1930s until the present in Europe, Asia, and Africa have followed this model. The United States continues to use this ploy in its War on Terrorism: in the current situation, judicial protection, including habeas corpus and due process, is withheld from those labeled "enemy combatants" by the administration and Congress.

Tribes were often duped or coerced into signing treaties resulting in their removal to Indian Territory. The Cherokee removal is an early example of this process. The forceful removal of the majority of the Cherokees in

1838 also reflects the duplicity of federal policy in its clandestine attempts to cause dissention within tribes by often legitimizing their people and authorizing them to sign away tribal lands. This practice of violating the federal role of *parens partriae* for political or monetary gain is still being adjudicated in federal courts in cases relating to Individual Indian Money trusts. The 1830 Indian Removal Act compelled all southeastern tribes to relocate to Indian Territory west of the Mississippi River. Georgia used this Act as a pretext for its intrusion into the Cherokee Nation, confiscating national property, including schools, council houses, printing presses, and other community facilities while, at the same time, condoning raids into Cherokee villages and onto plantations by white vigilantes known as "Pony Clubs." The Pony Clubs were a forerunner of the Ku Klux Klan formulated in response to reconstruction following the Civil War. No federal protection was afforded the Cherokees during those trying times despite treaties and Supreme Court decisions guaranteeing their rights. Georgia intensified its actions because they felt President Jackson condoned them despite the recent U.S. Supreme Court decisions.

The Trail of Tears

Weary of these abuses, a group of Cherokees known as the Treaty Party signed the Treaty of New Echota, also known as Schermerhorn's Treaty, in 1835. This action reflected a wide division in the tribal leadership, resulting in two rival delegations petitioning Washington on behalf of the Cherokees. One group wanted to remain in their traditional home; the other felt that the best solution was to go to Indian Territory. The delegation opposed to removal was headed by Principal Chief John Ross; the other delegation was led by The Ridge. The Ross faction consisted of a sizeable mixed-blood (white/Indian) population and represented many of those who held leadership positions within the newly revised Cherokee Nation. The Ridge faction, on the other hand, consisted of mostly traditional full-bloods who wanted to revive their aboriginal ways without confrontation with whites. They felt they could do this best in Indian Territory.

It was no secret that President Jackson also favored the removal party. Consequently, he had the principal chief jailed while final arrangements were being forged by Schermerhorn and the Ridge party. The Treaty of New Echota ceded all Cherokee territory east of the Mississippi River to the United States for approximately seven million acres in Indian Territory along with a settlement of $5 million. This treaty was signed by only twenty Cherokees, all members of the Ridge faction. This dealt with the last major obstacle to the removal of all the southeastern tribes. Most went peacefully; only the Cherokee and a contingent of Seminole resisted removal. Most of the other tribes made it to Indian Territory, although some found other areas to settle west of the Mississippi River. Among these groups were a band of Choctaw residing in Louisiana known as the Jena Band of Choctaw Indians and a group of Cherokees, under Chief Bowles, who went to Spanish Mexico (now Texas).

Under the conditions of the Treaty of New Echota, the Cherokees had two years to move to Indian Territory; otherwise they would be forcefully removed by the U.S. Army. Most Cherokees refused to believe that they would have to vacate their traditional homes, and they were even given support in Washington by liberal senators such as Bell, Calhoun, Clay, and Webster. But two months after the treaty's ratification by the U.S. Senate, the U.S. Army under General Wool was dispatched to disarm the Cherokees. Even then, only one-eighth of the Cherokee Nation elected to move voluntarily to Indian Territory to join the eight thousand already there. The twenty thousand who remained pinned their hopes on the mercy of the new U.S. president, but Van Buren refused to rescind the Removal Act and a petition by 15,665 Cherokees to the U.S. Congress was also rejected.

Thus, on May 23, 1838, two years to the day from the signing of the New Echota treaty, the detainment of the Cherokees began. They were forced to leave their homes with only those possessions they could carry and placed into stockades. By the end of June, General Winfield Scott's men had rounded up more than ten thousand Cherokees. As soon as Cherokees were forced from their homes, farms, plantations, and businesses, thousands of whites, primarily Georgia lottery holders, confiscated Cherokee property. Some Cherokees sought refuge in the Appalachian Mountains under the influence of a local leader, Tsali. Tsali, a member of the National Council from the Tawquohee district, finally surrendered, only to be summarily executed along with his brother and two elder sons on the orders of the U.S. Army. Even then, some thousand Cherokees hid out in the mountains to avoid removal, making up the Eastern Band of Cherokee Indians, who reside in North Carolina on the Qualla Boundary.

After witnessing the hardships and brutality associated with forced removal, the remaining Cherokees agreed to move west without military assistance. This last detachment of thirteen thousand left in October 1838, in a caravan of more than six hundred wagons. Former president Jackson protested when he heard that Principal Chief John Ross was designated Superintendent of Cherokee Removal and Subsistence and tried to get him arrested, but Attorney General Felix Grundy refused. Nonetheless, the cost of the Cherokee removal was great in terms of human lives and suffering. More than four thousand Cherokees died as a direct result of removal, about one-fifth of the entire Cherokee population. Some died in the stockades under the supervision of the U.S. Army, and thousands more died en route along the Trail of Tears. Hundreds more died upon arrival in Indian Territory as a result of illnesses and exposure during the thousand-mile trek. Once he was rid of the eastern tribes, President Van Buren, in a message to both houses of Congress, praised the Cherokee removal as a positive event for America. The Cherokees expressed their own sentiments, in line with aboriginal blood vengeance, in June 1839, when The Ridge, his son John, and Elia Boudinot, all signatories of the New Echota treaty, were executed for their role in destroying the original Cherokee Nation.[15]

Chapter Three

Manifesting America's Destiny through Indian Wars and Cultural Genocide

Establishing Anglo-American Ethnocentrism as the Foundation of U.S. Indian Policy

During the 19th century, the United States demonstrated not only that it was a major colonial power in its own right but also that it was a harsh colonizer, rejecting the concessions agreed upon by its European contemporaries.

The U.S. government found that if it could not obtain Indian lands through treaties and deceit it could do so merely by labeling uncooperative tribes as "enemies of the United States," thus justifying the use of force in order to subdue, manipulate, or eliminate them. Nevertheless, the "right to occupancy" clause rooted in colonial rule and inherited from Great Britain continued to be problematic given that the concept of collectively owned tribal lands is contra to the Protestant Ethnic and the foundations of the U.S. capitalist society. Essentially, the conflict over obtaining Indian lands represents the United States earliest *anti-Communism* campaign. Clearly, race was one factor relevant to the discrimination against American Indians, but their lifestyle was equally important, playing a significant role in efforts to transform tribalism so that it conformed to Western-style societies. Enforcement of the dictates of capitalism and individual ownership of property was also a devious method of generating "surplus lands" for white settlement. To American Indians these efforts spelled *cultural genocide* and little else.

The roots of cultural genocide as U.S. policy were articulated by the first Indian commissioner, Elbert Herring, in his first report to the secretary of war in November 1832:

> On the whole, it may be a matter of serious doubt whether, even with the fostering care and assured protection of the United States, the preservation and perpetuity of the Indian race are at all attainable, under the form of government and rude civil regulations subsisting among them. These were perhaps well enough suited to their condition, when hunting was their only employment, and war gave birth to their strongest excitements. The unrestrained authority of their chiefs, and the irresponsible exercise of power, are of the simplest elements of despotic rule; while the ab-

sence of the *meum* and *tuum* in the general community of possessions, which is the grand conservative principle of the social state, is a perpetual operating cause of the *vis inertiae* of savage life. The stimulus of physical exertion and intellectual exercise, contained in this powerful principle, of which the Indian is almost entirely void, may not unjustly be considered the parent of all improvements, not merely in the arts, but in the profitable direction of labor among civilized nations. Among them it is the source of plenty; with the Indians, the absence of it is the cause of want, and consequently of decrease of numbers. Nor can proper notions of the social system be successfully inculcated, nor its benefits be rightly appreciated, so as to overcome the habits and prejudices incident to savage birth, and consequently associations of matured years, except by the institution of separate and secure rights in the relations of property and person. It is therefore suggested, whether the formation of a code of laws on this basis, to be submitted for their adoption, together with certain modifications of the existing political system among them, may not be of very salutary effect, especially as co-operating with the influences derivable from the education of their youth, and the introduction of the doctrines of the Christian religion; all centering in one grand object—the substitution of the social for the savage state....[1]

The Native American perspective on the era preceding the U.S. Civil War was that the federal government employed a number of laws and coercive treaties during the 1830s to the 1850s to gain new lands by forcing more tribes into Indian Territory. Duane Champagne noted, in the *Reference Library of Native North America*, that part of the enticement for removal was the promise that the land set aside for tribes in Indian Territory would never become part of a state or territory without their consent. Nonetheless, by the end of the 19th century the government had broken all these treaties by transforming Indian Territory into Oklahoma Territory and later the state of Oklahoma, opening the floodgates to white settlers.[2]

Many other tribes were forcefully removed to Indian Territory during the forty years following Congressional authorization of Indian removal. Many tribes experienced hardships equal to or greater than that suffered by the Cherokees in 1838. Indeed, the era preceding the U.S. Civil War was one of blatant expansionism with designs on controlling a swath of North America from the Atlantic to the Pacific oceans. Racism played a major role in U.S. expansionism, beginning in 1836 with the creation of the surrogate state—the Republic of Texas. The declaration of independence by Texas from Mexico had less to do with *freedom* from despotism than it did with opportunism by slave owners and land speculators. Encouraged by supporters in the United States, Anglo settlers in what is now Texas were upset with the young Republic of Mexico's anti-slavery laws and its support of Indian tribes. The Republic of Texas also perfected the concept of a racist state police force with the Texas Rangers, who killed Indians, *mestizos*, and Mexicans indiscriminately during its 100-year independent reign of terror. Texas's blatant minority human rights violations directed toward black slaves, Native American tribes (Cherokee, Comanche, and so on), and the peasant *mestizos* denied the Republic of Texas the recognition it sought among world leaders at the time. Sam Houston, twice president of the Republic of Texas, former governor of Tennessee, and U.S. congressman and close friend of Andrew Jackson, was instrumental in getting the United States to annex Texas.

Texas formally became a part of the United States on February 19, 1846, less than a decade after its declaration of independence from Mexico. This act also precipitated the Mexican–American War, known as the War of Northern Aggression in Mexico. The United States invaded Mexico in January 1846, under the pretext of a conflict over the border between Texas and Mexico. Mexico claimed the Nueces River as the border, as stipulated by the Treaty of Velasco, while the United States wanted the border expanded to the Rio Grande River. President Polk requested a declaration of war with Mexico in May 1846, and Congress concurred, resulting in a two-year conflict that ended in the United States taking 55 percent of Mexico to create new territory in the southwest, including Arizona, California, New Mexico, and parts of Colorado, Nevada, and Utah. The 1848 Treaty of Guadalupe Hidalgo also established the Rio Grande as the southern border of Texas. Five years later, President Pierce forced Mexico to cede more lands, expanding U.S. territory in New Mexico and Arizona in a deal called the Gadsden Purchase.[3] Inherent in these territorial gains were numerous tribes, who engaged the U.S. Army for another forty years in an era known as the Indian wars.

The War with Mexico, especially the division in the country over slavery, further edged the United States toward the Civil War from 1861 to 1865. This conflict provided the United States with a fresh crop of military leaders to replace those who fought in the Revolutionary War and the War of 1812. These leaders included Ulysses S. Grant, Ambrose Burnside, Stonewall Jackson, George Meade, and Robert E. Lee. The conflict also provided a generation of U.S. presidents and presidential candidates, such as Zachary Taylor, Franklin Pierce, Winfield Scott, Ulysses S. Grant, and Jefferson Davis. American Indian groups suffered greatly during the Civil War, with many of their guaranteed protections eliminated under the guise of martial law or reconstruction.

The Post–Civil War Era of Punitive Indian Policy: Increased Physical and Cultural Genocide

The Five Civilized Tribes were punished for siding with the Confederacy. During reconstruction they were forced to cede their western lands in Indian Territory for the post-war removal of Plains tribes including the Kaw, Osage, Pawnee, Tonkawa, Ponca, Oto-Missouri, Iowa, Sac and Fox, Kickapoo, Pottawatomie, Shawnee, Cheyenne, Arapaho, Caddo, Comanche, and Kiowa Apache. Another infamous deed was the mass execution of thirty-eight Santee Sioux warriors who were hanged together on December 26, 1862. Later, the Santee Sioux leader, Little Crow, was killed along with his son. The white hunters earned a $500 reward from the U.S. government for Little Crow, and his scalp and skull were preserved and publicly displayed. And in 1864, the Navajo were rounded up by Colonel Kit Carson and forced on a deadly march known as the Long Walk.[4] Rupert Costo and Jeannette Henry, executive directors of the now-defunct Indian Historian Press, noted in their 1977 book *Indian Treaties: Two Centuries of Dishonor* that the United States made 394 treaties with Indian tribes between 1778 and 1868.[5]

Federal responsibility for these policies was established by the 1830 Removal Act, when the president of the United States was made the Superintendent of the newly designated federal Indian wards. Tribal leaders acknowledged this by referring to the president as the "great White Father."

> The President is authorized to exercise general superintendence and care over any tribe or nation which was removed upon an exchange of territory under authority of the act of May 28, 1830, "to provide for an exchange of lands with the Indians residing in any States or Territories, and for their removal west of the Mississippi; and to cause such tribe or nation to be protected, at their new residence, against all interruption or disturbance from any other tribe or nation of Indians, or from any other persons or persons whatever.[6]

Presidential authority over Indian affairs was modified in 1851 after the conclusion of the War with Mexico, allowing for the appointment of additional superintendents and agencies and the extension of the Trade and Intercourse Acts in this newly acquired territory. New treaties, such as the Treaty of Fort

Laramie, were also made so as to constrain the movement of the western tribes, allowing for road development and lands for white settlers.

The idea of generating more surplus Indian lands through *allotment* in the newly expanded United States was put forth by President Lincoln's commissioner of Indian affairs, William P. Dole. He also alluded to future policies of termination of federal ward status:

> In very many instances the reservation is entirely surrounded by white settlements, and however much the fact is to be regretted, it is, nevertheless, almost invariably true that the tracts of land still remaining in the possession of the Indians, small and insignificant as they are when compared with the broad domain of which they were once the undisputed masters, are the objects of the cupidity of their white neighbors; they are regarded as intruders, and are subject to wrongs, insults, and petty annoyances, which, though they may be trifling in detail, are, in the aggregate, exceedingly onerous and hard to be borne.
>
> They find themselves in the pathway of a race they are wholly unable to stay, and on whose sense of justice they can alone rely for a redress of their real or imaginary grievances. Surrounded by this race, compelled by inevitable necessity to abandon all their former modes of gaining a livelihood, and starting out in pursuits which to them are new and untried experiments, they are brought in active competition with their superiors in intelligence and those acquirements which we consider so essential to success. In addition to these disadvantages, they find themselves amenable to a system of local and federal laws, as well as their treaty stipulations, all of which are to the vast majority of them wholly unintelligible. If a white man does them an injury, redress is often beyond their reach; or, if obtained, is only had after delays and vexations which are themselves cruel injustice. If one of their number commits a crime, punishment is sure and swift, and oftentimes is visited upon the whole tribe. Under these circumstances, it is not surprising that very many of them regard their future prospects as utterly hopeless, and consequently cannot be induced to abandon their vicious and idle habits. It is gratifying that so many of them are steadily and successfully acquiring the arts of civilization, and becoming useful members, and, in some instances, ornaments of society.
>
> Very much of the evil attendant upon the location of Indians within the limits of State might be obviated, if some plan could be devised whereby a more hearty co-operation with government on the part of the States might be secured. It being a demonstrated fact that Indians are capable of attaining a high degree of civilization, it follows that the time will arrive, as in the case of some of the tribes it has doubtless now arrived, when the peculiar relations existing between them and the federal government may cease, without detriment to their interests or those of the community or State in which they are located; in other words, that the time will come when, in justice to them and to ourselves, their relations to the general government should be identical with those of the citizens of the various States. . . .[7]

Another ploy to renege on treaties was put forth by Commissioner of Indian Affairs Dennis N. Cooley, who advocated reversing treaty responsibilities to the eastern tribes removed to Oklahoma, including the Five Civilized Tribes, because they had made treaties with the Confederates during the Civil War: "The following named nations and tribes have by their own acts, by making treaties with the enemies of the United States at the dates hereafter named, forfeited all rights to annuities, lands, and protection by the United States."[8] Collectively, these actions led to President Grant's peace initiative and the plan to further reduce Indian Country through homestead allotments much like those awarded white settlers.

Following the U.S. Civil War, Congress ended treaty making through the Indian Appropriations Act of 1871. This represented a post–Civil War militaristic tendency in U.S. Indian policies. Events leading to the termination of treaty making with Indian tribes included the comments made by Indian Commissioner Ely S. Parker in his Annual Report of the Commissioner of Indian Affairs submitted to Congress in December 1869:

> It has become a matter of serious import whether the treaty system in use ought longer to be continued. In my judgment it should not. A treaty involves the idea of a compact between two or more sovereign powers, each possessing sufficient authority and force to compel a compliance with the obligations incurred. The Indian tribes of the United States are not sovereign nations, capable of making treaties, as none of them have an organized government of such inherent strength as would secure a faithful obedience of its people in the observance of compacts of this character. They are held to be the wards of the government, and the only title the law concedes to them to the lands they occupy or claim is a mere possessory one. But, because treaties have been made with them, generally for the extinguishment of their supposed absolute title to land inhabited by them, or over which they roam, they have become falsely impressed with the notion of national independence. It is time that this idea should be dispelled, and the government cease the cruel farce of thus dealing with its helpless and ignorant wards. Many good men, looking at this matter only from a Christian point of view, will perhaps say that the poor Indian has been greatly wronged and ill treated; that this whole country was once his, of which he has been despoiled, and that he has been driven from place to place until he has hardly left to him a spot where to lay his head. This indeed may be philanthropic and humane, but the stern letter of the law admits of no such conclusion, and great injury has been done by the government in deluding this people into the belief of their being independent sovereignties, while they were at the same time recognized only as its dependents and wards. As civilization advances and their possessions of land are required for settlement, such legislation should be granted to them as a wise, liberal, and just government ought to extend to subjects holding their depend-

ent relation. In regard to treaties now in force, justice and humanity require that they be promptly and faithfully executed, so that the Indians may not have cause of complaint, or reason to violate their obligations by acts of violence and robbery. . . .[9]

A year later, President Ulysses S. Grant proposed his peace policy in his Second Annual Message to Congress, whereby he established the first "Faith-Based Initiative," over 130 years before President George W. Bush. Grant's intent was the forced resocialization of American Indians from their traditional ways into Western Christianity:

> The Act of Congress reducing the Army renders army officers ineligible for civil positions. Indian agencies being civil offices, I determined to give all the agencies to such religious denominations as had heretofore established missionaries among the Indians, and perhaps to some other denominations who would undertake the work on the same terms—i.e., as a missionary work. The societies selected are allowed to name their own agents, subject to the approval of the Executive, and are expected to watch over them and aid them as missionaries, to Christianize and civilize the Indian, and to train him in the art of peace. The Government watches over the official acts of these agents, and requires of them as strict an accountability as if they were appointed in any other manner. I entertain the confident hope that the policy now pursued will in a few years bring all the Indians upon reservations, where they will live in houses, and have schoolhouses and churches, and will be pursuing peaceful and self-sustaining avocations, where they may be visited by the law-abiding white man with the same impunity that he now visits the civilized white settlements.[10]

Taking advantage of these sentiments, the U.S. Congress again asserted its authority over Indian matters and Indian Country by adding a rider to the Indian Appropriations Act on March 3, 1871. By this action the House eliminated the Senate as the major influence over Indian policy by taking from them their sole authority to ratify Indian treaties. As a replacement to treaties, "agreements" with tribes were established that required ratification by both houses of Congress. But soon Executive Orders and statutes became the norm for regulating Indian Country. What was clear from 1870 on was the diminished role of tribes in forging policy in Indian Country. Federal influence was now dictated without the pretense of reciprocal input, consent, or agreement. Moreover, these new political avenues did much to obviate existing treaties. By reversing the long-held colonial tenet of the "aboriginal right of occupancy," the United States could now classify uncooperative tribes and individual Indians as outlaws, renegades, savages, and so on, allowing them to be hunted down like dangerous criminals by the military, militias, and vigilantes. This policy did much to increase the level of conflict and genocide in the newly acquired territories and states. The process of cultural genocide, on the other hand, was carried out by the religious groups mandated to educate, domesticate, and *civilize* the tribes. The two competing Indian policies for gaining aboriginal lands—physical genocide (Indian wars and concentration camps) and cultural genocide (Christianization and allotment)—continued until the end of the 19th century, culminating in the first Wounded Knee massacre of December 1890. The extent of physical genocide could have been much worse if efforts to transfer Indian Affairs (the Indian Bureau) from the Department of the Interior (effective March 3, 1849) back to the War Department (currently the Department of Defense) following the Civil War had succeeded. General Sherman, of Civil War fame, was one of the strongest proponents of returning the Indian Bureau to the War Department.

Indian Education and the Mechanisms of Cultural Genocide

Attempts at resocialization via education had a long history extending back to the colonial era. Even then only a small percentage of Native Americans ever matriculated in these programs. For example, an Indian college was established as part of Harvard in 1654, but at the time of the Revolutionary War, 120 years later, only one Indian had earned an undergraduate degree. Dr. Eleazer Wheelock, a Congregational minister and Yale graduate, is known for establishing the first separate Indian college, called Moor's Charity School, which later became Dartmouth College and which started in Lebanon, Connecticut, and later moved to Hanover, New Hampshire. His model for a separate boarding school for Indians provided the blueprint for missionary/boarding schools that later emerged during the 19th century.

In the emerging United States, the role of *civilizing* and *Christianizing* American Indians was assigned to educational institutions, with oversight provided by the Bureau of Indian Affairs (BIA). The 1976 Indian Education Task Force addressed the progression of this phenomenon:

> The educational efforts of the federal government during these early years were directed towards civilizing the Indians, with the hope of eventually integrating them into the American way of life. This was considered the best way to preserve peace and maintain friendship with the tribes. However, in 1817, a bill was introduced into Congress which was specifically designed to provide for the civilization of the Indians adjoining the frontier settlements. It was a proposal to alleviate the Indian

problems by establishing schools among the frontier tribes, hastening their acceptance of civilized life. As eventually passed on March 3, 1819, this bill established the Civilization Fund which offered interested individuals who would work and teach among the Indians.[11]

The task force's report states that the sentiment concerning American Indians at the time of removal was that "[t]he Indians are not now, what they once were. . . . They must be civilized, or exterminated; no other alternatives exist."[12] The Five Civilized Tribes, as well as numerous eastern tribes and nations, adapted to the Western perception of civilization, including providing Anglo-style education. The Five Civilized Tribes continued to maintain these endeavors even following removal. However, more tribes were being displaced and either removed to Indian Territory or forced into restricted concentration camps. And with the repeal of the Civilization Fund in 1873 education now became the responsibility of the newly created Board of Indian Commissioners. The Board of Indian Commissioners relied heavily on religious groups as the primary education agencies. In all, thirteen religious groups served some two hundred thousand Indians in seventy-three agencies: American Board of Commissions for Foreign Missions, Baptist, Catholic, Christian, Congregational, Dutch Reformed, Episcopalian, Hicksite Friends, Lutheran, Orthodox Friends, Presbyterian, Methodist, and Unitarian. Here, vocational education and studies in Christian morality comprised the reservation education plan. The basic mandate of federally controlled Indian education was "to kill the Indian to save the child."

This epistemological model was illustrated by the Hampton/Carlisle model, one that closely resembled that developed for newly freed blacks (freedmen). In 1866, Civil War brevet Brigadier General Samuel Chapman Armstrong received an appointment as an agent of the Freedmen's Bureau and was placed in charge of the freedmen's camp at Hampton, Virginia, where he developed the Hampton Normal and Industrial Institute in 1868. A decade later the War Department sent the first Indian students to the Hampton Normal and Industrial Institute—seventeen Indians transferred from the federal Indian prison in St. Augustine, Florida.

Once it became apparent that black and Indian students were not compatible at Hampton, a separate Indian school, one based on the Hampton model, was established at Carlisle in 1878. Carlisle was situated on a four-hundred-acre campus near Hampton in Pennsylvania and became known as the Indian Branch of the Hampton Institute. The first Indian students at

Hampton came from the Kiowa, Comanche, Arapahoes, Caddos, and Cheyenne prisoners. At Carlisle, Sioux Indians became the first students. Numerous tribes were represented at Carlisle during its forty-year existence, including members of Geronimo's imprisoned Apache band, the Chiracahua.

Once the Indian Bureau was transferred from the War Department to the Department of the Interior admission was still coerced but not by first imprisoning tribal members. By the early 1880s, over a hundred Indian schools existed, including a dozen boarding schools. Following the Carlisle model, Congress made other abandoned military posts available for Indian schools. These included the Haskell Indian School at Lawrence, Kansas, and the Moravian Mission School in Bethel, Alaska. Cultural genocide was a major goal of Indian education, and Indian children were transformed with haircuts and a strict dress code. English was the only language allowed, and the practice of traditional rituals was strictly forbidden. Discipline was severe and instilled through corporal punishment or imprisonment. The exclusive use of English was instituted by Indian Commissioner J.D.C. Atkins and reported to Congress in his Annual Report of September 1887:

> Every nation is jealous of its own language, and no nation ought to be more so than ours, which approaches nearer than any other nationality to the perfect protection of its people. True Americans all feel that the Constitution, laws, and institutions of the United States, in their adaptation to the wants and requirements of man, are superior to those of any other country; and they should understand that by the spread of the English language will these laws and institutions be more firmly established and widely disseminated. Nothing so surely and perfectly stamps upon an individual a national characteristic as language. So manifest and important is this that nations the world over, in both ancient and modern times, have ever imposed the strictest requirements upon their public schools as to the teaching of the national tongue. Only English has been allowed to be taught in the public schools in the territory acquired by this country from Spain, Mexico, and Russia, although the native populations spoke another tongue. . . . Deeming it for the very best interest of the Indian, both as an individual and as an embryo citizen, to have this policy strictly enforced among the various schools on Indian reservations, orders have been issued accordingly to Indian agents, and the texts of the orders and of some explanations made thereof are given below:
>
> December 14, 1886.
>
> In all schools conducted by missionary organizations it is required that all instructions shall be given in the English language.
>
> February 2, 1887.
>
> In reply I have to advise you that the rule applies to all schools on Indian reservations, whether they be Government or mission schools. The instruction of the In-

dian in the vernacular is not only of no use to them, but is detrimental to the cause of their education and civilization, and no school will be permitted on the reservation in which the English language is not exclusively taught.

July 16, 1887.

Your attention is called to the regulation of this office which forbids instruction in schools in any Indian language. This rule applies to all schools on an Indian reservation, whether Government or mission schools. The education of Indians in the vernacular is not only of no use to them, but is detrimental to their education and civilization.

You are instructed to see that this rule is rigidly enforced in all schools upon the reservation under your charge.

No mission school will be allowed upon the reservation which does not comply with the regulation.

The following was sent to representatives of all societies having contracts with this bureau for the conduct of Indian schools:

July 16, 1887.

Your attention is called to the provisions of the contracts for educating Indian pupils, which provides that the school shall "teach the ordinary branches of an English education." This provision must be faithfully adhered to, and no books in any Indian language must be used or instruction given in that language to Indian pupils in any school where this office has entered into contract for the education of Indians. The same rule prevails in all Government Indian schools and will be strictly enforced in all contracts and other Indian schools.

The instruction of Indians in the vernacular is not only of no use to them, but is detrimental to the cause of their education and civilization, and it will not be permitted in any Indian school over which the Government has any control, or in which it has any interest whatever.

This circular has been sent to all parties who have contracted to educate Indian pupils during the present fiscal year.

You will see that this regulation is rigidly enforced in the schools under your direction where Indians are placed under contract. . . .

It is believed that if any Indian vernacular is allowed to be taught by the missionaries in schools on Indian reservations, it will prejudice the youthful pupil as well as his untutored and uncivilized or semi-civilized parent against the English language, and, to some extent at least, against Government schools in which the English language exclusively has always been taught. To teach Indian school children their native tongue is practically to exclude English, and to prevent them from acquiring it. This language, which is good enough for a white man and a black man, ought to be good enough for the red man. It is also believed that teaching an Indian youth in his own barbarous dialect is a positive detriment to him. The first step to be taken toward civilization, toward teaching the Indians the mischief and folly of continuing in their barbarous practices, is to teach them the English language. The impracticability, in not impossibility, of civilizing the Indians of this country in any other tongue than our own would seem to be obvious, especially in view of the fact

that the number of Indian vernaculars is even greater than the number of tribes. . . .
If we expect to infuse into the rising generation the leaven of American citizenship, we must remove the stumbling blocks of hereditary customs and manners, and of these language is one of the most important elements. . . .[13]

As the United States edged toward allotment and the further reduction of lands in Indian Country, the idea of separating Indian youth from their traditional culture was established by militarizing boarding school. Moreover, tribes were penalized for nonattendance of their children and youth in federal resocialization schools:

Vacant military posts or barracks for schools; detail of Army officers (July 1882)
The Secretary of the Army is authorized to set aside, for use in the establishment of normal and industrial training schools for Indian youth from the nomadic tribes having educational treaty claims upon the United States, any vacant posts or barracks, so long as they may not be required for military occupation, and to detail one or more officers of the Army for duty in connection with Indian education, under the direction of the Secretary of the Interior, at each such school so established. Provided, That monies appropriated or to be appropriated for general purposes of education among the Indians may be expended, under the direction of the Secretary of the Interior, for the education of Indian youth at such posts, institutions, and schools as he may consider advantageous, or as Congress from time to time may authorize and provide.[14]

Regulations for withholding rations for nonattendance at schools (March 1893)
The Secretary of the Interior may in his discretion, establish such regulations as will prevent the issuing of rations or the furnishing of subsistence either in money or in kind to the head of any Indian family for or on account of any Indian child or children between the ages of eight and twenty-one years who shall not have attended school during the preceding year in accordance with such regulations. This provision shall not apply to reservations or part of reservations where sufficient school facilities have not been furnished nor until full notice of such regulations shall have been given to the Indians to be affected thereby.

The amount and value of subsistence so withheld shall be credited to the tribe or tribes from whom the same is withheld, to be issued and paid when in the judgment of the Secretary of the Interior they shall have fully complied with such regulations. The Secretary of the Interior may in his discretion withhold rations, clothing and other annuities from Indian parents or guardians who refuse or neglect to send and keep their children of proper school age in some school a reasonable portion of the year.[15]

The late U.S. Supreme Court justice William O. Douglas summed up the Indian boarding school phenomenon in his 1973 analysis:

The express policy (of the schools was that of) stripping the Indian child of his cultural heritage and identity: Such schools were run in a rigid military fashion, with heavy emphasis on rustic vocational education. They were designed to separate a child from his reservation and family, strip him of his tribal lore and morés, force the complete abandonment of his native language, and prepare him for never again returning to his people.[16]

Jurisprudence and Cultural Genocide: Outlawing Traditionalism

Duane Champagne, providing the Native American perspective, notes that the shift during the second half of the 19th century was to further concentrate tribes so as to free up reservation lands for white settlers. Part of the rationale for placing Indians on white-regulated, concentrated reservations was purportedly to "civilize" and assimilate these wards of the federal government. However, the latent purpose of this policy was to dominate, weaken, and drive underground tribal government and legal systems. Part of this control mechanism was the establishment of the Courts of Indian Offenses and the Indian police. These actions were setting the stage for even further reduction of treaty-based reservations—the pretense of "full assimilation" via allotment.[17]

In a similar fashion, Getches, Wilkinson, and Williams, in their work *Cases and Materials on Federal Indian Law*, posit that the concentration reservation system was due not to a magnanimous and far-sighted federal government but to a desire to generate surplus lands and further destroy Indian traditionalism.[18] In their long history, the Trade and Intercourse Laws were concerned primarily with regulating the activities of whites interacting with tribes and had little to do with internal indigenous controls, folkways, and morés. The establishment of externally controlled (BIA) Indian police forces was based on the success of John Clum, agent of the San Carlos Apache reservation in what is now Arizona. Due to Clum's success, Indian Commissioner Ezra A. Hayt in 1877 recommended that Congress authorize Indian police forces for other BIA-controlled reservations. Toward this end, the U.S. Congress authorized pay for 430 Indian privates and 50 white officers in 1878, raising the figures to 800 privates and 100 officers in 1879.[19]

At the same time Indian tribes were struggling for legal parity during this era of diminished tribal authority and increased control and regulations placed upon them—a process which was clearly one-sided, with non-Indians having a substantial legal advantage over Indian clients. A landmark case reflecting this phenomenon was that of Standing Bear, who filed a writ of habeas corpus before the U.S. courts questioning his forced incarceration in Indian Territory (Oklahoma). The Ponca tribe was removed from its traditional home in eastern Nebraska so as to make room for the forcefully removed Santee (Dakota) Sioux following their uprising in Minnesota in the early 1860s, which resulted in the largest federally sanctioned execution in U.S. history: the group hanging of thirty-eight Sioux warriors on December 26, 1862. A group of Ponca under the leadership of Standing Bear left the horrid conditions of their new reservation and headed home to Nebraska. After leaving the reservation, they were subsequently arrested by General George Crook's forces. Following his arrest Standing Bear filed his appeal. The case was heard in the United States Circuit Court, District of Nebraska, by Judge Elmer S. Dundy. He ruled in the Poncas' favor on May 12, 1879. This ruling finally established that American Indians were human beings and not some subspecies who could be treated like wild animals or savages.

> Dundy, District Judge. During the fifteen years in which I have been engaged in administering the laws of my country, I have never been called upon to hear or decide a case that appealed so strongly to my sympathy as the one now under consideration. On the one side, we have a few of the remnants of a once numerous and powerful, but now weak, insignificant, unlettered, and generally despised race; on the other, we have the representative of one of the most powerful, most enlightened, and most Christianized nations of modern times. On the one side, we have the representatives of this wasted race coming into this national tribunal of ours, asking for justice and liberty to enable them to adopt our boasted civilization, and to pursue the arts of peace, which have made us great and happy as a nation; on the other side, we have this magnificent, if not magnanimous, government, resisting this application with the determination of sending these people back to the country which is to them less desirable than perpetual imprisonment in their own native land. But I think it is creditable to the heart and mind of the brave and distinguished officer who is made respondent herein to say that he has no sort of sympathy in the business in which he is forced by his position to bear a part so conspicuous; and, so far as I am individually concerned, I think it not improper to say that, if the strongest possible sympathy could give the relators title to freedom, they would have been restored to liberty the moment the arguments in their behalf were closed. No examination or further thought would then have been necessary or expedient. But in a country where liberty is regulated by law, something more satisfactory and enduring than mere sympathy must furnish and constitute the rule and basis of judicial action. It follows that this case must be examined and decided on principles of law, and that unless the relators are entitled to their discharge under the constitution or laws of the United States, or some treaty made pursuant thereto, they must be remanded to the custody of the officer who caused their arrest, to be returned to the Indian Territory, which they left without the consent of the government. . . .
>
> I have searched in vain for the semblance of any authority justifying the commissioner in attempting to remove by force any Indians, whether belonging to a tribe

or not, to any place, or for any other purpose than what has been stated. Certainly, without some specific authority found in an act of congress, or in a treaty with the Ponca tribe of Indians, he could not lawfully force the relators back to the Indian Territory, to remain and die in that country, against their will. In the absence of all treaty stipulations or laws of the United States authorizing such removal, I must conclude that no such arbitrary authority exists. It is true, if the relators are to be regarded as a part of the great nation of Ponca Indians, the government might, in time of war, remove them to any place of safety so long as the war should last, but perhaps no longer, unless they were charged with the commission of some crime. This is a war power merely, and exists in time of war only. Every nation exercises the right to arrest and detain an alien enemy during the existence of a war, and all subjects or citizens of the hostile nations are subject to be dealt with under this rule.

But it is not claimed that the Ponca tribe of Indians are at war with the United States, so that this war power might be used against them; in fact, they are amongst the most peaceable and friendly of all the Indian tribes, and have at times received from the government unmistakable and substantial recognition of their long-continued friendship for the whites. In time of peace the war power remains in abeyance, and must be subservient to the civil authority of the government until something occurs to justify its exercise. No facts exist, and nothing has occurred, so far as the relators are concerned, to make it necessary or lawful to exercise such an authority over them. If they could be removed to the Indian Territory by force, and kept there in the same way, I can see no good reason why they might not be taken and kept by force in the penitentiary at Lincoln, or Leavenworth, or Jefferson City, or any other place which the commander of the forces might, in his judgment, see proper to designate. I cannot think that any such arbitrary authority exists in this country.

The reasoning advanced in support of my views, leads me to conclude:

(a) That an Indian is a "person" within the meaning of the laws of the United States, and has, therefore, the right to sue out a writ of habeas corpus in a federal court, or before a federal judge, in all cases where he may be confined or in custody under the color of authority of the United States, or where he is restrained of liberty in violation of the constitution or laws of the United States.

(b) That General George Crook, the respondent, being commander of the military department of the Platte, has the custody of the relators, under color of authority of the United States, and in violation of the laws thereof.

(c) That no rightful authority exists for removing by force any of the relators to the Indian Territory, as the respondent has been directed to do.

(d) That the Indians possess the inherent right of expatriation, as well as the more fortunate white race, and have the inalienable right to "life, liberty, and the pursuit of happiness," so long as they obey the laws and do not trespass on forbidden ground. And,

(e) Being restrained of liberty under of color of authority of the United States, and in violation of the laws thereof, the relators must be discharged from custody, and it is so ordered.[20]

Efforts to enforce laws within federal jurisdictions were first established by the Trade and Intercourse Acts of 1790. In the 1834 version, following passage of the Removal Act of 1830, Congress authorized federal Indian agents and administrators with the arrest and adjudication of not only non-Indians in Indian Country but all Indians or non-Indians accused of committing any crime, offense, or misdemeanor within any state or territory who then fled to Indian Country. This was partly in response to the enactment of the Federal Crimes Act of 1825. The Federal Enclaves and Assimilative Crimes Acts were the norm in Indian Country following the Civil War and the ensuing Indian wars in the newly acquired western territories. In 1883, the Courts of Indian Offenses were established. Here, pro-Christian Indian judges were appointed by the white Indian agent with the intent of enforcing Anglo-style laws on the Indian populace in Indian Country. Clearly, these courts and their codes did not subscribe to indigenous trial rituals and practices. Instead, the Courts of Indian Offenses imposed the federal dictates of Christian civilization. Subsequently, traditional native spiritual dances and customary practices, including purification rituals, vision quests, sun dances, and plural marriages were outlawed.

The secretary of the interior at this time, Henry M. Teller, initiated the Courts of Indian Offenses in order to rid Indian Country of its "heathenish practices." These courts adjudicated minor offenses in Indian Country already defined by the Federal Enclaves and Assimilative Crime Acts:

> Many of the agencies are without law of any kind, and the necessity for some rule of government on the reservations grows more and more apparent each day. If it is the purpose of the Government to civilize the Indians, they must be compelled to desist from the savage and barbarous practices that are calculated to continue them in savagery, no matter what exterior influences are brought to bear on them....
>
> The Government furnishes the teachers, and the charitable people contribute to the support of missionaries, and much time, labor, and money is yearly expended for their elevation, and a few non-progressive, degraded Indians are allowed to exhibit before the young and susceptible children all the debauchery, diabolism, and savagery of the worst state of the Indian race. Every man familiar with Indian life will bear witness to the pernicious influence of these savage rites and heathenish customs....

In accordance with the suggestions of this letter, the Commission of Indian Affairs established a tribunal at all agencies, except among the civilized Indians, consisting of three Indians, to be known as the Court of Indian Offenses. The members of this tribunal consist of the first three officers in rank of the police force, if such selection is approved by the agency; otherwise, the agent may select from among the members of the tribe three suitable persons to constitute such tribunal.

The Commissioner of Indian Affairs, with the approval of the Secretary of the Interior, promulgated certain rules for the government of this tribunal, defining offenses of which it was to take cognizance. It is believed that such a tribunal composed as it is of Indians, will be a step in the direction of bringing the Indians under the influence of law.[21]

During this same time, attempts at maintaining traditional tribal customs within Indian Country were being played out in the U.S. courts in the Crow Dog incident. Preliminary to this case was the anti-Indian sentiment generated throughout the United States following Custer's Last Stand at Little Big Horn in 1776.[22] The Crow Dog case was equally sensational in that in 1881 a federally sponsored Sioux leader, Spotted Tail, was killed in an altercation by another Sioux leader, Crow Dog. Both were Brulé Sioux from the Rosebud Reservation. The case was adjudicated according to traditional restorative justice customs in line with the Sioux Harmony Ethos. Both Spotted Tail and Crow Dog were respected warriors and leaders among their people, with the former being the head chief of the Brulé at the time of the treaties of the 1860s establishing the Great Sioux Reservation. Spotted Tail's status was elevated by the United States when he kept the Brulé Sioux out of the 1876 uprising that led to Custer's defeat.

The Crow Dog Case and the Major Crimes Act
Crow Dog was a traditional Sioux leader who had once been the chief of the Orphan Band of Brulé Sioux. He remained the leader of the survivors of Big Raven's band following the massacre of Big Raven and all his warriors in the 1844 conflict with the Shoshone. Crow Dog was a close associate of Crazy Horse, accompanied him when he surrendered in 1877, and was credited with preventing bloodshed when soldiers attempted to assassinate Crazy Horse at the time of his surrender. Crow Dog was also an associate of Sitting Bull and had contact with him while he and his band were in exile in Canada following Custer's defeat.

Both Spotted Tail and Crow Dog were vying for leadership positions within the new Rosebud agency following its creation in 1878. Spotted Tail, who adopted the agency's accommodative stance, was preferred by the United States over Crow Dog, who represented the old, traditional Sioux ways. These ideological differences aside, the actual altercation was probably over a woman, Light-in-the-Lodge. Here, Spotted Tail was seen as enticing Light-in-the-Lodge away from her disabled elderly husband, and Crow Dog took it upon himself to right this wrong. Thus, on August 5, 1881, the forty-seven-year-old Crow Dog shot fifty-eight-year-old Spotted Tail as they approached each other on a road near the agency.

Since this was seen as an intra-tribal matter, it was presumed to be exempt from federal or territorial jurisdiction under the existing Federal Enclave/General Crimes Act regulating Indian Country. The matter was subsequently resolved by the respective clans. According to Brulé traditional restorative justice, Crow Dog's clan compensated Spotted Tail's clan with a restitution of $600, eight horses, and a blanket. While this restored balance to the Sioux, it did not resonate well with the federal Indian agents and the U.S. Army. Crow Dog was arrested by orders of the Indian agent and brought to Fort Niobrara in Nebraska for trial. In a quick response, the U.S. attorney general and the secretary of the interior concluded that the Federal Enclaves Act, as modified by the Assimilative Act, allowed Crow Dog to be eligible for the death sentence at his trial.

Crow Dog's trial came to represent a number of similar cases working their way through the federal courts. Crow Dog was portrayed as a *bad Indian* like his colleagues Crazy Horse and Sitting Bull and as deserving to be killed, if only to send a message to other renegades. There was little doubt that the all-white jury would find Crow Dog guilty, dismissing his claim of self-defense. Interestingly, during jury selection, his defense attorney, A. J. Plowman, questioned the jurors on how they felt about testimony from Indian witnesses. The general consensus was that the testimony of a white greatly outweighed that of an Indian, one stating 100 to 1. Nonetheless, the jury was quickly selected.

The lead prosecution witness, the Brulé Indian agent, John Cook, was not even on the reservation when the incident occurred but was allowed to give hearsay testimony as if it was a valid representation of the events that transpired. Witnesses for the defense included the agency Indian police chief, Eagle Hawk, who testified that Spotted Tail had a pistol and had a history of violence, having killed another competitor, Big Mouth, in 1869. Contrary to this depiction of Spotted Tail's character by his own people, white officials provided exemplary portrayals of Spotted Tail, noting his cooperation with the U.S. government and the agency. All efforts by the defense to introduce local customs of the Brulé tribe were suppressed by the prosecution. In the end, the jury convicted Crow Dog on capital murder and the judge sentenced him to be executed by hanging. Crow Dog's attorney appealed, only to have the decision upheld by the First Judicial District Court of Dakota, with the same sentencing judge, G.C. Moody, presiding over the original and appeal decisions. The case then went to the U.S. Supreme Court, which upheld Crow Dog's petition and released him from incarceration. This decision of December 17, 1883, became known as *Ex parte Crow Dog*:

> The petitioner is in the custody of the marshal of the United States for the Territory of Dakota, imprisoned in the jail of Lawrence County, in the First Judicial District of that Territory, under sentence of death, adjudged against him by the district court for that district, to be carried into execution January 14th, 1884. That judgment was rendered upon a conviction for the murder of an Indian of the Brulé Sioux band of the Sioux Nation of Indians, by the name of Sin-ta-ge-le-Scka, or in English, Spotted Tail, the prisoner also being an Indian, of the same band and nation, and the homicide having occurred as alleged in the indictment in Indian country, within a place and district of country under the exclusive jurisdiction of the United States and within the said judicial district. The judgment was affirmed, on a writ of error, by the Supreme Court of the Territory. It is claimed on behalf of the prisoner that the crime charged against him, and of which he stands convicted, is not an offense under the laws of the United States; that the district court had no jurisdiction to try him, and that its judgment and sentence are void. He therefore prays for a writ of habeas corpus, that he may be delivered from an imprisonment which he asserts to be illegal.
> . . .
> To give to the clauses in the treaty of 1868 and the agreement of 1877 effect, so as to uphold the jurisdiction exercised in this case, would be to reverse in this instance the general policy of the government towards the Indians, as declared in many statutes and treaties, and recognized in many decisions of this court, from the beginning to the present time. To justify such a departure, in such a case, requires a clear expression of the intention of Congress, and that we have not been able to find.
> It results that the First District Court of Dakota was without jurisdiction to find or try the indictment against the prisoner, that the conviction and sentence are void, and that his imprisonment is illegal.[23]

The U.S. Congress responded to the U.S. Supreme Court *Crow Dog* decision by enacting the Major Crimes Act in 1885. The Major Crimes Act represented a significant encroachment on tribal authority and autonomy. It provided overlapping jurisdiction with the Federal Enclaves Act by applying these rules to any offender, Indian or non-Indian, in Indian Country. More interestingly, the Major Crimes Act became the basis for federal police intervention in local criminal jurisdictions, notably under J. Edgar Hoover's leadership of the Federal Bureau of Investigation.

> *Major Crimes Act—March 3, 1885*
> That immediately upon and after the date of the passage of this act all Indians, committing against the person or property of another Indian or other person any of the following crimes, namely, murder, manslaughter, rape, assault with intent to kill, arson, burglary, and larceny within any Territory of the United States, and either within or without an Indian reservation, shall be subject therefor to the laws of such Territory relating to such crimes, and shall be tried therefor in the same courts and in the same manner and shall be subject to the same penalties as are all other persons charged with the commission of said crimes, respectively; and the said courts are hereby given jurisdiction in all such cases; and such Indians committing any of the above crimes against the person or property of another Indian or other persons within the boundaries of any State of the United States, and within the limits of any Indian reservation, shall be subject to the same laws, tried in the same courts and in the same manner, and subject to the same penalties as are all other persons committing any of the above crimes within the exclusive jurisdiction of the United States.[24]

The Major Crimes Act was challenged in 1886 in *United States v. Kagama* and upheld by the U.S. Supreme Court.[25] An obvious problem with this law was that American Indians did not have equal weight before the courts, especially when cases were being adjudicated by white judges and their fate decided by white juries. It would be another thirty-nine years before American Indians were granted federal citizenship. Even then, this did not guarantee equal legal status in local jurisdictions, notably those where they did not enjoy state citizenship. The Major Crimes Act, initially known as the "seven Index Crimes," also set the stage for the current situation where the FBI polices Indian Country.

Rules for the Courts of Indian Offenses (BIA courts) were modified in 1892 following the end of the Ghost Dance movement and the massacre at Wounded Knee in December 1890. Indian judges had to be assimilated into the dominant white American society. Appointed by the commissioner of Indian affairs, Indian judges served in districts within Indian Country hearing non–Index Crime offenses such as violations of the prohibitions against traditional rituals and customs, including the practice of traditional dances or similar celebrations, plural or polygamous marriages, and medicine men practices in addition to property destruction, immorality (prostitution or cohabitation), possession of alcohol or intoxication, and all misdemeanor offenses defined by the Assimilative Crimes Act. The district courts also served as appellate courts. These were known as Courts of Cultural Genocide by traditional Indians.

Serious crimes, the Index Crimes defined by the Major Crimes Act, were adjudicated by white judges within the federal district court system. In March 1893, U.S. attorneys were provided original jurisdiction in representing all federal Indian wards of the United States in "all suits at law and in equity." This policy clearly established the superior weight of U.S. and white interests compared with the interests of Indians in Indian Country. This practice continued until the Eisenhower administration and the institution of Public Law 280 allocating certain states primary legal authority in Indian Country existing within their boundaries.[26] The imposition of the white-dominated law enforcement apparatus in Indian Country set the stage for allotment and the end of Indian Territory.

Allotment: The Era of Forced Acculturation
Allotment actually began during the early years of the Civil War when Congress passed an act to protect Indians desiring civilized life. Here, federal legal protection was promised to those tribal members in Indian Country who elected to adopt the ways of the dominant society:

> Whenever any Indian, being a member of any band or tribe with whom the Government has or shall have entered into treaty stipulations, being desirous to adopt the habits of civilized life, has had a portion of the lands belonging to his tribe allotted to him in severalty, in pursuance of such treaty stipulations, the agent and superintendent of such tribe shall take such measures, not inconsistent with law, as may be necessary to protect such Indian in the quiet enjoyment of the lands so allotted to him.[27]

From the Native American perspective, Duane Champagne noted that the manifest purpose of allotment (the Dawes Act) was to diminish tribal control in Indian Country. Through the division of communal tribal lands into individual allotments, supposedly protected by federal trust, tribal authority would be greatly diminished. Moreover, "excess" or "surplus" lands could then be assigned to white settlers. The protective trust aspect of allotment failed, and many allotted plots were taken over by unscrupulous whites in collusion with the white-run courts, resulting in a substantial number of non-Indians living within the tribal boundaries yet not subject to tribal authority. In the end, over 60 percent of Indian Country (86 million acres) was lost during the allotment era, 1886–1934.[28]

Wilcomb E. Washburn of the Smithsonian Institution, in his work *The Assault on Indian Tribalism*, contends that allotment reflected the nation's growing frustration over the Indian problem. Thus, a number of options were available to the federal government in the 1880s: (1) renege on existing treaty obligations and pursue an intense program of physical genocide; (2) preserve the status quo and all treaty obligations to protect Indian Country from unwanted white encroachment; (3) entice tribes to agree voluntarily to individual allotment of lands and the adoption of "civilized" ways, e.g., to become farmers; (4) destroy tribal authority and force allotment upon Indians as well as subject them to the larger dominant society's laws; or (5) take whatever actions were deemed necessary to appease the demands of white settlers, farmers, ranchers, miners, and railroad companies for coveted tribal resources. The last option was what eventually emerged, regardless of how it was presented to the tribes, the nation, or the world.[29]

The General Allotment Act of 1887 (The Dawes Act)—February 8
An Act to Provide for the Allotment of Lands in Severalty to Indians on the Various Reservations, and to Extend the Protection of the Laws of the United States and the Territories Over the Indians, and for Other Purposes.

BE IT ENACTED *by the Senate and House of Representatives of the United States of America in Congress assembled,* That in all cases where any tribe or band of Indians has been, or shall hereafter be, located upon any reservation created for their use, either by treaty stipulation or by virtue of an act of Congress or executive order setting apart the same for their use, the President of the United States be, and he hereby is, authorized, whenever in his opinion any reservation or any part thereof of such Indians is advantageous for agricultural and grazing purposes, to cause said reservation, or any part thereof to be surveyed, or resurveyed if necessary, and to allot the lands in said reservation in severalty to any Indian located thereon in quantities as follows:

To each head of a family, one-quarter of a section;

To each single person over eighteen years of age, one-eighth of a section;

To each orphan child under eighteen years of age, one-eighth of a section; and

To each other single person under eighteen years now living, or who may be born prior to the date of the order of the President directing an allotment of the lands embraced in any reservation, one-sixteenth of a section:

Provided, That in case there is not sufficient land in any of said reservations to allot lands to each individual of the classes above named in quantities as above provided, the lands embraced in such reservation or reservations shall be allotted to each individual of each of said classes pro rata, in accordance with the provisions of this act:

And provided further, That where the treaty or act of Congress setting apart such reservation provides for the allotment of lands in severalty in quantities in excess of those herein provided, the President, in making allotments upon such reservation, shall allot the lands to each individual Indian belonging thereon in quantity as specified in such treaty or act: *And provided further,* That when the lands allotted are only valuable for grazing purposes, an additional allotment of such grazing lands, in quantities as above provided, shall be made to each individual.

SECTION II
That all allotments set apart under the provisions of this act shall be selected by the Indians, heads of families selecting for their minor children, and the agents shall select for each orphan child, and in such manner as to embrace the improvements of the Indian making the selection. Where the improvements of two or more Indians have been made on the same legal subdivision of land, unless they shall otherwise agree, a provisional line may be run dividing said lands between them, and the amount to which each is entitled shall be equalized in the assignment of the remainder of the land to which they are entitled under this act. *Provided,* That if any one entitled to an allotment shall fail to make a selection within four years after the President shall direct that allotments may be made on a particular reservation, the Secretary of the Interior may direct the agent of such tribe or band, if such there be, and if there be no agent, then a special agent appointed for that purpose, to make a selection for such Indian, which election shall be allotted as in cases where selections are made by the Indians, and patents shall issue in like manner.

SECTION III
That the allotments provided for in this act shall be made by special agents appointed by the President for such purpose, and the agent in charge of the respective reservations on which the allotments are directed to be made, under such rules and regulations as the Secretary of the Interior may from time to time prescribe, and shall be certified by such agents to the Commissioner of Indian Affairs, in duplicate, one copy to be retained in the Indian Office and the other to be transmitted to the Secretary of the Interior for his action, and to be deposited in the General Land Office.

SECTION IV
That where any Indian not residing upon a reservation, or for whose tribe no reservation has been provided by treaty, act of Congress, or executive order, shall make settlement upon any surveyed or unsurveyed lands of the United States not otherwise appropriated, he or she shall be entitled, upon application to the local land-office for the district in which the lands are located, to have the same allotted to him or her, and to his or her children, in quantities and manner as provided in this act for Indians residing upon reservations; and when such settlement is made upon unsurveyed lands, the grant to such Indians shall be adjusted upon the survey of the lands so as to conform thereto; and patents shall be issued to them for such lands in the manner and with the restrictions as herein provided. And the fees to which the officer of such local land-office would have been entitled had such lands been entered under

the general laws for the disposition of the public lands shall be paid to them, from the moneys in the Treasury of the United States not otherwise appropriated, upon a statement of an account in their behalf for such fees by the Commissioner of the General Land Officer, and a certification of such account to the Secretary of the Treasury by the Secretary of the Interior.

SECTION V
That upon the approval of the allotments provided for in this act by the Secretary of the Interior, he shall cause patents to issue therefor in the name of the allottees, which patents shall be of the legal effect, and declare that the United States does and will hold the land thus allotted, for the period of twenty-five years, in trust for the sole use and benefit of the Indian to whom such allotment shall have been made, or, in case of his decease, of his heirs according to the laws of the State or Territory where such land is located, and that at the expiration of said period the United States will convey the same patent to said Indian, or his heirs as aforesaid, in fee, discharged of said trust and free of all charge or incumbrance whatsoever: *Provided,* That the President of the United States may in any case in his discretion extend the period. And if any conveyance shall be made of the lands set apart and allotted as herein provided, or any contract made touching the same, before the expiration of the time above mentioned, such conveyance or contract shall be absolutely null and void: *Provided,* That the law of descent and partition in force in the State or Territory where such lands are situate shall apply thereto after patents therefor have been executed and delivered except as herein otherwise provided; and the laws of the State of Kansas regulating the descent and partition of real estate shall, so far as practicable, apply to all lands in the Indian Territory which may be allotted in severalty under the provisions of this act: *And provided further,* That at any time after lands in the Indian Territory which may be allotted to all the Indians of any tribe as herein provided, or sooner if in the opinion of the President it shall be for the best interests of said tribe, it shall be lawful for the Secretary of the Interior to negotiate with such Indian tribe for the purchase and release by said tribe, in conformity with the treaty or statute under which such reservation is held, of such portions of its reservation not allotted and such tribe shall, from time to time, consent to sell, on such terms and conditions as shall be considered just and equitable between the United States and said tribe of Indians, which purchase shall not be complete until ratified by Congress, and the form and manner of executing such release shall be prescribed by Congress. *Provided however,* That all lands adapted to agriculture, with or without irrigation or sold or released to the United States by any Indian tribe shall be held by the United States for the sole purpose of securing homes to actual settlers only in tracts not exceeding one hundred and sixty acres to any one person, on such terms as Congress shall prescribe, subject to grants which Congress may make in aid of education: *And provided further,* That no patents shall issue therefor except to the person so taking the same as and for a homestead, or his heirs, and after the expiration of five years occupancy thereof as such homestead; and any conveyance of said lands so taken as a homestead, or any contract touching the same, or lien thereon, created

prior to the date of such patent, shall be null and void. And the sums agreed to be paid by the United States as purchase money for any portion of any such reservation shall be held in the Treasury of the United States for the sole use of the tribe or tribes of Indians; to whom such reservations belonged; and the same, with interest thereon at three percent per annum, shall be at all times subject to appropriation by Congress for the education and civilization of such tribe or tribes of Indians or the members thereof. The patents aforesaid shall be recorded in the General Land Office, and afterwards delivered, free of charge, to the allottee entitled thereto. And if any religious society or other organization is now occupying any of the public lands to which this act is applicable, for religious or educational work among the Indians, the Secretary of the Interior is hereby authorized to confirm such occupation to such society or organization, in quantity not exceeding one hundred and sixty acres in any one tract, so long as the same shall be so occupied, on such terms as he shall deem just; but nothing herein contained shall change or alter any claim of such society for religious or educational purposes heretofore granted by law. And hereafter in the employment of Indian police, or any other employees in the public service among any of the Indian tribes or bands affected by this act, and where Indians can perform the duties required, those Indians who have availed themselves of the provisions of this act and become citizens of the United States shall be preferred.

SECTION VI
That upon the completion of said allotments and the presenting of the lands to said allottees, each and every member of the respective bands or tribes of Indians to whom allotments have been made shall have the benefit of and be subject to the laws, both civil and criminal, of the State or Territory in which they may reside; and no Territory shall pass or enforce any law denying any such Indian within its jurisdiction the equal protection of the law. And every Indian born within the territorial limits of the United States to whom allotments shall have been made under the provisions of this act, or under any law or treaty, and every Indian born within the territorial limits of the United States who has voluntarily taken up, within said limits, his residence separate and apart from any tribe of Indians therein, and has adopted the habits of civilized life, is hereby declared to be a citizen of the United States, and is entitled to all the rights, privileges, and immunities of such citizens, whether said Indians have been or not, by birth or otherwise, a member of any tribe of Indians within the territorial limits of the United States without in any manner impairing or otherwise affecting the right of any such Indian to tribal or other property.

SECTION VII
That in cases where the use of water for irrigation is necessary to render the lands within any Indian reservation available for agricultural purposes, the Secretary of the Interior be, and he is hereby, authorized to prescribe such rules and regulations as he may deem necessary to secure a just and equal distribution thereof among the Indians residing upon any such reservation; and no other appropriation or grant of water

by any riparian proprietor shall be authorized or permitted to the damage of any other riparian proprietor.

SECTION VIII
That the provisions of this act shall not extend to the territory occupied by the Cherokees, Creeks, Choctaws, Chickasaws, Seminoles, and Osage, Miamies and Perorias, and Sacs and Foxes, in the Indian Territory, nor to any of the reservations of the Seneca Nation of New York Indians in the State of New York, nor to that strip of territory in the State of Nebraska adjoining the Sioux Nation on the south added by executive order.

SECTION IX
That for the purpose of making the surveys and resurveys mentioned in section two of this act, there be, and hereby is, appropriated, out of moneys in the Treasury not otherwise appropriated, the sum of one hundred thousand dollars, to be repaid proportionately out of the proceeds of the sales of such land as may be acquired from the Indians under the provisions of this act.

SECTION X
That noting in this act contained shall be so construed as to affect the right and power of Congress to grant the right of way through any lands granted to an Indian, or tribe of Indians, for railroads or other highways, or telegraph lines, for the public use, or to condemn such lands to public use upon making just compensation.

SECTION XI
That nothing in this act shall be so construed as to prevent the removal of the Southern Ute Indians from their present reservation in Southwestern Colorado to a new reservation by and with the consent of a majority of the adult male members of said tribe.
Approved, February 8, 1887.[30]
The 1977 Final Report of the American Indian Policy Review Commission provided the following assessment of the Dawes Act:

Land Allotment—Disaster in the Making
That the allotment policy was a mistake was apparent shortly after its authorization. The effect of the legislation was almost exactly what its critics anticipated—it became an efficient device for separating Indians from their land and pauperizing them. Reservation after reservation was surveyed and allotted, even where insufficient rainfall made farming a precarious enterprise at best. So-called surplus lands, often at the behest and sometimes as a result of the coercion of Indian Service officials, was sold without tribal consent to the Federal Government and opened to white settlement. Funds from the sale of these lands were held in the U.S. Treasury and used by the Government to purchase farm and ranch equipment and supplies, provide education and welfare and sundry other purposes which in many cases, were

to have been provided under treaties still in effect between the tribes and the United States.

When Indians particularly in the Plains States resisted the effort to convert them into farmers on their allotted acres, Congress amended the Dawes Act to permit the leasing of lands not being farmed or grazed. Enterprising white farmers and ranchers took advantage of the allottees who might not be aware of the worth of their lands and negotiated leases at ridiculously low prices. This action prompted another layer of bureaucratic control to regulate and oversee Indian land leasing procedures.

The Burke Act of 1906 further amended the Dawes Act to permit the Secretary of Interior to bypass the trust period restrictions and issue "certificates of competency" to Indians declared by him to be "competent." As soon as the amendment became law, anxious creditors and land buyers were on hand to help allottees make out applications and prepare the necessary affidavits, showing competency in land matters and evidence of habits of civilized life. And when the certificates were issued, the same creditors and land-buyers were on hand to purchase the land from the Indian owners.

In this way and through other devices in the law, the best of Indian land passed into white ownership. First to be lost were agricultural and grasslands, virgin timber acreage, and land with potential water and mineral resources. As William T. Hagan has observed: "Severalty may not have civilized the Indian but it definitely corrupted most the white men who had any contact with it."

In 1887, Indian tribes collectively owned about 140 million acres of land. The Dawes Act as amended in succeeding years set up the mechanisms whereby some 90 million acres passed into white ownership before the policy was abandoned some 45 years later.[31]

The Dawes Act was followed with a number of similar acts leading to the creation of the State of Oklahoma and the dissolving of Indian Territory, that was created as a refuge for removed tribes. As a method of more stringent control in Indian Country, Congress in July 1892 allowed for the president of the United States to appoint officers of the U.S. Army to serve as Indian agents. The 1898 Curtis Act effectively destroyed tribal governments and opened tribal lands to outsiders for mineral exploitation. And, as mentioned, in May 1906, the Burke Act further reduced the length of federal protection for Indian allottees, making their holdings ripe for white exploitation. Then in March 1907, Congress, through the Lacey Act, authorized the allotment and distribution of Indian tribal funds. Eleven months later, Oklahoma became the 46th state. In November 1919 Congress allowed American Indians who fought in World War I to petition for federal citizenship. In June 1924 Congress granted federal citizenship to all Indians born in the

United States who were not already citizens. The federal government now felt that it had finally rid itself of the pesky Indian problem.[32]

The Individual Indian Money Fund Scandal

One of the major Indian issues and scandals today is that of the mismanagement of the Individual Indian Money (IIM) fund, which was an outgrowth of the Dawes Act. In 1996, Eloise Pepion Cobell, a member of the Blackfeet tribe, initiated one of the largest class-action suits in the United States. The suit was filed with the aid of the Native American Rights Fund (NARF) on June 10, 1996. In describing the suit, John Echohawk, executive director of NARF, noted: "The Bureau of Indian Affairs has spent more than 100 years mismanaging, diverting and losing money that belongs to Indians. They have no idea how much has been collected from the companies that use our land and are unable to provide even a basic, regular statement to Indian account holders. Every day the system remains broken, hundreds of thousands of Indians are losing more and more money."[33]

What complicates this matter is that the Department of the Interior approves all leases of both individual and tribal resources in Indian Country. The law also requires Indians to use the federal government as their bank, creating a situation where these transactions occur without Indian input or oversight. This issue was addressed in the introduction to the memorandum decision in *Eloise Pepion Cobell, et al. v. Bruce Babbitt, Secretary of the Interior, Lawrence Summers, Secretary of the Treasury, and Kevin Gover, Assistant Secretary of the Interior*:

> It would be difficult to find a more historically mismanaged federal program than the Individual Indian Money (IIM) trust. The United States, the trustee of the IIM trust, cannot say how much is or should be in the trust. As the trustee admitted on the eve of the trial, it cannot render an accurate accounting to the beneficiaries, contrary to a specific statutory mandate and the century-old obligation to do so. More specifically, as Secretary Babbitt testified, an accounting cannot be rendered for most of the 300,000-plus beneficiaries, who are now plaintiffs in this lawsuit. Generations of IIM trust beneficiaries have been born and raised with the assurance that their trustee, the United States, was acting properly with their money. Just as many generations have been denied any such proof, however. "If courts were permitted to indulge their sympathies, a case better calculated to excite them could scarcely imagined." *Cherokee Nation v. Georgia*, 30 U.S. (5 Pet.) 1, 15 (1831) (Marshall, C.J.).[34]

The court-appointed monitor reported to the court that the then secretary of the interior, Gale Norton, had presented compulsory reports that were untruthful, leading to a contempt charge being leveled against her that placed her in the same situation as her predecessor, Bruce Babbitt. NARF also notified the presiding Judge, Royce C. Lamberth, that sixteen Federal Reserve Banks, including the New York Federal Reserve Bank, had been destroying Indian trust account documents in violation of the federal court order.

Since the 1996 IIM fund class action, other tribes have looked at their trust funds for evidence of corruption and shady deals between U.S. corporations and the federal government. The Navajo Nation discovered secret deals between the Department of the Interior and Peabody Coal on their reservation. The Navajo claim in their suit that these illegal actions greatly restricted fair market royalties for coal taken from the Navajo Nation. This suit involves some $600 million. These issues have led to considerable distrust of the federal government and its trust responsibilities in Indian Country. Many tribes see these blatant abuses as contributing factors to the social and health problems long plaguing Indian Country. It is felt by many Native Americans that inadequately funded programs are due to a severe shortfall of resources guaranteed by treaties and Acts of Congress, including the IIM fund. A 2006 NARF update on the Indian class-action suit states:

> The government has appealed Judge Lamberth's structural injunction requiring the Interior defendants to conduct a historical accounting of the IIM trust and to provide plaintiffs with an accurate accounting of all funds held in trust. In light of certain recent developments, plaintiffs took an uncommon approach to this appeal. In recent filings, the government admitted, for the first time, that it was impossible for the government to provide the complete and accurate accounting by law. This, of course, has been our position for years—that as a result of the massive destruction of trust documents in breach of fundamental fiduciary duties and other malfeasance, it is simply not possible for the government to ever provide the accounting required by law. When the government confessed this, there was no longer a reason or justification to require the Interior Department to perform an act of futility. Accordingly, we asked that the Court of Appeals to remand the case to the District Court for a determination of whether an accounting is even possible in light of the overwhelming evidence that it is not. Such a determination would permit the District Court sitting in equity to utilize a methodology consistent with trust law to correct and restate account balances for each IIM Trust Beneficiary. The Court of Appeals for the District of Columbia heard oral argument on September 16, 2005. We await a decision.
> . . .

On July 20, Chairman McCain introduced a bill that he called a starting point for discussion. Among other things, it called for a settlement fund in the billions of dollars—but did not specify a number for the historical accounting claim. Chairman McCain stated that the future discussions would be held with the parties and hopefully reach a consensus number for the settlement. There are some serious deficiencies with the bill as currently structured, but NARF continues to work with Hill staff to address these concerns and create a bill that will lead to resolution in a fair manner. Plaintiffs continue to seek prompt resolution of the Cobell case, but we will not sacrifice fairness on the altar of political expediency to the detriment of the plaintiff class of 500,000 individual Indians.[35]

Chapter Four
Indian Reorganization
Preserving Indian Country

Introduction: The Pueblo Land Scandal as a Catalyst for Government Reform in Indian Country

Report on Allotment by the Indian Policy Review Commission
The 1977 Indian Policy Review Commission summed up the corruption and failures associated with the Dawes (Allotment) Act:

> The greatest threat to Indian survival resulted from the land policy imposed by the General Allotment Act of 1887, which in the years following its enactment reduced Indian land holdings in total disregard of future Indian needs. The damage was not confined to a shrinking land base, however; Indian social organization, belief systems, and moral vigor were all related to land, to a universe defined by myth and ritual.
>
> In brief summary: The preceding 100 years had wrought incalculable damage to Indians, their property, and their societies. Tribes had been moved about like livestock until, in some cases, the original homeland was no more than a legend in the minds of old men and women. Children had been removed from the family, by force at times, and kept in close custody until they lost their mother tongue and all knowledge of who they were, while parents often did not know where the children had been taken or whether they even lived. Tribal religious practices, when they were not proscribed outright, were treated as obscenities. Land losses, as noted, were catastrophic, while the failure of Government to provide economic tools and training for proper land use left the remaining holdings untenable or leased to white farmers at starvation rates. The bureaucratic structure had penetrated the entire fabric of Indian life, usurping the tribal decision making function, demeaning local leadership, obtruding into the family—and yet was totally oblivious of its inadequacies and its inhumanity.

Stirrings of Conscience
The failure of the Federal Government as trustee had become so notorious by the 1920's as to compel public action. The Pueblo Lands Board Act of 1924 and Osage Guardianship Act of 1925 gave notice of a new mood in Congress. Both Acts came about in response to public outcry against intolerable exploitation of Indian resources. This was followed by a more general demand for reform, which in 1926 led President Coolidge's Secretary of the Interior, Hubert Work, to request the privately endowed Institute for Government Research (later the Brookings Institution) to in-

vestigate the conditions of Indian life. The investigation resulted in the report of Lewis Meriam and Associates, entitled—"The Problem of Indian Administration"—published in 1928.[1]

The Pueblo tribes of New Mexico played a major role in forcing a reexamination of federal Indian policies following the abuses associated with allotment. The Pueblo Indians were the only tribe to successfully drive back European colonists in North America, doing so during the revolt of 1680. Here, the Pueblo tribes of New Mexico and the Hopi Pueblo tribe of Arizona, with the exception of the Piros Pueblo tribe, drove the Spanish from their traditional lands. This impasse with the Spanish lasted twelve years, resulting in, first, Spanish and, later, Mexican recognition of their autonomy. The Spanish Crown solidified this pact by issuing the Pueblos land grants. Mexico not only continued to recognize the Pueblo Indian land grants; they proclaimed all residents of Mexico, regardless of race, to hold citizen status. The Treaty of Guadalupe Hidalgo that settled the United States' land grab from Mexico in 1848 cited in Article 8 that residents of the newly acquired territory ceded to the United States had one year either to retain their Mexican citizenship status or to become U.S. citizens. None of the Pueblo Indian tribes elected to retain Mexican citizenship since they felt that they were autonomous Indians living on traditional lands that existed long before European or American occupation. Complicating matters, the Pueblo Indian tribes were exempt from the dictates of allotment, setting the stage for the U.S. Supreme Court decision in 1913 in *United States v. Sandoval*, which was filed initially over a law concerning the State of New Mexico's authority to regulate liquor laws in Indian Country:

The Sandoval decision regarding Federal authority over Pueblo tribes
The Court overruled a federal district court decision that a law making it a crime to introduce intoxicating liquor into Indian country was inapplicable to New Mexico Pueblos. The question was whether the Pueblo lands were "Indian country" over which the legislative authority of Congress extends. The Pueblos' lands, unlike Indian reservations, were owned communally in fee simple by the Pueblos under grants from the Spanish government, later confirmed by Congress.

The question to be considered, then, is, whether the status of the Pueblo Indians and their lands is such that Congress competently can prohibit the introduction of intoxicating liquor into those lands notwithstanding the admission of New Mexico to statehood.

The people of the pueblos, although sedentary rather than nomadic in their inclinations, and disposed to peace and industry, are nevertheless Indians in race, custom, and domestic government. Always living in separate and isolated communities, adhering to primitive modes of life, largely influenced by superstition and fetishism, and chiefly governed according to the crude customs inherited from their ancestors, they are essentially a simple, uninformed and inferior people. . . .

It is not necessary to dwell specially upon the legal status of this people under either Spanish or Mexican rule, for whether Indian communities within the limits of the United States may be subjected to its guardianship and protection as dependent wards turns upon other considerations. Not only does the Constitution expressly authorize Congress to regulate commerce with the Indian tribes, but long continued legislative and executive usage and an unbroken current of judicial decisions have attributed to the United States as a superior and civilized nation the power and the duty of exercising a fostering care and protection over all dependent Indian communities within its borders, whether within it original territory or territory subsequently acquired, and whether within or without the limits of a State. . . .

As before indicated, by a uniform course of action beginning as early as 1854 and continued up to the present time, the legislative and executive branches of the Government have regarded and treated the Pueblos of New Mexico as dependent communities entitled to its aid and protection, like other Indian tribes, and considering their Indian lineage, isolated and communal life, primitive customs and limited civilization, this assertion of guardianship over them cannot be said to be arbitrary but must be regarded as both authorized and controlling.

It is said that such legislation cannot be made to embrace the Pueblos, because they are citizens. As before stated, whether they are citizens is an open question, and we need not determine it now, because citizenship is not in itself an obstacle to the exercise by Congress of its power to enact laws for the benefit and protection of tribal Indians as a dependent people. . . . Considering the reasons which underlie the authority of Congress to prohibit the introduction of liquor into the Indian country at all, its seems plain that this authority is sufficiently comprehensive to enable Congress to apply the prohibition to the lands of the Pueblos.[2]

As stated, the nineteen Pueblo tribes were initially exempt from allotment. When it was granted statehood in 1912, New Mexico attempted to change their status so as to create more surplus land and to exploit the timber and other natural resources located on the Indian pueblos. The 1913 *Sandoval* decision made it clear that federal status now applied to the Pueblo tribes. This opened the door for a New Mexican land baron, Albert Bacon Fall, in his capacity as secretary of the interior under President Warren G. Harding, to attempt to dissolve the Pueblo tribes so that he and his colleagues could gain access to their lands and resources. Fall and the commissioner of Indian affairs, Charles H. Burke, attempted to get Congress to force the Pueblo tribes to forfeit their aboriginal lands under the pretext of attacking their traditional ritual and customs as being evil, anti-Christian beliefs. This plan was devised by Secretary of the Interior A.B. Fall and Holm O. Bursum. U.S. Senator from New Mexico. The Fall/Bursum ploy was spelled out in the 1922 *Bursum Bill:*

The Fall/Bursum Pueblo land grab scam
Be it enacted . . ., Jurisdiction of the District of the United States for the District of New Mexico over criminal and civil cases involving the Pueblos.

Section 7. That all persons or corporations who, prior to and since the date of the ratification and proclamation of the treaty of Guadalupe Hidalgo, July 4, 1848 either in person or through their predecessors, in claim of interest, grantors, privies, or agents, have had actual, open, notorious, exclusive, and continuous possession, under color of title, of, in or to any lands included within the exterior boundaries of any grant of land confirmed or patented to any of the pueblos hereinbefore named by the United States of America, shall be entitled to a decree in their respective favor for all of the lands so possessed, and the district court shall, by its decree, segregate the said land from the said pueblo grant, and shall ascertain and adjudicate the true boundaries and extent thereof, in the proof of which character of possession and of the boundaries and extend thereof secondary evidence shall be admissible and competent. Upon the entry of any decree segregating any of the lands of any pueblo grant pursuant to the provisions and requirements of this paragraph, the clerk of the said court shall forthwith send to the Secretary of the Interior of the United States a certified copy of said decree, and the said tract of land so segregated having been surveyed by or under his direction, according to the boundaries and extent as set forth in said decree, said Secretary of the Interior shall cause patent therefor to be issued to said person, his heirs or assigns, or to such corporation or its successors in interests. In all cases arising under the provisions of this act wherein the original title and the adverse possession thereunder antedates the dates of ratification and proclamation of the treaty of Guadalupe Hidalgo, the remedy, relief, and procedure in this paragraph provided shall be exclusive and either party to any suit brought pursuant to the provisions of this act may made proof of data and source of title and the possession thereunder.

Section 8. That all persons who, or corporations which, for more than 10 years prior to June 20, 1910, either in person or through their respective predecessors in claim of interests, grantors, privies, or agents, have had actual, open notorious, exclusive and continuous possession, with or without color of title, of any land falling or included within the exterior boundaries of any grant confirmed or patented to any of the pueblos in this act specified, and all persons who or corporations which in person or through their respective predecessors in claim of interest or grantors claim any such lands lying within the exterior boundaries of any of said pueblo grants under valid grant from the Government of Spain or Mexico, or under any grant, act of confirmation of patent of the United States of America, shall be entitled to a decree in their favor respectively for the whole of the lands so claimed, and the district court shall in its decree segregate the said land from the said pueblo grant and shall ascertain and adjudicate the area and extend thereof and the value of the said lands without improvement if any there shall be thereon, as of the date of the decree, and upon the entry of any decree provided for in this paragraph segregating any of the lands of any pueblo grant therefrom, the clerk of the district court shall forthwith send to the Secretary of the Interior of the United States of America a certified copy of the final decree, and, thereupon, the Secretary of the Interior shall cause to be surveyed from the public lands of the United States of America a tract or tracts of land as nearly adjacent to the said pueblo as possible, equal in area and value or equal in value to the lands so segregated in said final decree and shall cause patent therefore to be issued to the pueblo entitled thereto: but if it be found that such lands are not available then the Secretary of the Interior shall place to the credit of the said pueblo the value of the said land so segregated in cash as provided in said adjudication, and shall disburse the same to the best advantage and interest of the said pueblo.

Section 9. That the Secretary of the Interior shall promulgate all necessary rules and regulations relative to the selection of such lieu lands to be patented to any pueblo as in this act provided, and all necessary surveys, field notes, and plats made or necessary in ascertaining the extent of any area of any land to be segregated from any pueblo shall be made under the direction of the surveyor general of the United States for New Mexico upon instructions to that effect from the Secretary of the Interior, without cost to litigants...

Section 15. That surveys of lands within pueblo grants and reservations held and occupied by persons not Indian, or corporations, as heretofore made under the supervision of the surveyor general for New Mexico, and plats and field notes of which have been filed in his office, shall be accepted as prima facie evidence of the boundaries of lands therein described.[3]

Bursum's bill passed the U.S. Senate, but public outcry caused it to fail in the U.S. House of Representatives. Fall came to represent the type of unscrupulous federal official who was willing to use his trust position for personal gain. Fall had a notorious reputation long before joining the Harding administration as secretary of the interior in 1921. Earlier he was implicated in the 1896 disappearance of one of his ranching competitors, Colonel Albert Jennings Fountain, and his son. This notoriety made him a favorite of the Anglo politicians in this highly Hispanic and Native American territory. He went on to serve as a Republican in the Territorial Legislature, was appointed an associate justice of the New Mexico Territorial Supreme Court, served as New Mexico's attorney general for two terms, and served as one of the new state's first senators (1912–1921). The Teapot Dome scandal overshadowed Fall's anti-Indian actions, making him the first cabinet-level official to be convicted and sentenced to prison for his actions. Here, Fall conspired with Harry F. Sinclair, head of the Mammoth Oil Corporation, and Edward L. Doheny, head of the Pan-American Petroleum and Transport Company, to get the lucrative Naval Reserve contract, with a kickback in the order of hundreds of thousands of dollars given to Fall. Fall served a year in prison but avoided paying the $100,000 fine, despite having a substantial ranch in southeastern New Mexico and a home in El Paso. A.B. Fall's actions led to the creation of Title 25 of the United States Code in 1926 spelling out legal procedures relevant to Indian Country. It also led to reforms initiated by his successor as secretary of the interior, Hubert Work, under President Calvin Coolidge.

New Deal Indian Policies: Establishing Contemporary Tribal Standards

The Meriam Report: Promoting Education as a Tool for Forced Assimilation
The Meriam Report, issued in 1928, was the result of a study Hubert Work initiated with the Institute for Government Research (now the Brookings Institution):

> The fundamental requirement is that the task of the Indian Service be recognized as primarily educational, in the broadest sense of that word, and that it be made an efficient educational agency, devoting its main energies to the social and economic advancement of the Indians, so that they may be absorbed into the prevailing civilization or to be fitted to live in the presence of that civilization at least in accordance with a minimum standard of health and decency.
>
> To achieve this end the Service must have a comprehensive, well-rounded educational program, adequately supported, which will place it at the forefront of organizations devoted to the advancement of a people. This program must provide for the promotion of health, the advancement of productive efficiency, the acquisition of reasonable ability in the utilization of income and property, guarding against exploitation, and the maintenance of reasonably high standards of family and community life. It must extend to adults as well as to children and must place special emphasis on the family and the community. Since the great majority of the Indians are ultimately to merge into the general population, it should cover the transitional period and should endeavor to instruct Indians in the utilization of the services provided by public and quasi public agencies for the people at large in exercising the privileges of citizenship and in making their contribution in service and in taxes for the maintenance of the government. It should also be directed toward preparing white communities to receive the Indians. By improving the health of the Indian, increasing his productive efficiency, raising his standard of living, and teaching him the necessity for paying taxes, it will remove the main objections now advanced against permitting Indians to receive the full benefit of services rendered by progressive states and local governments for their populations. By actively seeking coopera-

tion with state and local governments and by making a fair contribution in payment for services rendered by them to untaxed Indians, the national government can expedite the transition and hasten the day when there will no longer be a distinctive Indian problem and when the necessary governmental services are rendered alike to whites and Indians by the same organization without discrimination.

In the execution of this program scrupulous care must be exercised to respect the rights of the Indian. This phrase "rights of the Indian" is often used solely to apply to his property rights. Here it is used in a much broader sense to cover his rights as a human being living in a free country. Indians are entitled to unfailing courtesy and consideration from all government employees. They should not be subjected to arbitrary action. Recognition of the educational leadership for the more dictatorial methods now used in some places will necessitate more understanding of and sympathy for the Indian point of view. Leadership will recognize the good in the economic and social life of the Indians in their religion and ethics, and will seek to develop it and build on it rather than to crush out all that is Indian. The Indians have much to contribute to the dominant civilization, and the effort should be made to secure this contribution, in part because of the good it will do the Indians in stimulating a proper race pride and self respect....

The Object of Work with or for the Indians. The object of work with or for the Indians is to fit them either to merge into the social and economic life of the prevailing civilization as developed by the whites or to live in the presence of that civilization at least in accordance with a minimum standard of health and decency. The first of these alternatives is apparently so clear on its face as to require no further explanation. The second, however, demands some further explanation.

Some Indians proud of their race and devoted to their culture and their mode of life have no desire to be as the white man is. They wish to remain Indians, to preserve what they have inherited from their fathers, and insofar as possible to escape from the ever increasing contact with and pressure from the white civilization. In this desire they are supported by intelligent, liberal whites who find real merit in their art, music, religion, form of government, and other things which may be covered by the broad term culture. Some of these whites would even go so far, metaphorically speaking, as to enclose these Indians in a glass case to preserve them as museum specimens for future generations to study and enjoy, because of the value of their culture and its picturesqueness in world rapidly advancing in high organization and mass production. With this view as a whole if not in its extremities, the survey staff has great sympathy. It would not recommend the disastrous attempt to force individual Indians or groups of Indians to be what they do not want to be, to break their pride in themselves and their Indian race, or to deprive them of their Indian culture. Such efforts may break down the good in the old without replacing it with compensating good from the new.

The fact remains, however, that the hands of the clock cannot be turned backward. These Indians are face to face with the predominating civilization of the whites. This advancing tide of white civilization has as a rule largely destroyed the economic foundation upon which the Indian culture rested. This economic foundation cannot be restored as it was. The Indians cannot be set apart away from contacts with the whites. The glass case policy is impracticable. . . .

The position taken, therefore, is that the work with and for the Indians must give consideration to the desires of the individual Indians. He who wishes to merge into the social and economic life of the prevailing civilization of this country should be given all practicable aid and advice in making the necessary adjustments. He who wants to remain an Indian and live according to his old culture should be aided in doing so. The question may be raised "Why aided? Just leave him alone and he will take care of himself." The fact is, however, as has been pointed out, that the old economic basis of his culture has been to a considerable extent destroyed and new problems have been forced upon him by contacts with the whites. Adjustments have to be made, economic, social and legal. Under social is included health. The advent of white civilization has forced on the Indians new problems of health and sanitation that they, unaided can no more solve that can a few city individuals solve municipal problems. The presence of their villages in close proximity to white settlements make the health and sanitary conditions in those villages public questions of concern to the entire section. Both the Indians and their white neighbors are concerned in having those Indians who want to stay Indians and preserve their culture, live according to at least a minimum standard of health and decency. Less than that means not only that they themselves will go through a long drawn out and painful process of vanishing. They must be aided for the preservation of themselves.

Whichever way the individual Indian may elect to face, work in his behalf must be designed not to do for him but to help him to do for himself. The whole problem must be regarded as fundamentally educational. However much the early policy of rationing may have been necessary as a defensive, preventive war measure on the part of the whites, it worked untold harm to the Indians because it was pauperizing and lacked any appreciable educational value. Anything else done for them in a way that neglects educating them to do for themselves will work in the same direction. Controlling the expenditure of individual Indian money, for example, is pauperizing unless the work is so done that the Indian is being educated to control his own. In every activity of the Indian Service the primary question should be, how is the Indian to be trained so that he will do this for himself. Unless this question can be clearly and definitely answered by an affirmative showing of distinct educational purposes and method the chances are that the activity is impeding rather than helping the advancement of the Indian. . . .[4]

Lauded as the prelude to humanistic reform in Indian Country, the Meriam Report was hardly the objective and balanced assessment it pretended to present. Indeed, it was a biased justification of white supremacy shrouded in the moral superiority of the Protestant Ethic and the inferiority of aboriginal traditionalism (the Harmony Ethos). These contradictory themes are woven throughout the assessment report. Individualism is flaunted as being superior to collectivism, hence providing unassailable support for the dominant white society at the expense of tribalism. Moreover, this moral imperative argument justifies the self-fulfilling prophecy of stealing Indian lands, breaking treaty promises, practicing cultural genocide, and destroying tribal culture and customs. Here, the Indian is blamed for this destruction leveled against tribalism and the ensuring dependency this practice fostered. The cultural attribution bias is most evident in the "glass case policy" discussion, where a lame attempt is made to pretend to seriously consider the argument put forth by whites that supported tribalism. This is evident in the following statement:

> The fact remains . . . that the hands of the clock cannot be turned backward. These Indians are faced with the predominating civilization of the whites. This advancing tide of white civilization has as a rule largely destroyed the economic foundation upon which the Indian culture rested. This economic foundation cannot be restored as it was. The Indian cannot be set apart away from contacts with the whites. The glass case policy is impracticable.[5]

Running throughout the report is the euphemism for forced assimilation with greater white control and exploitation in Indian Country—education. Through Euro-American-style education the Indian can be psychologically separated from his/her collective tribal conscience and held accountable for taxes and laws before an obviously biased white justice system.

Clearly, the end result of this form of education is to inculcate within American Indians the fact that they are inferior to whites as well as to foster a sense of their limited capacity to manage their own lives, hence further justifying outside control over their living standards, value systems, and resources. This manifesto set the stage for the "progressive" actions under the Indian Reorganization Act—actions that ultimately served to save tribalism from the destructive abuses associated with the combined forces of removal and allotment. Ironically, it also provided the basis for the devastating attempts at cultural genocide during the Eisenhower presidency—termination and relocation.

The Johnson–O'Malley Act

The Johnson–O'Malley Act set the stage for the institution of viable, ongoing health, education, and social welfare programs in Indian Country. This was a federal–state initiative. It preceded the Wheeler–Howard Indian Reorganization Act, the foundation piece of the F.D. Roosevelt administration, by two months.

Be it enacted..., That the Secretary of the Interior is hereby authorized, in his discretion, to enter into a contract or contracts with any State or Territory having legal authority so to do, for the education, medical attention, agricultural assistance, and social welfare, including the relief of distress, of Indians in such State or Territory, through the qualified agencies of such State or Territory, and to expend under such contract or contracts moneys appropriated by Congress for the education, medical assistance, agricultural assistance, and social welfare, including the relief of distress, of Indians in such State.

Section 2. That the Secretary of the Interior, in making any contract herein authorized with any State or Territory, may permit such State or Territory to utilize for the purpose of this Act, existing school buildings, hospitals, and other facilities, and all equipment therein or appertaining thereto, including livestock and other personal property owned by the Government, under such terms and conditions as may be agreed upon for their use and maintenance.

Section 3. That the Secretary is hereby authorized to perform any and all acts and to make such rules and regulations, including minimum standards of service, as may be necessary and proper for the purpose of carrying the provisions of this Act into effect. *Provided,* That such minimum standards of service are not less than the highest maintained by the States or Territories with which said contract or contracts, as herein provided, are executed.

Section 4. That the Secretary of the Interior shall report annually to the Congress any contract or contracts made under the provisions of this Act, and the moneys expended thereunder.

Section 5. That the provisions of this Act shall not apply to the State of Oklahoma.[6]

John Collier's Legacy: The Indian Reorganization Act

The path to reform in Indian Country was initiated by Coolidge's secretary of the interior, but it was F.D. Roosevelt's selection of John Collier as Indian commissioner under interior secretary Harold Ickes that forged dramatic changes designed to save what remained of the Indian tribes in America. F.D.R.'s sentiments differed from those of his distant relative and former president Theodore Roosevelt, who saw general allotment as a "mighty pulverizing engine to break up the tribal mass."[7] Collier saw that the sole purpose of the allotment policy was to undermine the tribal sovereignty principles established under Chief Justice Marshall. The Indian Reorganization Act attempted to reverse these attempts at tribal annihilation:

An Act to conserve and develop Indian lands and resources; to extend to Indians the right to form business and other organizations; to establish a credit system for Indians; to grant certain rights of home rule to Indians; to provide for vocational education for Indians; and for other purposes.

Be it enacted . . ., That hereafter no land of any Indian reservation, created or set apart by treaty or agreement with the Indians, Act of Congress, Executive order, purchase, or otherwise, shall be allotted in severalty to any Indian....

Section 2. The existing periods of trust placed upon any Indian lands and any restriction on alienation thereof are hereby extended and continued until otherwise directed by Congress.

Section 3. The Secretary of the Interior, if he shall find it to be in the public interest, is hereby authorized to restore to tribal ownership the remaining surplus lands to any Indian reservation heretofore opened, or authorized to be opened, to sale, or any other form of disposal by Presidential proclamation, or by any of the public land laws of the United States: *Provided, however,* That valid rights or claims of any persons to any lands so withdrawn existing on the date of the withdrawal shall not be affected by this Act....

Section 4. Except as herein provided, no sale, devise, gift, exchange or other transfer of restricted Indian lands or of shares in the assets of any Indian tribe or corporation organized hereunder, shall be made or approved: *Provided, however,* That such lands or interests may, with the approval of the Secretary of the Interior, be sold, devised, or otherwise transferred to the Indian tribe in which the lands or shares are located or from which the shares were derived or to a successor corporation; and in all instances such lands or interests shall descend or be devised, in accordance with the then existing laws of the State, or Federal laws where applicable, in which said lands are located or in which the subject matter of the corporation is located, to any member of such tribe or of such corporation or any heirs of such member: *Provided further,* That the Secretary of the Interior may authorize voluntary exchanges of lands of equal value and the voluntary exchange, in his judgment, is expedient and beneficial for or compatible with the proper consolidation of Indian lands and for the benefit of cooperative organizations.

Section 5. The Secretary of the Interior is hereby authorized, in his discretion, to acquire through purchase, relinquishment, gift, exchange, or assignment, any interest in lands, water rights or surface rights to lands, within or without existing reservations, including trust or otherwise restricted allotments whether the allottee be living or deceased, for the purpose of providing land for Indians....

Title to any lands or rights acquired pursuant to this Act shall be taken in the name of the United States in trust for the Indian tribe or individual Indian for which the land is acquired, and such lands or rights shall be exempt from State and local taxation.

Section 6. The Secretary of the Interior is directed to make rules and regulations for the operation and management of Indian forestry units on the principle of sustained yield management, to restrict the number of livestock grazed on Indian range units to the estimated carrying capacity of such ranges, and to promulgate such other rules and regulations as may be necessary to protect the range from deterioration, to prevent soil erosion, to assure full utilization of the range, and like purposes.

Section 7. The Secretary of the Interior is hereby authorized to proclaim new Indian reservations on lands acquired pursuant to any authority conferred by this

Act, or to add such lands to existing reservations: *Provided,* That lands added to existing reservations shall be designated for the exclusive use of Indians entitled by enrollment or by tribal membership to residence at such reservations.

Section 8. Nothing contained in this Act shall be construed to relate to Indian holdings of allotments or homesteads upon the public domain outside of the geographic boundaries of any Indian reservation now existing or established hereafter.

Section 9. There is hereby authorized to be appropriated, out of any funds in the Treasury not otherwise appropriated, such sums as may be necessary, but not to exceed $250,000 in any fiscal year, to be expended at the order of the Secretary of the Interior, in defraying the expenses of organizing Indian chartered corporations or other organizations created under this Act.

Section 10. There is hereby authority to be appropriated, out of any funds in the Treasury not otherwise appropriated, the sum of $10,000,000 to be established as a revolving fund from which the Secretary of the Interior, under such rules and regulations as he may prescribe, may make loans to Indian chartered corporations for the purpose of promoting the economic development of such tribes and of their members, and may defray the expenses of administering such loans. Repayment of amounts loaned under this authorization shall be available for the purposes for which the fund is established. A report shall be made annually to Congress of transactions under this authorization.

Section 11. There is hereby authorized to be appropriated, out of any funds in the United States Treasury not otherwise appropriated, a sum not to exceed $250,000 annually, together with any unexpended balances of previous appropriations made pursuant to this section, for loans to Indians for the payment of tuition and other expenses in recognized vocational and trade schools: *Provided,* That not more than $50,000 of such sum shall be available for loans to Indian students in high schools and colleges. Such loans shall be reimbursable under rules established by the Commissioner of Indian Affairs.

Section 12. The Secretary of the Interior is directed to establish standards of health, age, character, experience, knowledge, and ability for Indians who may be appointed, without regard to civil-service laws, to the various positions maintained, now or hereafter, by the Indian Office, in the administration of functions or services affecting any Indian tribe. Such qualified Indians shall hereafter have the preference to appointment to vacancies in any such position.

Section 13. The provisions of this Act shall not apply to any of the Territories, colonies, or insular possessions of the United States, except that sections 9, 10, 11, 12, and 16, shall apply to the Territory of Alaska: *Provided,* That Sections 2, 4, 7, 16, 17, and 18 of this Act shall not apply to the following named Indian tribes, the members of such Indian tribes, together with members of such Indian tribes, together with members of other tribes affiliated with such named tribes located in the State of Oklahoma, as follows: Cheyenne, Arapaho, Comanche, Kiowa, Caddo, Delaware, Wichita, Osage, Kaw, Otoe, Tonkawa, Pawnee, Ponca, Shawnee, Ottawa, Quapaw, Seneca, Wyandotte, Iowa, Sac and Fox, Kickapoo, Potawatomi,

Cherokee, Chickasaw, Choctaw, Creek, and Seminole. Section 4 of this Act shall not apply to the Indians of the Klamath Reservation in Oregon.

Section 14. [Similarly worded provision dealing with Sioux allotments.]

Section 15. Nothing in this Act shall be construed to impair or prejudice any claim or suit of any Indian tribe against the United States. It is hereby declared to be the intent of Congress that no expenditures for the benefit of Indians made out of appropriations authorized by this Act shall be considered as offsets in any suit brought to recover upon any claim of such Indians against the United States.

Section 16. Any Indian tribe, or tribes, residing on the same reservation, shall have the right to organize for its common welfare, and may adopt an appropriate constitution and bylaws, which shall become effective when ratified by a majority vote of the adult members of the tribe, or of the adult Indians residing on such reservation, as the case may be, at a special election authorized and called by the Secretary of the Interior under such rules and regulations as he may prescribe. Such constitution and bylaws when ratified as aforesaid and approved by the Secretary of the Interior shall be revocable by an election open to the same voters and conducted in the same manner as hereinabove provided. Amendments to the constitution and bylaws may be ratified and approved by the Secretary in the same manner as the original constitution and bylaws.

In addition to all powers vested in any Indian tribe or tribal council by existing law, the constitution adopted by said tribe shall also vest in such tribe or its tribal council the following rights and powers: To employ legal counsel, the choice of counsel and fixing of fees to be subject to the approval of the Secretary of the Interior; to prevent the sale, disposition, lease, or encumbrance of tribal lands, interests in lands, or other tribal assets without the consent of the tribe; and to negotiate with the Federal, State, and local Governments. The Secretary of the Interior shall advise such tribe or its tribal council of all appropriation estimates or Federal projects for the benefit of the tribe prior to the submission of such estimates to the Bureau of the Budget and the Congress.

Section 17. The Secretary of the Interior may, upon petition by at least one-third of the adult Indians, issue a charter of incorporation to such tribe: *Provided,* That such charter shall not become operative until ratified at a special election by a majority vote of the adult Indians living on the reservation. Such charter may convey to the incorporated tribe the power to purchase, take by gift, or bequest, or otherwise own, hold, manage, operate, and dispose of property of every description, real and personal, including the power to purchase restricted Indian lands and to issue in exchange therefor interests in corporate property, and such further powers as may be incidental to the conduct of corporate business, not inconsistent with law, but no authority shall be granted to sell, mortgage, or lease for a period exceeding ten years any of the land included in the limits of the reservation. Any charter so issued shall not be revoked or surrendered except by Act of Congress.

Section 18. This Act shall not apply to any reservation wherein a majority of the adult Indians, voting at a special election duly called by the Secretary of the Interior, shall vote against its application. It shall be the duty of the Secretary of the Interior, within one year after the passage and approval of this Act, to call such an election which election shall be held by secret ballot upon thirty days notice.

Section 19. The term "Indian" as used in this Act shall include all persons of Indian descent who are members of any recognized Indian tribe now under Federal jurisdiction, and all persons who are descendants of such members who were, on June 1, 1934, residing within the present boundaries of any Indian reservation and shall further include all other persons of one-half or more Indian blood. For the purposes of this Act, Eskimos and other aboriginal peoples of Alaska shall be considered Indians. The term "tribe" wherever used in this Act shall be construed to refer to any Indian tribe, organized band, pueblo, or the Indians residing on one reservation. The words "adult Indians" wherever used in this Act shall be construed to refer to Indians who have attained the age of twenty-one years.[8]

The Indian Reorganization Act (IRA, or Wheeler–Howard Act) established the rules for tribal government, standards that continue to the present. First and foremost the IRA cancelled the division of Indian Country into individual plots outside the traditional protection of tribal collectivism (see Sections 1–3). Section 4 placed curbs on reducing the remaining tribe-held lands, guaranteeing established boundaries along with federal trust protection against outside encroachment. Ironically, this section also reinforced the Department of the Interior's fiscal trust responsibilities for leased lands and mineral rights in Indian Country to outside interests, inadvertently contributing to the current trust suits against the federal government.

Section 7 is unique in that it authorized the secretary of the interior to purchase lands to add to existing tribal lands or to return prior tribal lands to tribes. The return of Standing Bear's original tribal lands to the Ponca in Nebraska is an example of the latter. Nonetheless, the significance of this section has sparked renewed interest since the 1980s and Congressional approval for Indian gaming.

Section 10 provided for federal support for Indian chartered corporations, yet another attempt at transforming tribal collectivism into Western capitalist corporate organizations—a concept seized upon by the Eisenhower administration in its attempt to dissolve Indian Country. Even then, it allowed tribes to establish gaming corporations so they could shelter this process from direct Department of the Interior and Bureau of Indian Affairs (BIA) interference.

Section 11 led to the establishment of Indian scholarships, a significant mechanism that led to the creation of an Indian middle class providing Indian teachers, doctors, and lawyers. This, plus the concept of "Indian preference" articulated in Section 12, has led to American Indians occupying many important positions in Indian Country at both the federal (BIA) and tribal levels. Today, we find increasing numbers of well-qualified Indian professionals working within the fields of Indian health, social services, Indian schools, law enforcement, and tribal law. The only similar federal employee advantage is that of "veteran's preference."

Sections 16–18 provided the framework for tribal government, a process modeled on the U.S. legislative format. While limited in its jurisdictional scope, tribal government became the norm, if only because it was compulsory for continued federal support. William Canby, in his *American Indian Law* primer, noted that the standard tribal or band constitution spelled out the governmental structure and its respective authority as well as allowances for developing tribe-specific amendments. The constitution also specified eligibility standards for membership. The basic unit of authority is a tribal council and its tribal chairman. Many tribes divided their constituency according to clan, town, or region. While the tribal chairman was the most common format of U.S.-approved tribal government under the IRA, chiefs, governors, and presidents also emerged in the tribal leadership format.[9]

The Cherokees adopted a U.S.-style constitution in the early 1800s prior to removal and continued with this format while in Indian Territory. The major difference here was that the federal government did not have ultimate authority over tribal governance as it does under IRA rules. Subsequently, the original Cherokee Nation's land-base was liquidated under allotment in 1887, and its form of government and judicial system was dissolved in 1898 under the Curtis Act. The Cherokees then became puppets of the federal government in that the Department of the Interior appointed their principal chief. Direct elections of their tribal leadership occurred in the 1970s under self-determination, with Ross Swimmer becoming the first tribally elected principal chief since allotment devastated the Cherokee Nation. His election was followed by that of the first Cherokee leader, Wilma Mankiller. The western Cherokees differ from most other tribes in that they do not have a minimum blood degree requirement for enrollment. You merely need to be related to someone on the official federal enrollment lists. This controversy continues to the present; in March 2006 the western Cherokees accepted as tribal members descendants of black slaves who were included in the Dawes Commission roll.

The Eastern Band of Cherokee Indians, those who managed to avoid the Trail of Tears, was one of the first Indian groups to adopt the IRA conditions, sans a constitution, doing so in 1934. The trust lands, known as the Qualla Boundary, consist of 56,571 acres in their traditional homeland in western North Carolina. All enrolled members qualified to vote (according to the U.S. age requirement) select a principal chief and vice chief at large for four-year terms. A twelve-member tribal council with two representatives from each of the six townships is elected for two-year terms. The tribal council elect, by vote, their tribal chairman. This division of tribal authority has continued since the adoption of IRA standards in 1934. In 1995, the Eastern Band elected their first female principal chief—Joyce C. Dugan. The Eastern Band currently requires one-eighth Qualla blood for membership in its rolls. In this they differ from their western counterparts, the United Keetoowha Band, those traditionalists who moved west prior to removal and who did not recognize the Cherokee Nation. They also accepted IRA conditions in 1934, electing their own chief and tribal council. They maintain a requirement of one-quarter blood from direct band descendants for membership.

The nineteen Pueblo tribes of New Mexico (Texas has one, as does Arizona) felt that their constitutional authority was vested in the Spanish land grants, which were later recognized by Mexico and then the United States (through the 1848 treaty ending the War with Mexico). Nonetheless, pressured by the federal government, the New Mexico Pueblo Indians finally agreed to IRA standards in 1965, when they adopted a collective All Indian Pueblo Council Constitution. Within this framework, each pueblo continues to elect its own governor, tribal council members, and religious leaders. The governors then select a chairman to represent the All Indian Pueblo Council. Delegates to the All Indian Pueblo Council are elected from the respective Pueblos at large.[10] They took this action after Indian Commissioner Collier forced a BIA-drafted constitution on their Hopi Pueblo neighbors in Arizona.

With tribal lands in Arizona, New Mexico, and Utah, the Navajo Nation government consists of three branches, the executive, legislative, and judicial. The executive branch is headed by an elected president and vice president, while the legislative branch consists of eighty-eight council members elected locally and representing the 110 local government subdivisions (chapters) in this, the largest component of Indian Country in the United States. The judicial branch consists of seven district courts, seven family courts, and a Supreme Court. A quarter-blood degree of Navajo descent is required for tribal membership.[11] The Navajo comprise the largest Indian population in the United States, followed by the western Cherokees. However, the western Cherokees have some of the most diluted and questionable Indian lineage of all Native Americans.

Finally, Section 19 of the IRA attempts to set the standard for "Indian" and "tribal" status for American Indians and Alaska Natives. As shown above, the 50 percent-blood degree requirement for Indian status has been greatly reduced by tribes as they struggle to maintain membership. Ironically, the 50 percent-blood degree once held the negative connotation of being a "half-breed." Today, many enrolled tribal members are not phenotypically Indian in any sense of the word. And many tribes do not recognize mixed tribal blood degrees. For instance, the Eastern Band of Cherokees do not recognize any western blood degrees, even though both groups once comprised the same Indian nation. Another problem is that tribal membership is often determined by federal rolls and not by tribal records. Moreover, tribal membership in Indian Country also requires federal recognition and is not necessarily based on native history, custom, or culture. This is a political process that has had great implications relevant to the Indian gaming controversy.

In *Cases and Materials on Federal Indian Law*, the Indian Reorganization Act is seen as providing the design for modern tribal government. It was finally realized that the attempts at forced assimilation of Indians through the Allotment Act actually had the effect of destroying Indians as individuals and Indian communities. The major premise of the IRA was that close supervision of the tribe, organized as a self-governing community, was a better model for dealing with the outside influences of the dominant society: "The reforms of the 1920s and 1930s thus were different from those previously employed by the United States in attempting to implement a final solution to the nation's *Indian problem*. The U.S. Government realized that Indian Country would be better served if tribal self-government were to be encouraged, rather than discouraged. During the two-year adoption period in which tribes could accept or reject the IRA standards, 258 Indian groups held elections, with 181 tribes accepting the Act and 77 tribes, including the Navajo, rejecting it. Overall, by 1946, 161 constitutions and 131 corporate charters had been adopted. Nonetheless, IRA standards for tribal government eventually became the norm for all federally recognized tribes, even if not all have their own specific constitution."[12]

Collier's successes as U.S. commissioner of Indian affairs during the Roosevelt administration were considerable not only in providing a model for tribal governance but also in the field of education. Clearly, the issue of tribal adaptation to segments of the larger dominant society was no longer a debate over retaining aboriginal customary, nonliterate education rather than adopting Western-style literacy. The world was changing due to the advent of telecommunications, making it difficult to remain isolated from the influence of others. Moreover, Native Americans already had a rich history of adaptation to the introduction of European influences such as the horse, steel implements, firearms, sheep herding, and wool rug weaving. Tribal groups soon followed the Cherokee model, having their traditional language transformed into a written format. Collier's contribution to this movement included closing off-reservation boarding schools while promoting both reservation day schools and public school programs (Johnson–O'Malley schools). Indeed, Indian school attendance was at its highest during Collier's tenure. Unfortunately, not everyone shared Collier's enthusiasm for culturally sensitive programs in Indian Country, and the same body that endorsed these programs, the U.S. Congress, also worked at curtailing and undermining them via appropriations.

John Collier later lamented the failure of Congress to fund the New Deal initiatives, a situation that continues to the present, setting the stage for the advent of Indian gaming in the 1980s. In his 1947 work *Indians of the Americas,* Collier noted that "land acquisition for Indians authorized by Congress, is blocked through the appropriation bills; the situation is similar with respect to the expansion of the Indian co-operative credit system." Collier said the same was true for support for technical advice and assistance. These latent actions have served to undermine every democratic, libertarian policy that Congress established as the law of the land. Collier went on to compare U.S. policy with Canadian Indian policy, noting that the latter continued the British model of respecting the Indian landholdings and tribal tradition: "Canada made Indian treaties thriftily and never broke them; neither did Canada drive the tribes at one another's throats to fight them. She formulated out of practice, a brief, flexible body of Canadian Indian law which is eminent for fairness of spirit and for common sense." Collier made these assessments just as the United States was to embark on yet another blatant attempt at cultural genocide.[13]

The American Indian Policy Commission on the IRA
It is important to note how the American Indian Policy Commission assessed this era in its 1977 Final Report:

> **Tribal Reorganization**
> The growing demand for reform resulted in the adoption of the Indian Reorganization Act of 1934, the first major legislation in this field since the enactment of the General Allotment Act. That earlier legislation was based on the premise that the individualizing of tribal land would expedite the process of transforming a tribal people into competitive, taxpaying, free citizens, in repudiation of their own values and traditions. The Indian Reorganization Act, in contrast, was designed to restore some measure of the resource base and the self-governance which tribes had enjoyed prior to 1887.
>
> Of the Allotment law the Meriam report had observed: "It almost seems as if the government assumed that some magic in individual ownership of property would in itself prove an educational civilizing factor, but unfortunately this policy has for the most part operated in the opposite direction. Individual ownership has in many instances permitted Indians to sell their allotment and to live for a time on the unearned income resulting from the sale." The report could have added that by the 1920's more than 100,000 Indians were landless. . . .
>
> *A Reversing Tide*
> By the 1930's it had become evident that the Indians would not vanish; indeed, the surprising fact was that the rate of net increase for the enumerated Indian population exceeded the growth rate of the general population. Between the years 1900 and 1950 the number of Indians increased by some 70 percent, by the end of that period the rate of increase for Indian the Indian population was 22 per 1,000, compared with a rate of 15 per 1,000 for the Nation. The Navajo tribe increased fivefold during the 60-year period 1870–1930.
>
> Survival was not in numbers alone. What came to be realized, reluctantly at times, was that Indian custom and tradition, Indian languages, Indian belief systems, Indian ways of rearing children, the Indian style of living in extended families, Indian sharing, all still prevailed. For the administrator, the educator, and the missionary worker this adherence to Indian ways seemed perverse and intolerable. On occasion it resulted in an intensified effort to obliterate the Indian past, as when Indian Commissioner Charles Burke, in 1923, instructed his field officers to require: (1) That Indian dances be limited to one each month in the daylight hours, in midweek, and at only one center in each district (except that during planting and harvesting no dances were to be allowed); (2) that no individuals under the age of 50

take part as dancers or as spectators and (3) that the field employees carry on an educational campaign against the dances.

The Meriam report made passing reference to "native ceremonies, such as celebrations, dances, games, and races," and found that such activities "tend to disappear under the general influence of white culture, or to take on the form of a spectacle and become commercialized, thus losing much of their original significance in group life."

In offering this observation the survey staff reflected the conventional wisdom of the period, which still held to the belief that Indian identity and tradition could not remain separate and distinct within the general society. The ultimate fate of the Indian people, according to this view, was assimilation into American Society.

This view, in fact, went unchallenged through the first half of the century; it was the basis of law and public policy. Meanwhile, evidence was accumulating that would seriously question these assumptions. While Indians in increasing numbers found employment in urban centers, especially after World War II, a relatively small percentage took up permanent residence in the city. A pattern of commuting between the reservation and the city began to emerge. Even highly skilled industrial workers, such as the Indians employed in "high steel" work on bridges and skyscrapers, remained closely attached to an Indian community. Intertribal and regional organizations came into existence, and Indians found themselves discussing shared problems and experiences. This was a new development, since with only a few exceptions tribes had no tradition of forming permanent alliances. Tribal ceremonies, of both ritual and social nature, attracted growing numbers, and individuals and families traveled to distant reservations to observe or to participate in local performances. A phenomenon referred to as the "pow wow circuit" began to flourish. Ceremonies that had not been performed for many years, were revived. The growth of the Native American Church after the 1930 accelerated. Tribal groups presumed to have been exterminated in the early years of settlement in the east and southeast, were rediscovered, often bearing a cryptic name and claiming Indian heritage, and moreover their numbers were increasing.[14]

Chapter Five

Termination and Relocation
The Last Major Effort at Cultural Genocide

Prelude to the Eisenhower Indian Policy

Ironically, certain elements of the Indian Reorganization Act set the stage for the devastating methods employed during the Eisenhower era to again dissolve Indian Country and impose the capitalist economic model. The vehicle here was the option for tribes to incorporate. Those that selected this Indian Reorganization Act (IRA) option had their tribal status transformed into that of a business corporation, where enrolled members constituted shareholders. A clause in the tribal corporation choice was for the tribe to terminate federal supervision. Clearly, few tribal groups were schooled in the economic and legal intricacies associated with corporate America, and conflicts soon emerged as to what authority the tribal corporation had to bring suit or be sued in civil litigation.

These and other legal issues in Indian Country led to the establishment of the Indian Claims Commission. The claims commission was originally mandated for a decade but has been extended over time to accommodate the increasing number of challenges American Indians are bringing against federal, state, and local governments as well as corporate interests which they feel have exploited Indians and Indian Country. These initiatives actually began under the Truman administration as part of streamlining the executive branch where the Hoover Task Force Commission included cuts in the Bureau of Indian Affairs (BIA). The Hoover Commission saw these measures as means of curtailing domestic spending in order to fund post-war rehabilitation programs for the defeated Axis nations (notably Germany and Japan). Ironically, these savings were to be at the expense of American Indians and their tribal holdings. This process began with the Zimmerman Plan, which surfaced in 1947, whereby the assistant commissioner of Indian affairs, William Zimmerman, and his committee ranked tribes in Indian Country according to their readiness to survive once federal trust was removed and they were entered into the state tax base. Donald Fixico, in his book *Termination and Relocation: Federal Indian Policy, 1945—1960*, noted that the Zimmerman Plan clearly provided the blueprint for the federal government to abrogate its trust responsibilities in Indian Country. In preparation for this process, Congress passed the Indian Claims Commission Act, thinking that they could easily buy off terminated tribes and end federal fiscal responsibilities to tribes.

The Indian Claims Commission Act
An Act to create an Indian Claims Commission, to provide for the powers, duties, and functions thereof, and for other purposes.
Be it enacted . . ., That there is hereby created and established an Indian Claims Commission, hereafter referred to as the Commission.
Section 2. The Commission shall hear and determine the following claims against the United States on behalf of any Indian tribe, band, or other identifiable group of American Indians residing within the territorial limits of the United States or Alaska: (1) claims in law or equity arising under the Constitution, law, treaties of the United States, and Executive orders of the President; (2) all other claims in law or equity, including those sounding in tort, with respect to which the claimant would have been entitled to sue in a court of the United States if the United States was subject to suit; (3) claims which would result if the treaties, contracts, and agreements between the claimant and the United States were revised on the ground of fraud, duress, unconscionable consideration, mutual or unilateral mistake, whether of law or fact, or any other ground cognizable by a court of equity; (4) claims arising from the taking by the United States, whether as the result of a treaty of cession or otherwise, of lands owned or occupied by the claimant without the payment for such lands of compensation agreed to by the claimant; and (5) claims based upon fair and honorable dealings that are not recognized by any existing rule of law or equity. No claim accruing after the date of the approval of this Act shall be considered by the Commission.

All claims hereunder may be heard and determined by the Commission notwithstanding any statute of limitations or laches, but all other defenses shall be available to the United States. . . .
Section 14. The Commission shall have the power to call upon any of the departments of the Government for any information it may deem necessary, and shall have the use of all records, hearings, and reports made by the committees of each House of Congress, when deemed necessary in the prosecution of its business. . . .

Section 15. Each such tribe, band, or other identifiable group of Indians may retain to represent its interests in the presentation of claims before the Commission an attorney or attorneys at law, of its own selection, whose practice before the Commission shall be regulated by its adopted procedure. . . . The Attorney General or his assistants shall represent the United States in all claims presented to the Commission. . . .[1]

This act served to spur Native Americans to organize to better represent their interests. Indeed, returning Indian World War II veterans established the National Congress of American Indians (NCAI) two years prior to the establishment of the Indian Claims Commission as a reaction to the trend toward dissolving federal protection of lands and minerals being sought by western state conservatives, notably the Mormons. Unforeseen, however, was the fact that American Indians were proliferating in numbers, and this, combined with their exposure to each other due to work and military experiences during the Great Depression (Civilian Conservation Corps, Works Projects Administration, etc.) and World War II, initiated a new wave of pan-Indianism. These events brought American Indians together to combat the political forces of Manifest Destiny and white supremacy. Although Indians were greatly outnumbered and had only a fraction of the funding available to those promoting cultural genocide, American Indian activism during this time, perhaps more than any other factor, was able to curtail the degree of devastation wrought by the Truman and Eisenhower administrations.

Getches, Wilkinson, and Williams, in their work *Federal Indian Law*, see the termination period as starting as early as 1945 with Collier's resignation. Immediately, Congress moved to repeal the IRA and its support of tribal self-government. The IRA movement lost another strong supporter when Felix Cohen left the Interior Department in 1948. Republicans were later energized by the 1949 Hoover Commission, with its recommendation for full integration of American Indians into U.S. society. Termination actually began under the Democratic presidency of Harry S. Truman, with his 1950 appointment of Dillon S. Myer, the notorious director of the War Relocation program during World War II, as commissioner for the Bureau of Indian Affairs. Clearly, Myer's plan was to terminate Indian Country under the pretense of making Indians independent of federal control. Myer petitioned Eisenhower to retain him in his position to see termination through to completion. But Myer proved to be too much of a liability to Eisenhower, who replaced him with Glenn L. Emmons, a western businessman and rancher from New Mexico. Nonetheless, Emmons shared Myer's plan of eliminating federal responsibility for Indian Country and opening up these lands to white exploitation.

Eisenhower needed his Republican conservatives in Congress to push his Korean conflict and Cold War agenda, thus allowing conservative senators such as Arthur V. Watkins, a Mormon from Utah, to push the termination process forward. Watkins did this in his capacity as chair of the Senate Interior Committee Subcommittee on Indian Affairs. The Mormons had another motive for rapid assimilation of American Indians in the West, and that was mineral exploitation. The Mormons own Peabody Coal and are accused in the current Individual Indian Money (IIM) fund scandal of cheating the Navajo and Hopi of tens of millions of dollars of royalties for their mining efforts in Indian Country. Moreover, the termination movement toward rapid assimilation and the removal of federal oversight in Indian Country provided the Eisenhower administration the impetus to again support a capitalist corporate model for Indian tribes in the hopes of dissolving their culture and communal lifestyle. This model even envisioned terminating the BIA itself and played well with the western state anti-Communist conservatives, many of whom viewed Indian Country and communal reservations as latent Communist entities.[2]

The Eisenhower Attempt at Purging Indian Country
The founders of the American Indian Historical Society, Rupert Costo and Jeannette Henry, noted that John Collier was later tasked by President F.D. Roosevelt with devising a plan for the removal of Japanese citizens and immigrants from their homes on the West Coast to concentration camps called "relocation camps." Costo and Henry claim that Roosevelt announced Collier was eminently qualified for this task due to his experience with working with reservation Indians. In 1953, the newly elected president Dwight D. Eisenhower reappointed Dillon Myer, the former head of the Japanese–American Relocation Centers, to be his BIA commissioner. Myer was noted for his dictatorial methods in both capacities, which were equated with those of General Scott during the forced removal of the Cherokees in 1838 or those of Colonel Kit Carson in the deadly forced removal of the Navajos in 1864. Termination was attempted prior to passage of House Concurrent Resolution 108 before the Eisenhower presidency. The example of termination of federal responsibilities for civil and criminal jurisdiction among the New York tribes illustrated this earlier attempt at introducing the dual impact of House Concurrent Resolution 108 and Public Law 280. Title 25 of the U.S. Code, section 232, notes that federal statutes recognized this authority in July 1948, five years prior to enactment of Public Law 280. Even the language is similar:

The State of New York shall have jurisdiction over offenses committed by or against Indians on Indian reservations within the State of New York to the same extent as the courts of the State have jurisdiction over offenses committed elsewhere within the State as defined by the laws of the State: Provided, That nothing contained in this section shall be construed to deprive any Indian tribe, band, or community, or members thereof, hunting and fishing rights as guaranteed them by agreement, treaty, or custom, nor require them to obtain State fish and game licenses for the exercise of such rights.[3]

The initiative of the new Eisenhower administration and his Republican Congress for the termination of Indian Country was begun in August 1953 with passage of two complementary Congressional Acts: House Concurrent Resolution 108, which ended federal responsibility among designated specific tribes, and Public Law 280, which replaced federal civil and criminal jurisdiction over Indian Country with that of the state in which the reservation was located.

House Concurrent Resolution 108 and Public Law 280

House Concurrent Resolution 108

Whereas it is the policy of Congress, as rapidly as possible, to make the Indians within the territorial limits of the United States subject to the same laws and entitled to the same privileges and responsibilities as are applicable to other citizens of the United States, and to grant them all of the rights and prerogatives pertaining to American citizenship; and

Whereas the Indians within the territorial limits of the United States should assume their full responsibilities as American citizens: Now, therefore, be it *Resolved by the House of Representatives (the Senate concurring),*

That it is declared to be the sense of Congress that, at the earliest possible time, all of the Indian tribes and the individual members thereof within the States of California, Florida, New York, and Texas, and all of the following named Indian tribes and individual members thereof, should be freed from Federal supervision and control and from all disabilities and limitations specially applicable to Indians: The Flathead Tribe of Montana, the Klamath Tribe of Oregon, the Menominee Tribe of Wisconsin, the Potowatamie Tribe of Kansas and Nebraska, and those members of the Chippewa Tribe who are on the Turtle Mountain Reservation, North Dakota. It is further declared to be the sense of Congress that, upon the release of such tribes and individual members thereof from such disabilities and limitations, all offices of the Bureau of Indian Affairs in the State of California, Florida, New York, and Texas and all other offices of the Bureau of Indian Affairs whose primary purpose was to serve any Indian tribe or individual Indian freed from Federal supervision should be abolished. It is further declared to be the sense of Congress that the Secretary of the Interior should examine all existing legislation dealing with such Indians, and treaties between the Government of the United States and each such tribe, and report to Congress at the earliest practicable date, but not later than January 1, 1954, his recommendations for such legislation as, in his judgment, may be necessary to accomplish the purposes of this resolution.[4]

Public Law 83-280
An Act to confer jurisdiction on the States of California, Minnesota, Nebraska, Oregon, and Wisconsin, with respect to criminal offenses and civil causes of action committed or arising on Indian reservations within such States, and for other purposes.
Section 2, Title 18, United States Code, is hereby amended by inserting in chapter 53 thereof immediately after section 1161 a new section, to be designated as section 1162, as follows:
1162: State jurisdiction over offenses committed by or against Indians in the Indian country.
(a) Each of the States listed in the following table shall have jurisdiction over offenses committed by or against Indians in the areas of Indian country listed opposite the name of the State to the same extent that such State has jurisdiction over offenses committed elsewhere within the State, and the criminal laws of such State shall have the same force and effect within such Indian country as they have elsewhere within the State:
State: Indian country affected:
California............All Indian country within the State.
Minnesota............All Indian country within the State, Except the Red Lake Reservation.
Nebraska.............All Indian country within the State.
Oregon...............All Indian country within the State, Except the Warm Springs Reservation.
Wisconsin............All Indian country within the State, Except the Menominee Reservation.
(b) Nothing in this section shall authorize the alienation, encumbrance, or taxation of any real or personal property, including water rights, belonging to any Indian or any Indian tribe, band, or community that is held in trust by the United States or is subject to a restriction against alienation imposed by the United States; or shall authorize regulation of the use of such property in a manner inconsistent with any Federal treaty, agreement, or statute or with any regulation made pursuant thereto; or shall deprive any Indian or any Indian tribe, band, or community of any right, privilege, or immunity afforded under Federal treaty, agreement, or statute with respect to hunting, trapping, or fishing or the control, licensing, or regulation thereof.
(c) Any tribal ordinance or custom heretofore or hereafter adopted by an Indian tribe, band, or community in the exercise of any authority which it may possess shall, if not inconsistent with any applicable civil law of the State, be given full force and effect in the determination of civil causes of action pursuant to this section.[5]

One of the most significant termination cases involved the Menominee Indians of Wisconsin, who were added to the list in 1954. Initiated in June 1954, but not fully implemented until 1961, the Menominee termination set the stage for the end of this destructive process, although the standards established under Public Law 280 continue to the present.

Termination of the Menominee Indians
An Act to provide for a per capita distribution of Menominee tribal funds and authorize the withdrawal of the Menominee Tribe from the Federal jurisdiction.
Be it enacted . . ., That the purpose of this Act is to provide for orderly termination of Federal supervision over the property and members of the Menominee Indian Tribe of Wisconsin.
Section 2. For the purposes of the Act:
(a) "Tribe" means the Menominee Indian Tribe of Wisconsin;
(b) "Secretary" means the Secretary of the Interior.
Section 3. At midnight of the date of enactment of this Act the roll of the tribe maintained pursuant to the Act of June 15, 1934 (48 Stat. 965), as amended by the Act of July 14, 1939 (53 Stat. 1003), shall be closed and no child born thereafter shall be eligible for enrollment: Provided, That applicants for enrollment in the tribe shall have three months from the date the roll is closed in which to submit applications for enrollment: Provided further, That the tribe shall have three months thereafter in which to approve or disapprove any application for enrollment: Provided further, That any applicant whose application is not approved by the tribe within six months from the date of enactment of this Act may, within three months thereafter, file with the Secretary an appeal from the failure of the tribe to approve his application, as the case may be. The decision of the Secretary on such appeal shall be final and conclusive. When the Secretary has made decisions on all appeals, he shall issue and publish in the Federal Register a Proclamation of Final Closure of the roll of the tribe and the final roll of the members. Effective upon the date of such proclamation, the rights or beneficial interests of each person whose name appears on the roll shall constitute personal property and shall be evidenced by a certificate of beneficial interest which shall be issued by the tribe. Such interests shall be distributable in accordance with the laws of the State of Wisconsin. Such interests shall be alienable only in accordance with such regulations as may be adopted by the tribe.
Section 4. Section 6 of the Act of June 15, 1934 (48 Stat. 965, 966) is hereby repealed.
Section 5. The Secretary is authorized and directed, as soon as practicable after the passage of this Act, to pay from such funds as are deposited to the credit of the tribe in the Treasury of the United States $1,500 to each member of the tribe on the rolls of the tribe on the date of the Act. Any other persons whose application for enrollment on the rolls of the tribe is subsequently approved, pursuant to the terms of section 3 hereof, shall, after enrollment, be paid a like sum of $1,500: Provided,

That such payments shall be made first from any funds on deposit in the Treasury of the United States to the credit of the Menominee Indian Tribe drawing interest at the rate of 5 per centum, and thereafter from the Menominee judgment fund, symbol 14X7142.

Section 6. The tribe is authorized to select and retain the services of qualified management specialists, including tax consultants, for the purpose of studying industrial programs on the Menominee Reservation and making such reports or recommendations, including appraisals of Menominee tribal property, as may be described by the tribe, and to make other studies and reports as may be deemed necessary and desirable by the tribe in connection with the termination of Federal supervision as provided for hereinafter. Such reports shall be completed not later than December 31, 1957. Such specialists are to be retained under contracts entered into between them and authorized by the Secretary. Such amounts of Menominee tribal funds as may be required for this purpose shall be made available by the Secretary.

Section 7. The tribe shall formulate and submit to the Secretary a plan or plans for the future control of the tribal property and service functions now conducted by or under the supervision of the United States, including, but not limited to, services in the fields of health, education, welfare, credit, roads, and law and order. The Secretary is authorized to provide such reasonable assistance as may be requested by officials of the tribe in the formulation of the plan or plans heretofore referred to, including necessary consultations with representatives of Federal departments and agencies, officials of the State of Wisconsin and political subdivisions thereof, and members of the tribe: Provided, That the responsibility of the United States to furnish all such supervision and services to the tribe and to the members thereof, because of their status as Indians shall cease on December 31, 1958, or on such earlier date as may be agreed upon by the tribe and the Secretary.

Section 8. The Secretary is hereby authorized and directed to transfer to the tribe, on December 31, 1958, or on such earlier date as may be agreed upon by the tribe and the Secretary, the title to all property, real and personal, held in trust by the United States for the tribe: Provided, however, That if the tribe obtains a charter for a corporation or otherwise organizes under the laws of a State or of the District of Columbia for the purpose, among any others, of taking title to all tribal lands and assets and enterprises owned by the tribe or held in trust by the United States for the tribe, and requests such transfer to be made to such corporation or organization, the Secretary shall make such transfer to such corporation or organization.

Section 9. No distribution of the assets made under the provisions of this Act shall be subject to any Federal or State income tax: Provided, That so much of any cash distribution made hereunder as consists of a share of any interest earned on funds deposited in the Treasury of the United States pursuant to the Supplemental Appropriation Act, 1952 (65 Stat. 736, 754), shall not be virtue of this Act be exempt from individual income tax in the hands of the recipients for the year in which paid. Following any distribution of assets made under the provisions of this Act, such assets and any income derived therefrom in the hands of any individual, or corporation or organization as provided in section 8 of this Act, shall be subject to the same taxes, State and Federal, as in the case of non-Indians, except that any valuation for purposes of Federal income tax on gains or losses shall take as the basis of the particular taxpayer the value of the property on the date title is transferred by the United States pursuant to section 8 of this Act.

Section 10. When title to the property of the tribe has been transferred, as provided in section 8 of this Act, the Secretary shall publish in the Federal Register an appropriate proclamation of that fact. Thereafter individual members of the tribe shall not be entitled to any of the services performed by the United States for Indians because of their status as Indians, all statutes of the United States which affect Indians because of their status as Indians shall no longer be applicable to the members of the tribe, and the laws of the several States shall apply to the tribe and its members in the same manner as they apply to other citizens or persons within their jurisdiction. Nothing in this Act shall affect the status of the members of the tribe as citizens of the United States.

Section 11. Prior to the transfer pursuant to section 8 of this Act, the Secretary shall protect the rights of members of the tribe who are less than eighteen years of age, non compos mentis, or in the opinion of the Secretary in need of assistance in conducting their affairs, by causing the appointment of guardians for such members in courts of competent jurisdiction, or by such other means as he may deem adequate.

Section 12. The Secretary is authorized and directed to promulgate such rules and regulations as are necessary to effectuate the purpose of this Act.

Section 13. If any provision of this Act, or the application thereof to any person or circumstance, is held invalid, the remainder of the Act and the application of such provision to other persons or circumstances shall not be affected thereby.[6]

Wilkinson and Biggs noted in a 1977 *American Indian Law Review* article that since House Concurrent Resolution 108 was a policy statement, specific Congressional acts were needed to terminate specific tribes, beginning with the Menominee Indians. Altogether some 190 tribes were affected, including 1,362,155 acres in Indian Country and 11,466 tribal members, resulting in the shrinkage of federal Indian trust lands by 3.2 percent. Common to these termination acts was the transformation of land ownership patterns from one of communally held tribal lands to a corporate or capitalist design. Here, tribal lands were appraised and sold by the U.S. government to a non-Indian bidder, often involving collusion, and the proceeds were then assigned to the tribe minus the processing fees determined by the secretary of the interior. This process ended the trust responsibility, including federal expertise for land and resource management and federal protection from tax or other liens against Indian lands. To fill this gap state jurisdiction was imposed on the tribes, with state legislatures and county boards given authority to impose their influence in the areas of law, education, land use, religion, and social and economic issues. This authority was granted via Public Law 280. Moreover, all exemptions from state taxing authority ended with termination, and, at the same time, all special federal programs to tribes were discontinued, placing the tribal members at the mercy of the white-dominated political and law enforcement apparatus. Essentially, with termination, tribal sovereignty was ended.[7]

Relocation of Indians to Urban Ghettos
The second component of this effort at eliminating Indian Country was relocation. Fixico noted that this effort had some merit initially, in that severe weather in 1947 and 1948 worsened the already devastated economies in Indian Country in the western United States, forcing the U.S. government to provide emergency assistance, notably to the Navajos. With Indian veterans returning from World War II, the government began resettlement programs in magnet cities surrounding the Navajo Nation, notably Denver, Salt Lake City, and Los Angeles. Using this as a model for the larger relocation effort, Commissioner of Indian Affairs Dillon S. Myer initiated the relocation program in 1951 as another component of the termination of Indian Country. In 1952 he requested $500,000 f or his relocation efforts. This figure jumped to $8.5 million for the following year.

The relocation initiative, like termination, was picked up by Myer's successor as commissioner of Indian affairs, Glenn Emmons. The majority of the first applicants came from the Great Plains tribes, followed by tribes from the southwestern regions. By 1954, additional offices had been opened in San Francisco, Oakland, San Jose, St. Louis, Dallas, Cleveland, Oklahoma City, and Tulsa. BIA figures indicate that by the end of 1954, over 6,000 American Indians had been resettled in these urban settings. Between 1952 and 1955 some 3,000 reservation Indians, mostly from the southwestern tribes, relocated in Chicago alone. But without adequate education and training, most of the jobs they took ended up being low-paying seasonal jobs and the Indian settlements poor ghettos.[8]

The Native American perspective on termination is expressed by Rupert Costo and Jeannette Henry in their 1977 book *Indian Treaties: Two Centuries of Dishonor*:

Religious groups and white-controlled humanitarian organizations generally embodied the worst of the growing paternalism toward the Natives. Finally, the federal government, jockeying precariously between policies of assimilation and the growing recognition that the tribes simply would not disappear together with their unique cultures, originated what has become known as the "Relocation Program." Indians were induced to go to the cities for training in the arts of the technological world. There they were dumped into housing that in most cases was ghetto-based, into jobs that were dead end, and training that failed to lead to professions and occupations. The litany of that period provides the crassest example of government ignorance of the Indian situation. The "Indian problem" did not go away. It worsened. The policies of the Eisenhower administration, which espoused the termination of federal-Indian relationships, was shown to be a failure, a gross injustice added to a history of injustice. . . . Tribes found that termination brought deeper poverty, hopelessness, despair, thrusting the Indian into the darkest regions between two worlds, that of the Native American and that of the Euroamerican.[9]

Another excellent assessment of the relocation programs is provided in the 1977 Final Report of the American Indian Policy Review Commission:

After World War II, Indian perceptions of reservations and cities began to change. The war showed many Indians a world they had never seen and seldom heard of. There were opportunities for achievement in the military service which they had never found on reservations. They proved themselves capable of using those opportunities and returned home with confident hopes that they could make their reservations better places to live. This hope soon turned to despair as they tackled the obstacles which impeded reservation development. Many Indians, however reluctant to leave their communities and families, decided that low quality subsistence was the only future for the reservations and set off for the cities to find work. By 1951, more than 17,000 Navajos worked away from the reservation, primarily on railroads and agriculture.

At the same time, the Federal policy of assimilation manifested itself in a new way. A theory that reservations were overpopulated gained credence. By 1954, a congressional report entitled, "Survey report on the BIA" generalized that "most of the reservations are overpopulated, and could not support the population at anything approaching a reasonable adequate standard of living." Rather than pursuing a way to make Indian homelands financially secure places to live, the Federal Government chose to follow a simpler approach: relocation of Indians away from the reservations. Thinning out the population of reservations, however, did not mean they were willing to stop being Indians; and whether or not reservations bred some social problems, it could not have been assumed that those problems would be shed at the reservation boundaries. Nevertheless, Federal policy followed exactly that simplistic an approach. Transportation funds were provided, but relocation services were not.

The Federal Government not only failed to provide needed services to the Indians it relocated, but actually refused to provide those services. The Federal relocation program was to be initiated by the BIA but was left to be implemented by local, State and county assistance programs, or churches or humanitarian organizations. The only thing that was shrugged off at reservation boundaries, it turned out, was Federal responsibility.

Indians affected by relocation were not given an opportunity to tell their side of the story until the National Council on Indian Opportunity held hearings in five major cities in 1968 and 1969. The numerous criticisms that were heard at this time fell into three categories: (1) The lack of orientation in relocation from reservations to cities; (2) the low quality of opportunities for work; (3) the confusion of where to turn for necessary services. Federal policy had ignored particular difficulties Indians faced in the cities, difficulties such as language barriers, questions of where to find services or help, and the most fundamental problems of daily survival.... To solve these problems which the Federal Government largely created and then totally ignored, Indian people themselves have contributed the most recent and the most constructive development of urban Indian service centers.[10]

The Backlash to Termination and Relocation

The Advent of Tribal Activism

As noted above, tribal members felt the need to organize in order to promote their own interests given that it was obvious that the federal government was delinquent in its trust responsibilities. Even worse were the numerous examples of the federal government exploiting American Indians and Indian Country for itself and its non-Indian constituents. Special Indian interest groups prior to the formation of the NCAI comprised predominantly whites advocates for Indian issues. The Association on American Indian Affairs (AAIA) began in 1922 as the Eastern Association on Indian Affairs; its members were outspoken critics of the Bursum/Fall Pueblo land swindle and are credited with getting Congress to reject the Bursum Bill. The organization then joined with the New Mexico Association on Indian Affairs to become the National Association on Indian Affairs in 1933 under the leadership of Oliver La Farge—the Pulitzer-winning author of *Laughing Boy*. The white leadership of the AAIA, however, led to suspicion of collusion with the BIA, especially during the Indian reorganization era. This reaction led to the establishment of the all-Indian National Congress of American Indians. The AAIA was reestablished in 1995 as an Indian-administered organization.

Both the AAIA and the NCAI were concerned with the monopoly the federal government had on Indian affairs without any external review or oversight. These unscrupulous relations surfaced again during the termination/relocation era. White lawyers petitioned the BIA for lucrative assignments, supposedly representing tribes who wanted to manage their affairs under the new corporate-style conditions. One example is that of John Boyden, a Mormon lawyer out of Salt Lake City, who received the rights to represent the Hopi in relation to their mineral rights. Boyden also represented the Mormon-owned Peabody Coal and served as a counsel for the Mormon Church; he was able to get Peabody Coal surface rights to the rich coal fields in the Hopi pueblo and in the Navajo Nation at a rate far below the fair market value. Even then, the Navajo claim that the BIA allowed Peabody to further cheat the tribes of their mineral revenues. This is part of the current IIM fund suit, which has been expanded to include tribal interests. The challenges facing the NCAI and the AAIA were numerous, with the trend being to stack Indian affairs committees with western state conservatives such as Arthur Watkins, who served on the U.S. Indian Claims Commission between 1959 and 1967.

Many urban Indians felt that the federal government deliberately caused chaos in Indian Country by playing tribes against one another, causing dissent within the ranks of the National Congress of American Indians. This dissatisfaction led to the creation of the National Indian Youth Council (NIYC) in Gallup, New Mexico, in 1961. The NIYC's membership was more radical than the more traditional leaders of the NCAI. It served as the parent organization for the even more radical American Indian Movement (AIM), much as Students for a Democratic Society fostered the more radical Weathermen. Not only was the National Indian Youth Council critical of the more conservative NCAI organization of the older World War II generation; they contested the idea that the NCAI allegedly spoke for most Native Americans. Indeed, the NIYC represented the new pan-Indianism that now included those Native Americans born off the reservation in the urban Indian ghettos. The NIYC's current mission statement is to ensure that every Native American has an equal opportunity to participate, excel, and become a viable member of and asset to his/her community by providing access to education, health care, social services, employment, housing, leadership in government, and economic development.

Clearly, its offspring, AIM, has gained more notoriety than any Indian movement since the Ghost Dance movement of the late 19th century, which resulted in the Wounded Knee massacre. AIM was the Indian counterpart to ethnic countercultural movements of the 1960s and 1970s such as the Black Panthers and La Rasa. The late Indian scholar Vine Deloria Jr. credited the emergence of AIM to the failed urban relocation programs and the repressive police actions against Indians fostered by Public Law 280. AIM was an urban militant organization founded in Minneapolis in 1968, and its actions quickly resulted in the NIYC distancing itself from its radical faction.[11]

The chronology of radical Indian actions drawing attention to their plight began in 1964, when Survival of American Indians initiated "fish-ins" to continue to use their off-reservation, treaty-guaranteed fishing rights in Washington state. This group, and not AIM, became involved in the occupation of Alcatraz. In March 1964, five Sioux Indians claimed the island under the 1868 Fort Laramie Treaty, which allowed Sioux Indians to take possession of surplus federal land. This occupation lasted only four hours. As AIM was founded in the summer of 1968 in Minneapolis, the United Native Americans, another pan-Indian group, was created in San Francisco. In December 1968, Mohawk Indians blockaded the Cornwall International Bridge connecting the U.S. (New York) and Canadian (Quebec) portions of their nation due to restrictions on the free movement of tribal members over the international boundary.

The year 1969 was another eventful one for American Indian activism, with the nineteen-month occupation of Alcatraz initiated in November. A month later, AIM leaders visited the Alcatraz group to lend their support for the occupation effort. In 1970, AIM painted Plymouth Rock in Massachusetts red and occupied the *Mayflower* replica on Thanksgiving Day. This was also the year when the Native American Rights Fund (NARF) was organized. It provided an Indian-run law firm for Indian issues in Indian Country. In June 1971, the remaining Indian occupiers of Alcatraz were taken off the island by U.S. Marshals and FBI agents, ending the island's occupation. In November 1972, AIM organized the Trail of Broken Treaties march on Washington, DC, occupying BIA headquarters for seven days and demanding that the United States recognize tribal self-determination.

AIM is probably best known for its involvement in the Pine Ridge Reservation occupation of Wounded Knee—the area where Big Foot's party was massacred on December 29, 1890. Here, AIM assisted Lakota tribe members who were attempting to remove Dick Wilson, the BIA-backed tribal leader who had his own private police force known as the GOON (Guardians of the Oglala Nation) squad. AIM leader Russell Means and a contingent of Sioux and other AIM followers seized the area around the Wounded Knee massacre site for 71 days. During this time, the U.S. military, FBI, and local and tribal police fired over 500,000 rounds into the AIM fortifications, resulting in the death of two occupying Indians and an FBI agent. Over 1,000 protesting Indians were arrested for this action, while many others hid on other reservations throughout the country in order to avoid being arrested. Indeed, the next three years witnessed increased FBI and local police harassment of young Indians throughout Indian Country and in their urban ghettos. American Indians refer to this era as the FBI's "Reign of Terror." Indeed, the FBI emboldened Wilson's GOON squads, resulting in 61 homicides among AIM supporters, most not investigated by the FBI. It was these circumstances that resulted in the murder of two FBI agents on June 26, 1975, when they encountered a large contingent of AIM supporters at the Jumping Bull Ranch on Pine Ridge. After an intense international manhunt, AIM leader Leonard Peltier was captured in Canada, extradited, and convicted for these murders by an all-white jury. Despite serious questions about his involvement in the murders and judicial improprieties in his trial, he is serving two life sentences at the federal military prison at Leavenworth, Kansas. The irony is that the Wounded Knee II battle occurred in the same region as the Crow Dog situation in the 1880s and under similar circumstances. Both situations pitted traditional Indians against a U.S.-backed puppet government and then used the resulting altercation as a pretext for more intense policing in Indian Country. This is the intensity of protest that was warranted to get Congress to establish an American Indian Policy Review Commission and for the establishment of Indian self-determination.

The Indian Civil Rights Act of 1965
President Lyndon Johnson's greatest contributions to U.S. society were his endeavors to get the Civil Rights Acts passed. While the primary focus of these Acts was the enfranchisement of Black Americans, he was the first to promote self-determination for American Indians. In his March 6, 1968, Special Message to Congress, President Johnson proposed a new direction in Indian programs: "A goal that ends the old debate about 'termination' of

Indian programs and stresses self-determination; a goal that erases old attitudes of paternalism and promotes partnership and self-help."

Self-Help and Self-Determination
The greatest hope for Indian progress lies in the emergence of Indian leadership and initiative in solving Indian problems. Indians must have a voice in making the plans and decisions in programs which are important to their daily life. . . . Passive acceptance of Federal service is giving way to Indian involvement. More than ever before, Indian needs are being identified from the Indian viewpoint—as they should be.

This principle is the key to progress for Indians—just as it has been for other Americans. If we base our programs upon it, the day will come when the relationship between Indians and the Government will be one of full partnership— not dependency. . . . We must affirm the right of the first Americans to remain Indians while exercising their rights as Americans. We must affirm their right to freedom of choice and self-determination. We must seek new ways to provide Federal assistance to Indians—with new emphasis on Indian self-help and with respect for Indian culture. And we must assure the Indian people that it is our desire and intention that the special relationship between the Indian and his government grow and flourish. For, the first among us must not be the last.[12]

A month later, Congress passed the Civil Rights Act of 1968, where Titles II–VII addressed American Indians. This was important legislation given that American Indians had been conferred federal citizenship in 1924 but this had not guaranteed them the right to vote in state and local elections. Two of the worst states in terms of Indian voting rights were Arizona and New Mexico—the home of the largest U.S. tribe, the Navajo, as well as the Pueblo and Apache tribes. The Civil Rights Act provided more freedoms to individual members of tribes, again obviating traditional clan influences, and empowered the tribes to accept or reject continued Public Law 280 influences. No tribe has agreed to Public Law 280 conditions after being given this opportunity. Moreover, most tribes that live under these imposed conditions would like the law rescinded.

An Act To provide penalties for certain acts of violence or intimidation, and for other purposes.

TITLE II—RIGHTS OF INDIANS
   Definitions
   Section 201. For purposes of this title, the term –

(1) "Indian tribe" means any tribe, band or other group of Indians subject to the jurisdiction of the United States and recognized as possessing powers of self-government;

(2) "powers of self-government" means and includes all governmental powers possessed by an Indian tribe, executive, legislative, and judicial, and all offices, bodies, and tribunals by and through which they are executed, including courts of Indian offenses; and

(3) "Indian court" means any Indian tribal court or court of Indian offense.

Indian Rights

Section 202. No Indian tribe in exercising powers of self-government shall—

(1) make or enforce any law prohibiting the free exercise of religion, or abridging the freedom of speech, or of the press, or the right of the people peaceably to assemble and to petition for a redress of grievances;

(2) violate the right of the people to be secure in their persons, houses, papers, and effects against unreasonable search and seizures, supported by oath or affirmation, and particularly describing the place to be searched and the person or thing to be seized;

(3) subject any person for the same offense to be twice put in jeopardy;

(4) compel any person in any criminal case to be a witness against himself;

(5) take any private property for a public use without just compensation;

(6) deny to any person in a criminal proceeding the right to a speedy and public trail, to be informed of the nature and cause of the accusation, to be confronted with the witnesses against him, to have compulsory process for obtaining witnesses in his favor and at his own expense to have the assistance of counsel for his defense;

(7) require excessive bail, impose excessive fines, inflict cruel and unusual punishment, and in no event impose for conviction of any one offense any penalty or punishment greater than imprisonment for a term of six months or a fine of $500, or both;

(8) deny to any person within its jurisdiction the equal protection of its laws or deprive any person of liberty or property without due process of law;

(9) pass any bill of attainder or ex post facto law; or

(10) deny to any person accused of an offense punishable by imprisonment the right, upon request, to a trial by jury of not less than six persons.

Habeas Corpus

Section 203. The privilege of the writ of habeas corpus shall be available to any person, in a court of the United States, to test the legality of his detention by order of an Indian tribe.

TITLE III—MODEL CODE GOVERNING COURTS OF INDIAN OFFENSES

Section 301. The Secretary of the Interior is authorized and directed to recommend to the Congress, on or before July 1, 1968, a model code to govern the administration of justice by courts of Indian offenses on Indian reservations. Such code shall include provisions which will (1) assure that any individual being tried for an offense by a court of Indian offenses shall have the same rights, privileges, and immunities under the United States Constitution as would be guaranteed any citizen of the United States being tried in a Federal court for any similar offense, (2) assure that any individual being tried for an offense by a court of Indian offenses will be advised and made aware of his rights under the United States Constitution, and under any tribal constitution applicable to such individual, (3) establish proper qualifications for the office of judge of the courts of Indian offenses, and (4) provide for the establishing of educational classes for the training of judges of courts of Indian offenses. In carrying out the provisions of this title, the Secretary of the Interior shall consult with the Indians, Indian tribes, and interested agencies of the United States.

Section 302. There is hereby authorized to be appropriated such sum as may be necessary to carry out the provisions of this title.

TITLE IV—JURISDICTION OVER CRIMINAL AND CIVIL ACTIONS

Assumption by state

Section 401. (a) The consent of the United States is hereby given to any State not having jurisdiction over criminal offenses committed by or against Indians in the areas of Indian country situated within such State to assume, with the consent of the Indian tribe occupying the particular Indian country or part thereof which could be affected by such assumption, such measure of jurisdiction over any or all of such offenses committed within such Indian country or any part thereof as may be determined by such State to the same extent that such State, and the criminal laws of such State shall have the same force and effect within such Indian country or part thereof as they have elsewhere within that State.

(b) Nothing in this section shall authorize the alienation, encumbrance, or taxation of any real or personal property, including water rights, belonging to any Indian or any Indian tribe, band, or community that is held in trust by the United States or is subject to a restriction against alienation imposed by the United States; or shall authorize regulation of the use of such property in a manner inconsistent with any Federal treaty, agreement, or statute or with any regulation made pursuant thereto; or shall deprive any Indian or any Indian tribe, band, or community of any rights, privilege, or immunity afforded under Federal treaty, agreement, or statute with respect to hunting, trapping, or fishing or the control, licensing, or regulation thereof.

Assumption by state or civil jurisdiction

Section 402. (a) The consent of the United States is hereby given to any State not having jurisdiction over civil causes of action between Indians or to which Indians are parties which arise in the areas of Indian country situation within such State to assume, with the consent of the tribe occupying the particular Indian country or part thereof which would be affected by such assumption, such measure of jurisdiction over any or all such civil causes of action arising within such Indian country or any part thereof as may be determined by such State to the same extent that such State has jurisdiction over other civil causes of action, and those civil laws of such State that are of general application to private persons or private property shall have the same force and effect within such Indian country or part thereof as they have elsewhere within that State.

(b) Nothing in this section shall authorize the alienation, encumbrance, or taxation of any real or personal property, including water rights, belonging to any Indian or Indian tribe, band, or community that is held in trust by the United States or is subject to a restriction against alienation imposed by the United States; or shall authorize regulation of the use of such property in a manner inconsistent with any Federal treaty, agreement, or statue, or with any regulation made pursuant thereto; or shall confer jurisdiction upon the State to adjudicate, in probate proceedings or otherwise, the ownership or rights to possession of such property or any interest therein.

(c) Any tribal ordinance or custom heretofore or hereafter adopted by an Indian tribe, band, or community in the exercise of any authority which it may possess shall, if not inconsistent with any applicable civil law of the State, be given full force and effect in the determination of civil causes of action pursuant to this section.

Retrocession of jurisdiction by State

Section 403. (a) The United States is authorized to accept a retrocession by any State of all or any measure of the criminal or civil jurisdiction, or both, acquired by such State pursuant to the provisions of section 1162 of title 18 of the United States Code, section 1360 of title 28 of the United States Code, or section 7 of the Act of August 15, 1953 (67 Stat. 588), as it was in effect prior to its repeal by subsection (b) of this section.

(b) Section 7 of the Act of August 1, 1953 (67 Stat. 588), is hereby repealed, but such repeal shall not affect any cession of jurisdiction made pursuant to such section prior to its repeal. . . .

Special Election

Section 406. State jurisdiction acquired pursuant to this title with respect to criminal offenses or civil causes of action, or with respect to both, shall be applicable in Indian country only where the enrolled Indians within the affected area of such Indian country accept such jurisdiction by a majority vote of the adult Indians voting in a special election held for that purpose. The Secretary of the Interior shall call such special election under such rules and regulations as he may prescribe, when requested to do so by the tribal council or other governing body, or by 20 per centum of such enrolled adults.

TITLE V—OFFENSES WITHIN INDIAN COUNTRY
Amendment
Section 501. Section 1153 of title 18 of the United States Code is amended by inserting immediately after "weapon," the following: "assault resulting in serious bodily injury,".

TITLE VI—EMPLOYMENT OF LEGAL COUNSEL
Approval
Section 601. Notwithstanding any other provision of law, if any application made by an Indian, Indian tribe, Indian council, or any band or group of Indians under any law requiring the approval of the Secretary of the Interior or the Commissioner of Indian Affairs of contracts or agreements relating to the employment of legal council (including the choice of counsel and the fixing of fees) by any such Indians, tribe, council, band, or group is neither granted nor denied within ninety days following the making of such application, such approval shall be deemed to have been granted.

TITLE VII—MATERIALS RELATING TO CONSTITUTIONAL RIGHTS OF INDIANS
Secretary of the Interior to prepare
Section 701. (a) In order that the constitutional rights of Indians might be fully protected, the Secretary of the Interior is authorized and directed to—

(1) have the document entitled "Indian Affairs, Laws and Treaties" (Senate Document Numbered 319, volumes 1 and 2, Fifty-eight Congress), revised and extended to include all treaties, laws, Executive orders, and regulations relating to Indian affairs in force on September 1, 1967, and to have such revised document printed at the Government Printing Office;

(2) have revised and republished thesis entitled "Federal Indian Law"; and

(3) have prepared, to the extent determined by the Secretary of the Interior to be feasible, an accurate compilation of the official opinions, published and unpublished, of the Solicitor of the Department of the Interior relating to Indian affairs rendered by the Solicitor prior to September 1, 1967, and to have such compilation printed as a Government publication at the Government Printing Office.

(b) With respect to the document entitled "Indian Affairs, Laws and Treaties" as revised and extended in accordance with paragraph (1) of subsection (a), and the compilation prepared in accordance with paragraph (3) of such subsection, the Secretary of the Interior shall take such action as may be necessary to keep such document and compilation current on an annual basis.

(c) There is authorized to be appropriated for carrying out the provisions of this title, with respect to the preparation but not included printing, such sum as may be necessary.[13]

Canby, in his book *American Indian Law*, states that the Civil Rights Act of 1968 was welcomed by the tribes because it amended Public Law 280 so that states could no longer assume civil and criminal jurisdiction in Indian County without tribal consent and special elections.[14] Many in Indian Country were disappointed because Congress did not rescind the existing

Public Law 280 jurisdictions. While the Indian Civil Rights Act (ICRA) was presented as a measure to increase tribal authority and self-determination, many in Indian Country saw it as yet another attempt to undermine tribal traditionalism while imposing Euro-American jurisprudence upon tribal courts. The ICRA did legally afford Indian defendants the basic "Bill of Rights" guarantees that other Americans have long enjoyed.

Prior to the ICRA, tribes were not subject to the federal Constitution; the IRA allowed them to design their own tribal constitutions incorporating traditional ways and customs. With the ICRA, tribal courts, many with white judges, are now held to Western-style laws and procedures, except for major crimes, where the U.S. Attorney and FBI still hold primary jurisdiction. Omitted from this refinement of tribal court jurisdiction are the areas of probate, juvenile justice, domestic relations, and housing matters. Clearly, the 1968 ICRA served notice to Indian Country that only the U.S. style of civil and criminal justice will be tolerated and that tribal authority is to be greatly curtailed.

A number of subsequent cases have refined the strengths and limitations of tribal authority in the realm of criminal justice. In 1978, the U.S. Supreme Court, in *United States v. Wheeler*, ruled that tribes and tribal courts held inherent criminal jurisdiction over only their enrolled members, even though this was not a salient issue in the case. That same year, the U.S. Supreme Court, in *Oliphant v. Suquamish Indian Tribe*, ruled that tribal jurisdiction did not extend to non-Indians arrested in Indian Country. Later, in *Merrion v. Jicarilla Apache Tribe*, the federal courts recognized the tribes' power of exclusion for unwanted persons, including member Indians, nonmember Indians, and non-Indians, as long as these individuals do not hold federally conferred rights to be in Indian Country. It was *Dura v. Reina*, however, that led to statutory changes relating to tribal judicial authority over nontribal Indians. In 1990, the U.S. Supreme Court, in *Dura*, stated that tribes do not hold criminal jurisdiction over nonmember Indians who commit crimes on the reservation. In 1991, the U.S. Congress exercised its authority as ultimate guardian in all matters within Indian Country, passing Public Law 102-137, an Act entitled "Criminal Jurisdiction over Indians" reinstating tribal judicial authority over all Indians in Indian Country, including nonmember Indians.[15]

Report on Indian Education

Native American activists have long criticized the U.S. government's handling of Indian education, especially the boarding schools. The American Indian Policy Review Commission cited the failures of the Eisenhower–Emmons Era in the 1976 Final Report of Task Force Five—Indian Education:

> The years of the Eisenhower administration from 1953 to 1961 were not brilliant ones for Indian education. This was the decade of House Concurrent Resolution 108 . . . which sought to terminate the government's role as trustee. Actually, termination was accomplished with the Menominee and Klamath tribes, and while termination was repudiated as national policy before the decade was out, the government continued to define its trusteeship very narrowly. For example, federal educational services, whether performed directly by the BIA or by contract with the states under the authority of the Johnson-O'Malley Act, were provided solely on the basis of the tax exempt status of Indian land held in trusteeship by the federal government. Thus, federal educational services were awarded only to Indians living on reservations and were denied to urban Indians, even though the latter might have moved to the city with the encouragement of the BIA's "relocation" branch, later renamed "employment assistance." Treaty obligations were considered to be of little effect.[16]

The task force on Indian education was the outgrowth of a 1969 Special Subcommittee on Indian Education initially chaired by Senator Robert Kennedy and subsequently chaired by his brother, Senator Edward Kennedy, following the his brother's murder. Following a comprehensive two-year investigation, the subcommittee members told Congress that they were shocked at what they had discovered, recommending that a White House Conference on American Indian Affairs be convened, along with a Senate Select Committee on the Human Needs of American Indians. They felt that this problem was so vast that it required an initiative similar to the Marshall Plan that revitalized post-war Europe. In their conclusions they stated: "it is sufficient to restate our basic finding: that our Nation's policies and programs for educating American Indians are a national tragedy."[17] Other studies at this time drew similar conclusions. Fuchs and Havinghurst, in their report on their National Study of Indian Education, published in their book, *To Live on This Earth*, were also critical of Indian education, notably the BIA boarding schools. Similarly, Costo and Henry noted concerns in Indian Country over BIA-directed education. The major concern here was that the BIA controlled the schools, the curriculum, the choice of textbooks, and the students themselves. BIA education up to the self-determination era was based on forced resocialization along with the derogation of Indian culture. Indeed, it was not until the mid-1960s that meaningful input was incorporated into the BIA's educational structure.[18]

The Nixon Initiative toward Reversing the Eisenhower Legacy

The initiatives on and investigations into U.S. Indian policies by the Kennedy and Johnson administrations obviously influenced President Nixon, who solidified the movement toward Indian self-determination. This seems out of context for Richard Nixon, who served eight years as Eisenhower's vice president and was one of the most outspoken opponents of "Communism." Indeed, we now know of his administration's complicity in the right-wing death squads operating in South America under the authority of the anti-Communist dictators of Argentina, Bolivia, Brazil, Chile, Paraguay, and Uruguay under *Plan Condor*. Clearly, the cold war reignited the United States' hemispheric police efforts under the Monroe Doctrine, with Nixon and Reagan being strong adherents of this policy. Anti-Communism here meant support for the rich elites of European descent at the expense of the poor Indians and *mestizos* of the region. Given this scenario, it is uncharacteristic for President Nixon to appear as a champion of the American Indian and the preservation of Indian Country. Nonetheless, this is the case and was articulated in his July 8, 1970 Special Message on Indian Affairs:

> To the Congress of the United States:
> The first Americans—the Indians—are the most deprived and most isolated minority group in our nation. On virtually every scale of measurement—employment, income, education, health—the condition of the Indian people ranks at the bottom.
> This condition is the heritage of centuries of injustice. From the time of their first contact with European settlers, the American Indians have been oppressed and brutalized, deprived of their ancestral lands and denied the opportunity to control their own destiny. Even the Federal programs which are intended to meet their needs have frequently proven to be ineffective and demeaning.
> But the story of the Indian in America is something more than the record of the white man's frequent aggression, broken agreements, intermittent remorse and prolonged failure. It is a record also of endurance, of survival, of adaptation and creativity in the face of overwhelming obstacles. It is a record of enormous

contributions to this country—to its art and culture, to its strength and spirit, to its sense of history and its sense of purpose.

It is long past time that the Indian policies of the Federal government began to recognize and build upon the capacities and insights of the Indian people. Both as a matter of justice and as a matter of enlightened social policy, we must begin to act on the basis of what the Indians themselves have long been telling us. The time has come to break decisively with the past and to create the conditions for a new era in which the Indian future is determined by Indian acts and Indian decisions.

Self-Determination without Termination

The first and most basic question that must be answered with respect to Indian policy concerns the historic and legal relationship between the Federal government and Indian communities. In the past, this relationship has oscillated between two equally harsh and unacceptable extremes.

On the one hand, it has—at various times during previous Administrations—been the stated policy objective of both the Executive and Legislative branches of the Federal government eventually to terminate the trusteeship relationship between the Federal government and the Indian people. As recently as August of 1953, in House Concurrent Resolution 108, the Congress declared that termination was the long-range goal of its Indian policies. This would mean that Indian tribes would eventually lose any special standing they had under Federal law: the tax exempt status of their lands would be discontinued; Federal responsibility for their economic and social well-being would be effectively dismantled. Tribal property would be divided among individual members who would then be assimilated into the society at large.

This policy of forced termination is wrong, in my judgment, for a number of reasons. First, the premises on which it rests are wrong. Termination implies that the Federal government has taken on a trusteeship responsibility for Indian communities as an act of generosity toward a disadvantaged people and that it can therefore discontinue this responsibility on a unilateral basis whenever it sees fit. But the unique status of Indian tribes does not rest on any premise such as this. The special relationship between Indians and the Federal government is the result instead of solemn obligations which have been entered into by the United States Government. Down through the years, through written treaties and through formal and informal agreements, our government has made specific commitments to the Indian people. For their part, the Indians have often surrendered claims to vast tracts of land and have accepted life on government reservations. In exchange, the government has agreed to provide community services such as health, education and public safety, services which would presumably allow Indian communities to enjoy a standard of living comparable to that of other Americans.

This goal, of course, has never been achieved. But the special relationship between Indian tribes and the Federal government which arises from these agreements continues to carry immense moral and legal force. To terminate this relationship would be no more appropriate than to terminate the citizenship rights of any other American.

The second reason for rejecting forced termination is that the practical results have been clearly harmful in the few instances in which termination actually has been tried. The removal of Federal trusteeship responsibility has produced considerable disorientation among the affected Indians and has left them unable to relate to a myriad of Federal, State and local assistance efforts. Their economic and social condition has often been worse after termination than it was before.

The third argument I would make against forced termination concerns the effect it has had upon the overwhelming majority of tribes which still enjoy a special relationship with the Federal government. The very threat that this relationship may someday be ended has created a great deal of apprehension among Indian groups and this apprehension, in turn, has had a blighting effect on tribal progress. Any step that might result in greater social, economic or political autonomy is regarded with suspicion by many Indians who fear that it will only bring them closer to the day when the Federal government will disavow its responsibility and cut them adrift.

In short, the fear of one extreme policy, forced termination, has often worked to produce the opposite extreme: excessive dependence on the Federal government. In many cases this dependence is so great that the Indian community is almost entirely run by outsiders who are responsible and responsive to Federal officials in Washington, D.C., rather than to the communities they are supposed to be serving. This is the second of the two harsh approaches which have long plagued our Indian policies. Of the Department of the Interior's programs directly serving Indians, for example, only 1.5 percent are presently under Indian control. Only 2.4 percent of HEW's [Health, Education and Welfare] Indian health programs are run by Indians. The result is a burgeoning Federal bureaucracy, programs which are far less effective than they ought to be, and an erosion of Indian initiative and morale.

I believe that both of these policy extremes are wrong. Federal termination errs in one direction, Federal paternalism errs in the other. Only by clearly rejecting both of these extremes can we achieve a policy which truly serves the best interests of Indian people. Self-determination among the Indian people can and must be encouraged without the threat of eventual termination. In my view, in fact, that is the only way that self-determination can effectively be fostered....

The Indians of America need Federal assistance—this much has long been clear. What has not always been clear, however, is that the Federal government needs Indian energies and Indian leadership if its assistance is to be effective in improving the conditions of Indian life. It is a new and balanced relationship between the United States government and the first Americans that is at the heart of our approach to Indian problems. And that is why we now approach these problems with new confidence that they will successfully be overcome."[19]

Clearly, the Johnson/Nixon doctrines, guided by the Kennedy Report, provided the foundation for Indian self-determination and the New Federalism whereby the federal government formed a partnership with tribes and Indian leaders in dealing with problems in Indian Country both on the reservation and in the urban Indian centers. President Nixon was true to his philosophy, helping the Taos Pueblo tribe of New Mexico get its traditional religious grounds, Blue Lake, returned to the tribe in December 1970. This was of tremendous cultural significance since President Nixon made specific mention of the religious importance of this land to the traditional worship of the Pueblo Indians. In June 1972, Congress acted on the 1969 Kennedy Report by passing the Indian Education Act, which provided for a special Indian desk within the Department of Health, Education, and Welfare.

Also in June 1972, the federal policy of Indian preference was extended to American Indians within the Bureau of Indian Affairs to cover all vacancies. This expansion of the original IRA law was later upheld in 1974 when a non-Indian challenged the Indian preference rule within the BIA saying that it did not comply with the provisions of the Equal Employment Opportunity Act of 1972. In *Morton v. Mancari*, the U.S. Supreme Court upheld Indian preference, stating that it was not based on racial discrimination but rather on the special legal status of American Indians.

A landmark event was the Menominee Restoration Act of December 22, 1973, which led to the repeal of the Termination Act of June 17, 1954. This Act restored the Menominee tribe to federal protective status. In October 1974, Indian students were afforded due process protection rights while attending either BIA or Johnson–O'Malley schools. However, perhaps the most significant event during the termination/relocation era was the establishment of the American Indian Policy Review Commission, authorized on January 2, 1975. The commission was authorized by a joint resolution of both the House of Representatives and the U.S. Senate. Nevertheless, strong opposition to Indian self-determination was evident in the conservative western states—those states that benefited most from taking lands from both Hispanics and American Indians. And while the partnership concept of American Indian policy finally placed tribes on the same playing field as other social, political, and business interests in the country, they still were disadvantaged in these endeavors until the advent of Indian gaming[20]

Chapter Six

Indian Self-Determination and the New Federalism

Establishing the American Indian Policy Review Commission

The American Indian Policy Review Commission set the stage for the contemporary scene in Indian Country. The crises involving Indian Country and Indian activism led certain members of Congress to question the status of Indian affairs in the early 1970s, causing them to look again at the recommendations of the Kennedy Report. Toward this end, James Abourezk, the U.S. senator from South Dakota, led the effort to establish the American Indian Policy Review Commission, which was authorized by a joint resolution on January 2, 1975. This comprehensive review addressed the following areas of Indian affairs: (1) trust responsibility and the federal–Indian relationship, including treaty review; (2) tribal government; (3) federal administration and structure of Indian affairs; (4) federal, state, and tribal jurisdiction; (5) Indian education; (6) Indian health; (7) reservation development; (8) urban, rural nonreservation, terminated, and non–federally recognized Indians; and (9) Indian law revision, consolidation, and codification. The commission's mandate and general recommendations are stated in its 1977 Final Report:

> A Policy for the Future
>
> This final report of the American Indian Policy Review Commission represents 2 years of intensive investigative work encompassing the entire field of Federal-Indian relations. The last such investigation occurred almost 50 years ago. The conclusions of that investigation and its condemnation of the policies which had governed Federal administration over the preceding 50 years brought an abrupt shift in the statutory policies governing the Federal-Indian relations, a complete repudiation of the policies which had controlled from the late 1800's to the mid-1930's. And yet the American Indian today finds himself in a position little better than that which he enjoyed in 1928 when the Meriam Report was issued.
>
> It has been the fortune of this Commission to be the first in the long history of this Nation to listen attentively to the voice of the Indian rather than the Indian expert. The findings and recommendations which appear in this report are founded on that Indian voice. It can only be hoped that this Commission will be seen as a

watershed in the long and often tarnished history of this Country's treatment of its original people.

What are the explanations for the circumstance in which the Indian finds himself today? First and foremost are the consistently damaging Federal policies of the past—policies which sought through the first three-quarters of the 19th century to remove the Indian people from the midst of the European settlers by isolating them on reservations; and policies which after accomplishing isolation were then directed toward breaking down their social and governmental structures and throwing their land, water, timber and mineral resources open to exploitation by non-Indians. These policies were repudiated by Congress with passage of the Indian Reorganization Act of 1934, but by this time severe damage had been done.

It is the legacy of these policies with which the Indian people attempt to cope today; it is the legacy of these policies which this Commission examines in this report; and it is the legacy of these policies which the people of the United States must resolve over the next years.

One of the greatest obstacles faced by the Indian today in his drive for self-determination and a place in this Nation is the American public's ignorance of the historical relationship of the United States with Indian tribes and the lack of general awareness of the status of the American Indian in our society today. To adequately formulate a future Indian policy it is necessary to understand the policies of the past. For this reason the Commission has included extensive discussion of law and history in order to provide a foundation for understanding matters which affect Indian people.

The relationship of the American Indian tribes to the United States is founded on principles of international law. It is a political relation: a relation of a weak people to a strong people; a relationship founded on treaties in which the Indian tribes placed themselves under the protection of the United States and the United States assumed the obligation of supplying such protection. It is a relationship recognized in the law of this Nation as that of a domestic, dependent sovereign.

It is a relationship which has sometimes in the past been honored but more frequently violated and at times even terminated. It is a relationship which can and should be nurtured and cherished by this Nation. The fact that the United States has not chosen to disavow this relationship, has not chosen to simply abrogate its treaty commitments, has not chosen to withdraw its recognition of Indians as separate and distinct peoples with cultures, land and governments of their own—these facts set the United States above other nations in its treatment of its native people, and provide a moral and legal setting from which a forward-looking policy of Federal-Indian relations must progress. No other course will do honor to this Nation; no other course can hold any future for the Indian people.

The fundamental concepts which must guide future policy determinations are:

    1.   That Indian tribes are sovereign political bodies, having the power to determine their own membership and power to enact laws and enforce them within the boundaries of their reservations, and

2. That the relationship which exists between the tribes and the United States is premised on a special trust that must govern the conduct of the stronger toward the weaker....

Certain broad concepts have been agreed upon which we believe should guide future policy in relationship to the trust doctrine:

1. The trust responsibility to American Indians extends from the protection and enhancement of Indian trust resources and tribal self-government to the provision of economic and social programs necessary to raise the standard of living and social well being of the Indian people to a level comparable to the non-Indian society.

2. The trust responsibility extends through the tribe to the Indian member, whether on or off the reservation.

3. The trust responsibility applies to all United States agencies and instrumentalities, not just those charged specifically with the administration of Indian affairs....

Finally, Indian project initiatives must be encouraged through a program, planning, and budget process which is guided by Indian priorities rather than to satisfy the needs of a self-perpetuating bureaucracy.

It is the conclusion of this Commission that:

1. The executive branch should propose a plan for a consolidated Indian Department or independent agency. Indian programs should be transferred to this new consolidated agency where appropriate.

2. Bureaucratic processes must be revised to develop an Indian budget system operating from a "zero" base, consistent with long-range Indian priorities and needs. Those budget requests by tribes should be submitted without interference to Congress.

3. Federal laws providing for delivery of domestic assistance to State and local governments must be revised to include Indian tribes as eligible recipients.

4. To the maximum extent possible, appropriations should be delivered directly to Indian tribes and organizations through grants and contracts; the first obligation being to trust requirements.[1]

An important outcome of the review commission was the establishment of the post of assistant secretary for Indian affairs under the secretary of the interior. This idea was first put forth by President Nixon, but it took the impact of the American Indian Policy Review Commission's Final Report recommendations for this action to take place, under President Carter's administration. This essentially established what is now commonly known as the "Indian desk" in the Department of the Interior. The assistant secretary is traditionally an enrolled American Indian. His or her main responsibility is to run and oversee the Bureau of Indian Affairs (BIA).[2]

Indian Self-Determination and Education Act

Two days following the authorization of the comprehensive American Indian Policy Review Commission, Congress passed the Indian Self-Determination and Education Assistance Act, laying the foundation for the new era of Indian self-determination. A major element of this Act was its provision for tribes to contract to run their own education and health programs and to have more control over curriculum matters.

An Act to provide maximum Indian participation in the Government and education of Indian people; to provide for the full participation of Indian tribes in programs and services conducted by the Federal Government for Indians and to encourage the development of human resources of the Indian people; to establish a program of assistance to upgrade Indian education; to support the right of Indian citizens to control their own educational activities; and for other purposes (Public Law 93-638)

Title 1—Indian Self-Determination Act
Section 101. This title may be cited as the "Indian Self-Determination Act."
Contracts by the Secretary of the Interior
Section 102. (a) The Secretary of the Interior is directed, upon the request of any Indian tribe, to enter into a contract or contracts with any tribal organization of any such Indian tribe to plan, conduct, and administer programs, or portions thereof, provided for in the Act of April 16, 1934 (48 Stat. 596), as amended by this Act, any other program or portion thereof which the Secretary of the Interior is authorized to administer for the benefit of Indians under the Act of November 21, 1921 (42 Stat. 208), and any Act subsequent thereto: Provided, however, That the Secretary may initially decline to enter into any contract requested by an Indian tribe if he finds that: (1) the service to be rendered to the Indian beneficiaries of the particular program or function to be contracted will not be satisfactory; (2) adequate protection of trust resources is not assured, or (3) the proposed project or function to be contracted for cannot be properly completed or maintained by the proposed contract: Provided further, That in arriving at his finding, the Secretary shall consider whether the tribe or tribal organization would be deficient in performance under the contract with respect to (A) equipment, (B) bookkeeping and accounting procedures, (C) substantive knowledge of the program to be contracted for, (D) community support for the contract, (E) adequately trained personnel, or (F) other necessary components of contract performance.

(b) Whenever the Secretary declines to enter into a contract or contracts pursuant to subsection (a) of this section, he shall (1) state his objections in writing to the tribe within sixty days, (2) provide to the extent practicable assistance to the tribe or tribal organization to overcome his stated objections, and (3) provide the tribe with a hearing, under such rules and regulations as he may promulgate, and the opportunity for appeal. . . .

Contracts by the Secretary of Health, Education, and Welfare

Section 103. (a) The Secretary of Health, Education, and Welfare is directed, upon the request of any Indian tribe, to enter into a contract or contracts with any tribal organization of any such Indian tribe to carry out any or all of his functions, authorities, and responsibilities under the Act of August 5, 1954 (68 Stat. 674), as amended....

Grants to Indian Tribal Organizations

Section 104. (a) The Secretary of the Interior is authorized, upon the request of any Indian tribe (from funds appropriated for the benefit of Indians pursuant to the Act of November 2, 1921 (42 Stat. 208), and any Act subsequent thereto) to contract with or make a grant or grants to any tribal organization for—

(1) the strengthening or improvement of tribal government (including, but not limited to, the development, improvement, and administration of planning, financial management, or merit personnel systems; the improvement of tribally funded programs or activities; or the development, construction, improvement, maintenance, preservation, or operation of tribal facilities or resources);

(2) the planning, training, evaluation of other activities designed to improve the capacity of a tribal organization to enter into contract or contracts pursuant to section 102 of this Act and the additional costs associated with the initial years of operation under such a contract or contracts:

(3) the acquisition of land in connection with items (1) and (2) above: Provided, That in the case of land within reservation boundaries or which adjoins on at least two sides land held in trust by the United States for the tribe or for individual Indians, the Secretary of Interior may (upon request of the tribe) acquire such land in trust for the tribe; or

(4) the planning, designing, monitoring, and evaluating of Federal programs serving the tribe.

(b) The Secretary of Health, Education, and Welfare may, in accordance with regulations adopted pursuant to section 107 of this Act, make grants to any Indian tribe or tribal organization for—

(1) the development, construction, operation, provision, or maintenance of adequate health facilities or services including the training of personnel for such work, from funds appropriated to the Indian Health Service for Indian health services or Indian health facilities; or

(2) planning, training, evaluation or other activities designed to improve the capacity of a tribal organization to enter into a contract or contracts pursuant to section 103 of this Act....

Effect on Existing Rights

Section 110. Nothing in this Act shall be construed as—

(1) affecting, modifying, diminishing, otherwise impairing the sovereign immunity from suit enjoyed by an Indian tribe; or

(2) authorizing or requiring the termination of any existing trust responsibility of the United States with respect to the Indian people.

Title II—The Indian Education Assistance Act

Section 201. This title may be cited as the "Indian Education Assistance Act."

Part A – Education of Indians in Public Schools. Section 202. .... Section 4. The Secretary of the Interior shall not enter into any contracts for the education of Indians unless the prospective contractor has submitted to, and has had approved by the Secretary of the Interior, an education plan, which plan, in the determination of the Secretary, contains educational objectives which adequately address the educational needs of the Indian students. . . .

Section 5. . . . Whenever a school district affected by a contract or contracts for the education of Indians pursuant to this Act has a local school board not composed of a majority of Indians, the parents of the Indian children enrolled in the school or schools affected by such contract or contracts shall elect a local committee from among their number. Such committee shall fully participate in the development of, and shall have the authority to approve or disapprove programs to be conducted under such contracts or contracts. . . .[3]

Not everyone was pleased with the movement toward Indian self-determination. Those states and industries that benefited most from termination and exploitation of resources in Indian Country were the most displeased. Indeed, most western states were in favor of full state rights over Indian Country regardless of whether they were included in the Public Law 280 termination scheme. Representing themselves as the Council of State Governments, they presented their objections to the findings of the American Indian Policy Review Commission, which legitimized and expanded the scope of the Indian Self-Determination and Education Assistance Act.

RESOLUTION ON THE AMERICAN INDIAN POLICY REVIEW COMMISSION

WHEREAS, the American Indian Policy Review Commission has recently completed its report to Congress; and

WHEREAS, the Commission Report has assumed as first principles that all policy and legal issues in contemporary Indian law should be resolved in favor of the Indians; and

WHEREAS, the Western Conference of The Council of State Governments believes that the Commission Report fails to recognize the following facts:

1. That the Constitution of the United States provides for only two sovereign powers—the United States and the several states within their spheres of influence.

2. Indian tribes are political subdivisions of the United States and are not sovereign in their own sphere.

3. Powers not specifically denied by treaty are not reserved to the tribes.

4. The intent of the Federal Congress in establishing Indian self-government was purposive in nature, to maintain tribal integrity and identity. Therefore, Congress did not intend Indian government to be general or territorial in nature.

5. There is no legal doctrine whereby one entering the land of another consents to general lawmaking and enforcing authority of the landowner.

6. The Commission Report fails to recognize that Indian tribes are no longer isolated communities; and

WHEREAS, the granting of sovereignty to Indian tribes and the necessary inclusion of non-Indians under their jurisdiction will destroy the ability of Indian peoples to make their own laws and be governed by them.

THEREFORE, BE IT RESOLVED, by the Western Conference of The Council of State Governments, that it agrees with the Minority Report of Congressman Lloyd Meeds, Vice Chairman of the American Indian Policy Review Commission, that Americans are justified in believing that 400 years have been sufficient to quiet title to the continent; and

BE IT FURTHER RESOLVED that the Western Conference also agrees with the following recommendations and opinions of the Minority Report:

1. That Congress should enact comprehensive legislation defining the scope and nature of tribal self-government, making clear that tribal governmental powers are limited.

2. Legislation should be enacted directly prohibiting Indian courts from exercising criminal jurisdiction or civil jurisdiction over any non-Indian or Indian who is not a member of the tribe which operated the court.

3. Congress should enact legislation allowing civil jurisdiction in state courts against Indian defendants in all cases where states would have jurisdiction were it not for Indian status of the defendant, and tribal government does not provide a judicial forum. Tribal interests could be protected by providing that rules of decision must be given appropriate weight in state court.

4. Congress should bar actions by Indians against non-Indians for claims arising on reservations where tribes have not provided forums for similar actions by non-Indians against Indians.

5. Congress should enact legislation confirming that states have the same power to levy taxes, the legal incidence of which falls upon non-Indian activities or property, on Indian reservations as they have off Indian reservations. The exemptions to this blanket state authority should come in instances where federal regulation of special subject matter would preempt state regulation.

6. Congress should expressly proscribe the authorization for tribal taxation of nonmembers or property of nonmembers.

7. With regard to the Indian Civil Rights Act of 1968, if Indian governments are to exercise governmental powers as licensees of the United States, it is imperative that they be fully answerable for the improper exercise of those powers.

8. To the extent that chosen national Indian policy entails financial burdens on persons other than Indians, it is neither fair nor rational for those burdens to be cast disproportionately on the taxpayers of the states in which Indian reservations are situated.

9. Congress should undertake to define "Indian Country" for the various purposes for which the term is used.

10. In regards to the operation of Public Law 280, if withdrawal from state jurisdiction is to be done on grounds of federal policy, the policy choices should be made by Congress, which can weigh fairly the cost of balkanizing state jurisdictions as well as the advantages to Indians.

11. In the Absence of ultimate authority over Indian land use planning lying with federal officials, the fairest system would be to place final authority in state planning agencies in which Indians would participate equally with other affected citizens; and

BE IT FURTHER RESOLVED, that copies of this resolution be delivered to the President of the United States, the President Pro Tempore of the United States Senate, the Speaker of the United States House of Representatives, the Secretaries of Agriculture and the Interior and to the Congressional Delegation of each of the member states of the Western Conference of The Council of State Governments and each of the six easterly adjoining states.

As Approved by the Western Conference of The Council of State Governments, September 28, 1977.[4]

The leaders of the American Indian Historical Society, Rupert Costo and Jeannette Henry, warned in 1977 that the Meeds minority report from the American Indian Policy Review Commission would provide fuel for those who wanted to continue the devastating effects of termination and Public Law 280. Indeed, Meeds and others in Congress proposed legislation that would further open up Indian Country for continued exploitation by non-Indian interests. Costo and Henry saw this movement as an attempt to emasculate tribal sovereignty and Indian rights while destroying federal treaty obligations. Charles Wilkinson, in his 2005 book *Blood Struggle*, described the conservative anti-Indian movement within the U.S. Supreme Court. Here, tribal sovereignty was assailed with respect to tribal self-determination and the tribe's authority to tax oil and gas companies that had lucrative deals with the U.S. Department of Interior to exploit natural resources in Indian Country, with impunity from prosecution by tribal governments.

Wilkinson cites the *Merrion v. Jicarilla Apache* case, which went to the U.S. Supreme Court in 1982. This case favored the tribes in their efforts to earn revenues in order to provide governmental services to their people. The

Court decided that tribes must have similar flexibility to other sovereign governmental entities to generate revenues for municipal services. Justice Thurgood Marshall, who wrote the opinion, noted the dire needs within Indian Country compared with the riches of the big corporations and concluded that there is nothing exceptional in these enterprises contributing via taxes to the general cost of tribal government. Wilkinson also noted that these sentiments in the Supreme Court changed once William Rehnquist arrived in 1972 and as the Court became more conservative and pro-state rights with the addition of Antonin Scalia in 1986 and Clarence Thomas in 1991.

Another element of the western governors' manifesto to exploit Indian Country was the issue of the state's right to tax tribal revenues, notably profits made by businesses in Indian Country that also serve non-Indian customers. Canby notes that state powers of taxation are severely restricted in Indian Country and that adherence to this exclusionary rule was a major factor in allowing western states admission to the Union. Ironically, Congress, in 1924, allowed states to tax royalties from mineral leases of Indian trust lands—the same function these very states have fought so hard to keep tribes from exercising. Hence, the general rule of thumb is that Indians residing in Indian Country, notably federally recognized reservations, are exempt from state income taxes and the like. However, Indians residing outside Indian Country are subject to state jurisdiction, including being taxed for taxable activity. Moreover, the state can even tax the income of tribal members working on the reservation if they reside off the reservation.[5]

Self-determination was also countered with increased federal criminal jurisdiction, especially following the Wounded Knee II incident. In the Indian Crimes Act of 1976, the Major Crimes Act of 1885 was expanded beyond the original seven Index Crimes to include exclusive federal jurisdiction over the following offenses committed within Indian Country: murder; manslaughter; kidnapping; rape; carnal knowledge by a man of any woman, not his wife, who has not attained the age of sixteen (statutory rape); assault with intent to commit rape; incest; assault with intent to commit murder; assault with a dangerous weapon (aggravated assault); assault resulting in serious bodily injury (aggravated assault and battery); arson; burglary; robbery; and larceny. This translates to the FBI and federal attorney having authority over tribal police and tribal courts in relation to these offenses in Indian Country. Moreover, in 1978, in *United States v.*

Wheeler, the U.S. Supreme Court upheld the right of the FBI and federal courts to charge Indian defendants with a major crime even when tribal courts had already ruled on the same incident as a lesser offense within their jurisdiction. This ruling means that Indians accused of crimes within Indian Country are subject to double jeopardy by virtue of this dual criminal justice system.[6]

As mentioned, in *Oliphant v. Suquamish Indian Tribe*, also heard in 1978, the U.S. Supreme Court ruled that tribal jurisdiction did not extend to non-Indians other than in enforcing decorum (contempt orders) against disruptive non-Indians in Indian Country. These restrictions on tribal courts and police continued until 1991, when the U.S. Congress finally curtailed Supreme Court interventions by strengthening tribal criminal jurisdiction with passage of Public Law 102-137—"Criminal Jurisdiction over Indians." Two years later, Congress passed the Indian Tribal Act of 1993, which attempted to bring tribal codes up to those of the Anglo-based U.S. system in general. With this Act came a new support system known as the Office of Tribal Justice Support. Taken together, these efforts have resulted in an increase in the number of tribal courts within Indian Country.[7]

Self-Determination, Indian Education, and Religious Freedom

Indian Education

In the previous chapter, it was noted that Indian education was addressed in the Kennedy Report. Indeed, the Senate Subcommittee on Indian Education, chaired by Senator Robert Kennedy, led to the National Study of Indian Education. This study in turn led to Indian education being part of the American Indian Policy Review Commission, resulting in Task Force Five—Indian Education. Interestingly, the four primary members of Task Force Five were American Indians representing the Lumbee, Blackfeet, Colville, and Missouri-Cherokee tribes. These tribal leaders articulated the Native American perspective on self-determination in relation to Indian education in the preface to their Final Report:

> Many hundreds of years ago, at the beginning of history, our wise men foretold of the coming of other people to this land. They foresaw a time of rapid change and confusion in which our youth would be growing into adulthood unprepared to cope with these new conditions. We the Native Americans people, are now at that very point in our history and we must take account of our responsibility to our young. Our ancient wise men never imagined that we would not or could not respond to

that responsibility. Responsibility for the welfare of the young is so much a part of Native American life that it is assumed.

Throughout most of history, Native Americans were the most free and the most responsible of peoples. We were free to make decisions and to deal with our own destiny. . . . Unfortunately, for most of the last hundred years, we have not been free, in the ultimate sense of the word, and thus we have not been able to exercise our responsibility. However, the situation of our young demands that we attend to their educational needs. We know that the development of our children must be not only the responsibility of the school, but also of parents, relatives, and the whole community. It must be a joint responsibility, as it is among all other Americans. Such a setting can only be provided by Indian controlled schools.

We see the function of the Indian controlled schools as two-fold. Firstly, it gives us, Native American adults, a chance to express our concern for our children and to help them in their education. Further, it is a place for us to learn, and to make a contribution. We have learned much about modern life by democratically electing school boards, by discussing budgets and curriculum, in negotiations with teachers, and by just being involved in the workings of a modern education. We want to help the school develop the student into a person who knows how to live in harmony with others and who has respect for himself and all men. . . . We know that education starts in the home and continues in the school. We must see to it that the home and the school complement one another and are consistent and mutually supportive. We feel that these goals can be realized only through Indian control of our schools.[8]

Tribal self-determination in education was also an important element of cultural preservation. In the past, education was a tool for forced resocialization and cultural genocide. Its main outcome was psychological marginalization and the birth of poverty and a host of mental and physical health problems in both Indian Country and the federally established urban Indian ghettos. A resurgence of traditional Indian ways was associated with Indians' input into their own education. Among the first groups to take advantage of Indian self-determination in Indian Country schools were the Navajo. Indeed, the Rough Rock Demonstration School became the first contemporary Indian-directed educational experiment sanctioned by the federal government in Indian Country.

It was significant that the Navajo took the initiative in self-determination in tribal education given that they were the prime target of Indian Commissioner Glenn Emmons's 1950s effort to detraditionalize Indian culture. This program was known as the Navajo Emergency Education Program (NEEP), or locally as the Borderline Program with borderline schools. The NEEP program comprised a federally subsidized public school system intended to accommodate thousands of Navajo youth. The schools were built off the reservation in borderline towns such as Gallup, New Mexico. An adjunct to this program was the Mormon program of placing Indian youth (Navajo, Ute, Pueblos) with white Mormon families during the nine-month school year so as to resocialize them into the Mormon socioreligious perspective. In addition to concerns about the Mormons robbing these youths of their language and traditions, American Indian traditionalists were concerned about the secretive nature of this program, which has continued to the present.

The Rough Rock Demonstration School was started in 1966 at Chinle, Arizona, in the Navajo Nation and was funded jointly through the BIA and the now-defunct Office of Economic Opportunity. Navajo input was through an organization called DINE (Demonstration in Navajo Education), a term spelled the same as their traditional name—the Diné. A local school board supervised the curriculum for some 250 students ranging from Head Start to the 10th grade. What was significant in this Indian-run curriculum was that Navajo culture and language were major elements. The Rough Rock school also exposed weaknesses that had to be overcome if more Indian-run schools were to be effective in Indian Country. One major factor was the heavy reliance on the traditional oral presentation of Navajo history and culture; another was the lack of state-approved Navajo teachers.

The first of these issues was addressed by the Navajo Curriculum Center that was established in 1967 from Title 1 of the Elementary and Secondary Education Act. Its main purpose was to provide material required for instruction in Navajo history, language, and culture. This project led to the written transcription of the Navajo language—a language very different from English. Indeed, the Athapaskan language is so different that it was used by the United States Marine Corps during World War II as a communications medium. Here, Navajo men were recruited by the Marine Corps to be "code talkers." The Japanese could not decode the Navajo language and the code talkers are credited with having played a significant role in the success of the Pacific campaigns. The original Navajo code talkers were subsequently recognized by President Clinton and eventually awarded the Congressional Gold Medal on July 26, 2001, by President George W. Bush. Other Navajos trained as code talkers were awarded the Congressional Silver Medal, including the long-serving tribal chairman Peter MacDonald.

The second issue was the lack of Navajos with a formal education to act as teachers, a requirement imposed by the three states within which the Navajo Nation resides—Arizona, New Mexico, and Utah. Again, the Navajo Nation took the lead in this effort, establishing on July 1, 1968, the Navajo Community College (NCC), the first Indian-run college in the country. While the college had to rely on non-Indian faculty during its developmental years, it required that the curriculum be presented from an Indian-centric perspective, with a focus on Navajo culture, history, and language.

In December, 1971, Congress passed the Navajo Community College bill assisting in the funding of the program. This led to passage of the Tribally Controlled Community College Assistance Act of October, 1978, which provided grants to tribes for the establishment of community colleges. A month later, Congress passed the Education Amendments Act of 1978 (Public Law 95-561—Title XI—Indian Education). This Act was a reaction to the greater influence of Indian-run school boards. The Act provided for cultural instruction as well as a more standardized curriculum in BIA schools. It also authorized funding for school facilities, including dormitories. Most significant, it freed BIA teachers from the constraints of the civil service system, providing more authority to Indian-run school boards to hire and fire teachers—most of whom were non-Indian at this time.[9]

Following the Navajo Community College lead, other tribes began to organize their own community colleges, including the Turtle Mountain Community College, Standing Rock Community College, and Fort Berthold Community College in North Dakota, the American Indian Satellite Community College in Nebraska, and the Sisseton-Community College in South Dakota. More tribal community colleges followed after passage of the 1975 Indian Self-Determination and Educational Assistance Act. Today, we see many of these two-year colleges transformed into four-year and graduate colleges and universities, including NCC, which is now Diné College. Other notable Indian four-year and graduate facilities are Sinte Gleska University on the Rose Bud Sioux Reservation, Oglala Lakota College on the Pine Ridge Sioux Reservation, and D-Q University (formerly Hehaka Sapa College) in California; even the notorious Haskell industrial boarding school in Kansas is now the inter-tribal Haskell Indian Nation University. Duane Champagne, in volume III of the *Reference Library of Native North America*, notes that there are now thirty-three tribally controlled community colleges, most of which hold membership, along with four-year/graduate programs, in the Tribal Colleges of the American Indian Higher Education Consortium. Other tribes, such as the Eastern Band of Cherokee Indians, have made arrangement with state colleges and universities to provide on-campus courses for tribal members. Another educational milestone was the emergence of Native Indian Studies or Native American Studies among the courses offered in the major colleges and universities in the United States. By 1985, over a hundred of these programs existed.[10]

In the mid-1990s the Navajo Nation Teacher Education Consortium (NNTEC) was created with the help of a Ford Foundation grant. Its goal was to prepare native Navajos to be teachers for their schools. It also hoped to establish a Navajo Department of Education so that Navajos could evaluate their own schools and be directly accredited by the U.S. Department of Education. As things stand now, teachers in the Navajo schools need to meet the Department of Education standards of the state where the school is located (Arizona, New Mexico, or Utah). The standards for teacher accreditation and program approval differ among these states. The NNTEC began to work with local public and private colleges and universities in its effort to produce Navajo teachers, especially teachers who were fluent in the Navajo language. This model, while not fully implemented even today, articulates the basic philosophical and epistemological differences existing between the dominant U.S. standards, based on the Protestant Ethic, and the traditional Native American Harmony Ethos. The NNTEC's stated purpose was outlined in 1991:

> The Navajo Nation has a great need to have more qualified Navajo teachers to teach its children. Currently the 242 schools (K-12) on or near the Reservation are staffed primarily by non-Navajo teachers. Teachers employed by the Navajo Nation schools typically are not Indians and when they are, they are not from the Reservation. These teachers are generally unprepared to work with children from a culture different from their own. Over 6,000 teachers make up the teaching force on the Navajo Nation with responsibility for the education of 70,000 Navajo children. Only approximately 8% of the teachers are Navajo, though virtually all of the teacher aides in the schools are Navajo.
>
> It is well documented in the literature that different cultures produce different learning styles. Cultural influences not only affect learning style, but the subtler aspects of perception and cognitive behavior as well. For example, in comparing non-western to western cultural groupings, non-western cultures (Native

Americans, Mexican Americans, etc.) emphasize group cooperation, value harmony with nature, approach time as relative, accept affective expression, and engage in holistic thinking. Western cultures, on the other hand, emphasize individual competition, achievement for the individual, mastery and control of nature, adhere to a rigid time schedule, limit affective expression, and promote dualistic thinking.[11]

In 1988, the Tribally Controlled Schools Act augmented the 1975 Indian Self-Determination and Education Assistance Act so that outright grants could now be made to tribes for their primary and secondary schools.

Religious Freedom

Traditional spiritualism is the foundation of Indian culture. It has been assaulted since the colonial days, with these attacks forming the basis of cultural genocide. Rooted in the cooperative aboriginal Harmony Ethos, traditional spiritualism was seen as the antithesis of the Euro-American Protestant Ethic and as the force that kept the American Indian cultural ways alive. Attempts to extinguish native languages, rites, and customs were harsh, with the dominant white cultural ways deemed to be superior. Indeed, white supremacy is the main tenet of Manifest Destiny and the ethnocentric policies that have justified the harsh treatment of the indigenous population of the Americas. While the military, militias, and police were responsible for carrying out physical genocide, Christian churches (Catholic, Protestant, Mormon) were the soldiers of cultural genocide surrounding the ever-diminishing Indian Country. While the military long ago withdrew from reservations (to be replaced by the FBI), the churches remain as the cultural police to curtail any aboriginal regression in Indian Country. Indeed, the first thing one is likely to see on entering an Indian reservation are the numerous churches surrounding all the entries, like the walls of a fort. Even then, aboriginal ways have survived to the present. As physical genocide and ethnic cleansing were not able to wipe out the American Indians, neither were attacks on their spirituality able to destroy their culture.

French, in a study of the Appalachian (Eastern Band) of Cherokees in the 1970s, when the reservation population was about 8,000 enrolled members, found that there were twenty-seven churches on or close to the main portion of the reservation (the Qualla Boundary): twenty-one Baptist, one Methodist (with three satellites), one Pentecostal Holiness, one Church of God, one Episcopal, one Latter Day Saints (Mormon), and one Roman Catholic. In assessing this phenomenon, French noted that the Christian influence among the Cherokees coincided with the rise of fundamentalism in America. During the early 1800s, when the Cherokee Nation was rapidly developing its "separate but similar" government, the United States saw the emergence of a rash of new fundamentalist sects, including the Mormons, Pentecostals, Shakers, and the Oneida Community, to mention a few. Many of these churches saw the Cherokees as a rich source of converts and quickly established a foothold on or near the reservation. Later, they were encouraged and rewarded by the government for their efforts at "civilizing" these Indians. The churches established among the Cherokee Nation followed them to Indian Territory (Oklahoma) and continued to proselytize new tribes as whites moved west in the 1800s.

Ten years after the Indian Civil Rights Act, Congress, in a joint resolution, passed a policy supportive of Indian cultural autonomy termed the American Indian Religious Freedom Act (AIRFA):

> Whereas the freedom of religion for all people is an inherent right, fundamental to the democratic structure of the United States and is guaranteed by the First Amendment of the United States Constitution;
>
> Whereas the United States has traditionally rejected the concept of a government denying individuals the right to practice their religion and, as a result, has benefited from a rich variety of religious heritages in this country;
>
> Whereas the religious practices of the American Indian (as well as Native Alaskan and Hawaiian) are an integral part of their culture, tradition and heritage, such practices forming the basis of Indian identity and value systems;
>
> Whereas the traditional American Indian religions, as an integral part of Indian life, are indispensable and irreplaceable;
>
> Whereas the lack of a clear, comprehensive, and consistent Federal policy has often resulted in the abridgment of religious freedom for traditional American Indians;
>
> Whereas such religious infringements result from the lack of knowledge or the insensitive and inflexible enforcement of Federal policies and regulations premised on a variety of laws;
>
> Whereas such laws were designed for such worthwhile purposes as conservation and preservation of natural species and resources but were never intended to relate to Indian religious practices and, therefore, were passed without consideration of their effect on traditional American Indian religions;
>
> Whereas such laws and policies often deny American Indian access to sacred sites required in their religions, including cemeteries;
>
> Whereas such laws at times prohibit the use and possession of sacred objects necessary to the exercise of religious rites and ceremonies;

Whereas traditional American Indian ceremonies have been intruded upon, interfered with, and in a few instances banned: Now, therefore be it

Resolved by the Senate and House of Representatives of the United States of America in Congress assembled, That henceforth it shall be the policy of the United States to protect and preserve for American Indians their inherent right of freedom to believe, express, and exercise the traditional religions of the American Indian, Eskimo, Aleut, and Native Hawaiians, including but not limited to access to sites, use and possession of sacred objects, and freedom to worship through ceremonies and traditional rites.

Section 2. The President shall direct the various Federal departments, agencies, and other instrumentalities responsible for administering relevant laws to evaluate their policies and procedures in consultation with native traditional religious leaders in order to determine appropriate changes necessary to protect and preserve Native American religions and cultural rights and practices. Twelve months after approval of this resolution, the President shall report back to Congress the results of his evaluation, including any changes which were made in administrative policies and procedures, and any recommendations he may have for legislative action.[12]

A companion to the Indian Religious Freedom resolution was passage of the Archaeological Resources Protection Act in October 1979, finally recognizing Indian burial sites as sacred places, just as burial sites are for non-Indians. For centuries, the looting of Indian sites, including burial sites, has been a lucrative cottage industry, with the U.S. government and major colleges and universities and museums being the main culprits in this market. Displaying Indian artifacts, including skeletal remains, did not rise to the same level of repulsion and illegality as grave robbing non-Indians. This Act recognized that "existing Federal laws do not provide adequate protection to prevent the loss and destruction of these archaeological resources and sites resulting from uncontrolled excavations and pillage." Even then, non-Indians could still apply to the Federal land manager for a permit to excavate or remove any archaeological resource located on public land or in Indian Country. Since passage of this law, tribes have fought to have artifacts, including body parts, returned to Indian Country. Religious artifacts are returned for spiritual rituals, while body parts are finally given a traditional burial. Nonetheless, Indian sites continue to be exploited to fuel the lucrative market in such items. Valuable artifacts being excavated today for profit include the burial bowls of the Mimbres and Anasazi tribes located in sites in Arizona and New Mexico.

Regarding the religious freedom resolution, a task force convened to research the incidence of restrictions on traditional spiritual ways noted 522 instances involving 70 tribes in 28 states. The AIRFA and the Archaeological Resources Protection Act did not have strong enforcement clauses, leaving enforcement to the discretion of land managers within the Department of the Interior. The use of eagle feathers and peyote came to symbolize the legal battles for American Indian groups to freely exercise their spiritual rights. Rueben Snake Jr., in Task Force Eleven: Alcohol and Drug Abuse, part of the 1976 Indian Policy Review Commission study, cited the negative effects of the imposition of prohibition in Indian Country: "An 1832 federal Indian law prohibiting the sale of liquor to Indian people remained in effect until 1953 and could have been instrumental in the formation of the 'hidden group,' 'drink until it's gone,' and 'quick' drinking patterns that Native American people exhibit."

These laws were initiated under the Trade and Intercourse Acts with the intention of keeping rumrunners out of Indian Country. But while the initial intention was to protect American Indians from unscrupulous white traders, this prohibition took on new meaning under the shroud of Manifest Destiny. Here, prohibition is linked to the legislation of morality whereby the fundamentalist Protestant sects and Mormons, those who preach abstinence from alcohol, attempted to legislate their moral superiority vis-à-vis the new immigrants into the United States, notably those of Irish, German, and East European descent who were Catholics or Jews—religions that used alcohol in their services. Nonetheless, these restrictions remained as federal policy in Indian Country years after repeal. Even today there is tremendous pressure for tribes to outlaw alcohol on the reservation.

Rueben Snake Jr. was also a strong advocate of religious freedom for the Native American Church and fought to have the 1978 American Indian Religious Freedom Act amended to accept the ritual use of peyote. Toward this end he established the Native American Religious Freedom project with the Native American Rights Fund (NARF). These efforts, with the assistance of both Peterson Zah, president of the Navajo Nation, and Senator Daniel K. Inouye, chairman of the Senate Committee on Indian Affairs, resulted in twelve Congressional hearings recommending the acceptance of the use of peyote by the Native American Church. These recommendations were initially blocked by President George W.H. Bush but were later made into law by President William J. Clinton. With President Clinton's signature, House Resolution 4230 became Public Law 103-344 amending the 1978 Act to legally protect the use, possession, or transportation of peyote in all fifty states and the District of Columbia. President Clinton also signed a directive in 1994 providing for the distribution of eagle feathers for Native American religious purposes. It authorized the Department of the Interior to maintain an adequate refrigerated repository of eagle feathers available to qualified Indian spiritual leaders.[13]

New Federalism, Self-Determination, and Indian Health

Indian Health Status and the Indian Health Service
Indian health has always been a serious concern in Indian Country. As a group, Indians continue to have high morbidity rates. These problems were addressed during the early years of Indian self-determination with the 1976 Final Report of Task Force Six: Indian Health of the American Indian Policy Review Commission and the ensuing passage of Public Law 94-437, the Indian Health Care Improvement Act.

> **Final Report on Task Force Six**
> *The History of Federal Involvement in Health Care to Indians* (Chapter 4)
> It is believed that the Indian race was remarkably disease free before European settlers came to the new world. But with the foreign invasion, Indian health began to deteriorate. The natives had no immunity to the disease germs carried by Europeans. Their health was further impaired when they were forcibly removed from their traditional habitat and denied the practice of their customs, one of which was the use of the medicine man and his herbs for healing.
> The federal government made sporadic attempts over the years to attend to the poor health of Indians, but the cumulative effects of confining, unsanitary reservation life, combined with government rations, put the population into a cycle of deteriorating health and increasing susceptibility to still further illness. Nothing short of a comprehensive, coordinated health program could have corrected the situation at any given time.
> But such a program was never designed. The health care which Indians actually received in the first 100 years was delivered in a piecemeal, inconsistent fashion, and the few appropriations made were never large enough to meet the overwhelming need. There was always an on-going shortage of hospitals, clinics, nursing homes, convalescent centers, equipment, doctors, nurses, dentists, technicians, administrative and maintenance personnel, and staff housing. Preventive or general health care was not possible under these circumstances. Generally, health service was solely of the crisis type. . . .
> *Health Status of American Indians* (Chapter 6)
> As mentioned elsewhere in this report, observers remarked that at the time of initial contact with Indians they enjoyed a remarkably good state of health. A study

of the status of Indian health in 1955, however, noted that the health of Indians was appalling, citing in decreasing order the following conditions as the most urgent: Tuberculosis, pneumonia and other respiratory diseases, diarrhea and other enteric diseases, accidents, eye and ear diseases and defects, dental disease and mental illness. It is prophetic perhaps that these same conditions, even though the rank may be altered, still remain the most urgent. . . .

Problems of Health Care of Urban Indians (Chapter 22)

About one-half of all Indians now reside in urban areas. The Indian Health Service (IHS) acknowledges that the law and the intent of Congress do not exclude urban Indians from receiving the same health care that the Indian Health Service provides to reservation-based Indians. IHS, however, denies direct services to urban Indians, and justifies its denial of these health services on the fact that it receives a woefully low budget, too low, in fact, to meet the needs of even the recognized tribes in their own communities. IHS considers itself to be "an agency of last resort" for Indians in urban areas. It often requires urban Indians to utilize Medicaid or Medicare (if they are eligible for them) before IHS benefits are provided. The programs of IHS are then used to deal with the problem not taken care of by the Medicaid and/or Medicare systems. The provision of health service to urban Indians who can travel to their "home" IHS facility is not pertinent to most urban Indians who may be hundreds of miles from the facility. . . .

In 1952, the Bureau of Indian Affairs (BIA), under a policy of termination of federal supervision of Indian activities, initiated relocation programs offering both direct job placement and vocational training that stimulated the massive city-wards influx of about one-third of the nation's Indian population. However, upon conclusion of BIA support, Indians were left to their own resources and encountered full force the handicaps that minority cultures have traditionally experienced in our modern competitive society.[14]

Given the obvious failure of the Indian Health Service since it replaced the Division of Indian Health in 1955 reported in the Task Force Six study, the 94th Congress acted immediately and passed Public Law 94-437 on September 30, 1976. This was known as the Indian Health Care Improvement Act and set the stage for the development of health facilities and services through Indian Country and through urban Indian centers.

Indian Health Care Improvement Act

Be it enacted by the Senate and House of Representatives of the United States of America in Congress assembled, That this Act may be cited as the "Indian Health Care Improvement Act."

Findings

Section 2. The Congress finds that—

(a) Federal health services to maintain and improve the health of the Indians are consonant with and required by the Federal Government's historical and unique legal relationship with, and resulting responsibility to, the American Indian people.

(b) A major national goal of the United States is to provide the quantity and quality of health services which will permit the health status of Indians to be raised to the highest possible level and to encourage the maximum participation of Indians in the planning and management of those services.

(c) Federal health services to Indians have resulted in a reduction in the prevalence and incidence of preventable illnesses among, and unnecessary and premature deaths of, Indians.

(d) Despite such services, the unmet health needs of the American Indian people are severe and the health status of the Indians is far below that of the general population of the United States. For example, for Indians compared to all Americans in 1971, the tuberculosis death rate was over four and one-half times greater, the influenza and pneumonia death rate over one and one-half times greater, and the infant death rate approximately 20 per centum greater.

(e) All other Federal services and programs in fulfillment of the Federal responsibility to Indians are jeopardized by the low health status of the American Indian people.

(f) Further improvement in Indian health is imperiled by –

(1) inadequate, outdated, inefficient, and undermanned facilities. For example, only twenty-four or fifty-one Indian Health Service hospitals are accredited by the Joint Commission on Accreditation of Hospitals; only thirty-one meet national fire and safety codes; and fifty-two locations with Indian populations have been identified as requiring either new or replacement health centers and stations, or clinics remodeled for improved or additional service;

(2) Shortage of personnel. For example, about one-half of the Service hospitals, four-fifths of the Service hospital outpatient clinics, and one-half of the Service health clinics meet only 80 per centum of staffing standards for their respective services;

(3) Insufficient services in such areas as laboratory, hospital inpatient and outpatient, eye care and mental health services, and services available through contracts with private physicians, clinics, and agencies....

(4) Related support factors. For example, over seven hundred housing units are needed for staff at remote Service facilities;

(5) Lack of access of Indians to health services due to remote residences, undeveloped or underdeveloped communication and transportation systems, and difficult, sometimes severe, climate conditions; and

(6) Lack of safe water and sanitary waste disposal services....

Section 3. The Congress hereby declares that it is the policy of this Nation, in fulfillment of its special responsibilities and legal obligation to the American Indian people, to meet the national goal of providing the highest possible health status to Indians and to provide existing Indian health services with all resources necessary to effect that policy.

Title V—Health Services for Urban Indians

Purpose

Section 501. The purpose of this title is to encourage the establishment of programs in urban areas to make health services more accessible to the urban Indian population.

Contracts with Urban Indian Organizations

Section 502. The Secretary, acting through the Service, shall enter into contracts with urban Indian organizations to assist such organizations to establish and administer, in the urban centers in which such organizations are situated, programs which meet the requirements set forth in sections 503 and 504.

Contract Eligibility

Section 503. (a) The Secretary, acting through the Service, shall place such conditions as he deems necessary to effect the purpose of this title in any contract which he makes with any urban Indian organization pursuant to this title. Such conditions shall include, but are not limited to, requirements that the organization successfully undertake the following activities:

(1) determine the population of urban Indians which are or could be recipients of health referral or care services;

(2) identify all public and private health service resources within the urban center in which the organization is situated which are or may be available to urban Indians;

(3) assist such resources in providing services to such urban Indians;

(4) assist such urban Indians in becoming familiar with and utilizing such resources;

(5) provide basic health education to such urban Indians;

(6) establish and implement manpower training programs to accomplish the referral and education tasks set forth in clauses (3) through (5) of this subdivision;

(7) identify gaps between unmet health needs of urban Indians and the resources available to meet such needs;

(8) make recommendations to the Secretary and Federal, State, local, and other resource agencies on methods of improving health service programs to meet the needs of urban Indians; and

(9) when necessary, provide or contract for health care services to urban Indians. . . ."[15]

While these initiatives were certainly needed, they did not totally ameliorate Indian health problems. Duane Champagne, providing the Native American perspective, notes that the health needs of American Indians remain in the critical stage in both Indian Country and urban Indian communities: "The Indian Health Service reports that Indian deaths due to alcoholism are more than four times greater than those reported for the general population, and death from accidents are double." He went on to state that American Indians are among the poorest, least educated, and most neglected of minority groups in the United States. American Indians have the highest mortality rate in the United States for tuberculosis, alcoholism, diabetes mellitus, accidents, homicide, pneumonia and influenza, and suicide. Heart disease continues to be the leading cause of death, followed by accidents and cancer (the major cause of death among Alaska Natives), with colon cancer and diabetes mellitus, especially Type II diabetes, being high and liver disease and cirrhosis being four times higher than among the general population. Moreover, accidents are the leading cause of death among Indian youths.[16]

An October 2006 National Institutes of Health report on the National Epidemiologic Survey on Alcohol and Related Conditions (NESARC) involved the largest and most comprehensive study to date, including the best minority representation in any study of its kind. The findings show that American Indians are still susceptible to mental health issues.

> Because NESARC included oversampling of minorities, it is now possible to examine the prevalence of comorbidity in subgroups that never before had been studied. For example, very few large national surveys have been able to examine the prevalence of psychiatric disorders among Asians and Native Americans in the United States. With NESARC, researchers have been able to study race/ethnic differences in the prevalence and co-occurrence of a variety of substance use and psychiatric disorders among Whites, Blacks, Asians, Native Americans, and Hispanics. Researchers reported that 12-month rates of mood, anxiety, and substance use disorders generally were greatest among Native Americans and lowest among Asians. On the other hand, alcohol dependence was associated most strongly with anxiety disorders among Whites, Blacks, and Asians but not among Native Americans.[17]

New Federalism and Indian Child Welfare

Another well-meaning initiative during the early self-determination years was passage of the Indian Child Welfare Act of 1978. The basic thrust of this Act was in reaction to programs that sanctioned white adoptions of Indian children, including the Mormon school-year resocialization scheme. This Act addressed increased concerns within Indian Country over the BIA and state authority to allow these adoptions and placements to occur without tribal authority. Now, tribes would have a say in getting Indian children placed with Indian families or with tribal-run foster care facilities: "An Indian tribe shall have jurisdiction exclusive as to any State over any child custody proceeding involving an Indian child who resides or is domiciled within the reservation of such tribe, except where such jurisdiction is otherwise vested in the State by existing Federal law (Public Law 280 States)." The Department of the Interior was also authorized to provide grants to Indian tribes for the establishment and operation of Indian child and family service programs on or near the reservation.[18]

Absent from the 1978 Indian Child Welfare Act were federal protections against Indian child abuse, including compulsory reporting laws that were imposed on all state jurisdictions at this time. These changes would come only following the 1989 Special Committee on Investigations of the 101st Congress in a 1989 report entitled *A New Federalism for American Indians*. The committee's Executive Summary articulates the nature and extent of these abuses of Indian children:

Executive Summary: A New Federalism for American Indians
The Committee found that the BIA also permitted a pattern of child abuse by its teachers to fester throughout BIA schools nationwide. For almost 15 years, while child abuse reporting standards were being adopted by all 50 states, the Bureau failed to issue any reporting guidelines for its own teachers. Incredibly, the BIA did not even require even a minimum background check into potential school employees. As a result, the BIA employed teachers who actually admitted past child molestation, including at least one Arizona teacher who explicitly listed a prior criminal offense for child abuse on his employment form.

At a Cherokee Reservation elementary school in North Carolina, the BIA employed Paul Price, another confessed child molester—even after his previous principal, who had fired him for molesting seventh grade boys, warned BIA officials that Price was an admitted pedophile. Shocked to learn several years later from teachers at the Cherokee school that Price continued to teach despite the warning, Price's former principal told several Cherokee teachers of Price's pedophilia and notified the highest BIA official at Cherokee. Instead of dismissing Price or conducting an inquiry, BIA administrators lectured an assembly of Cherokee teachers on the unforeseen consequences of slander.

The Committee found that during his 14 years at Cherokee, Price molested at least 25 students while the BIA continued to ignore repeated allegations—including an eyewitness account by a teacher's aide. Even after Price was finally caught and the negligence of BIA supervisors came to light, not a single official was ever disciplined for tolerating the abuse of countless students for 14 years. Indeed, the negligent Cherokee principal who received the eyewitness report was actually promoted to the BIA Central Office in Washington—the same office which, despite the Price case, failed for years to institute background checks for potential teachers or reporting requirements for instances of suspected abuse. Another BIA Cherokee school official was promoted to the Hopi Reservation in Arizona without any inquiry into his handling of the Price fiasco.

Meanwhile at Hopi, a distraught mother reported to the local BIA principal a possible instance of child sexual abuse by the remedial reading teacher, John Boone. Even though five years earlier the principal had received police records of alleged child sexual abuse by Boone, the principal failed to investigate the mother's report or contact law enforcement authorities. He simply notified his superior, who also took no action. A year later, the same mother eventually reported the teacher to the FBI, which found that he had abused 142 Hopi children, most during the years of BIA's neglect. Again, no discipline or censure of school officials followed: the BIA simply provided the abused children with one counselor who compounded their distress by intimately interviewing them for a book he wished to write on the case.

Sadly, these wrongs were not isolated incidents. While in the past year the Bureau has finally promulgated some internal child abuse reporting guidelines, it has taken the Special Committee's public hearing for the BIA to fully acknowledge its failures.[19]

Both Price and Boone were sentenced to prison in North Carolina for their offenses. In reaction to the select committee's findings, Congress passed The Indian Child Abuse Prevention and Treatment Act in 1990. This bill established mandatory reporting procedures for certain professionals working in Indian Country by amending Title 18 of the U.S. Code, providing criminal penalties for failure to report cases of child abuse or neglect—holding Indian Country to the same rules regulating child protection as had been long held in all state jurisdictions. Child abuse reporting was the major element of the Indian Child Protection and Family Violence Prevention Act (Title IV of Public Law 101-630—Miscellaneous Indian Legislation). The law:

1. require that reports of abused Indian children are made to the appropriate authorities in an effort to prevent further abuse;
2. authorize such actions as are necessary to ensure effective child protection in Indian country;
3. establish the Indian Child Abuse Prevention and Treatment Grant Program to provide funds for the establishment on Indian reservations of treatment programs for victims of child sexual abuse;
4. provide for the treatment and prevention of incidents of family violence; and

5. authorize other actions necessary to ensure effective child protection on Indian reservations.

The Eastern Band of Cherokee Indians passed their own Tribal Resolution to further keep child predators like Price off reservation lands. Tribal Resolution No. 59, passed on December 5, 1991, authorizes the tribal council to issue a banishment order removing from the reservation anyone, including enrolled tribal members, who is convicted of a sexual offense against a minor.[20]

Indian Gaming

The link between Indian gaming and Indian self-determination was the tribes' attempt to shore up their often-inadequate federal monies promised via treaty obligations. While this would certainly appear to be a "win–win" situation all around, strong opposition emerged on a number of fronts. One was the religious front, with the Mormons taking the lead. Not only does the Mormon theocracy view Indian culture in a negative light; it also is adamantly opposed to gaming of any sort within the Mormon-dominated political domains of Utah and much of Arizona, Hawaii, and New Mexico. The exceptions are their profitable enterprises in Las Vegas and Reno, Nevada. Indeed, Utah and Hawaii are the only two states that prohibit any form of legalized gaming. The other sources of contention include those who profit from nonreservation gaming, such as Donald Trump, and those advocating states' rights to tax Indian Country, especially Public Law 280 states.

The dilemma around Indian gaming is entwined in these obstacles, resulting in only some tribes benefiting from this industry while others continue to suffer in poverty. Thus, while it has emerged as the largest revenue source for those tribes with gaming, it is foolhardy to pretend that this wealth is shared across Indian Country. And as more tribes attempt to gain gaming concessions, there is the reality of an eventual saturation of this market. Moreover, states are increasingly entering this lucrative market in off-reservation endeavors.

Nonetheless, the battle for Indian gaming was intense and drawn out, with legal challenges continuing to the present. These legal battles began during the Reagan presidency and with his policy of Reaganomics, a cost-cutting plan that again reduced federal monies for Indian Country, much as the Eisenhower administration did with termination and relocation.

President Ronald Reagan's statement on Indian Policy (January 24, 1983)
This administration believes that responsibilities and resources should be restored to the governments which are closest to the people served. This philosophy applies not only to State and local governments but also to federally recognized American Indian tribes.

When European colonial powers began to explore and colonize this land, they entered into treaties with sovereign Indian nations. Our new nation continued to make treaties and to deal with Indian tribes on a government-to-government basis. Throughout our history, despite periods of conflict and shifting national policies in Indian affairs, the government-to-government relationship between the United States and Indian tribes has endured. The Constitution, treaties, laws, and court decisions have consistently recognized a unique political relationship between Indian tribes and the United States which this administration pledges to uphold.

In 1970 President Nixon announced a national policy of self-determination for Indian tribes. At the heart of the new policy was a commitment by the Federal Government to foster and encourage tribal self-government. That commitment was signed into law in 1975 as the Indian Self-Determination and Education Assistance Act.

The principle of self-government set forth in this act was a good starting point. However, since 1975 there has been more rhetoric than action. Instead of fostering and encouraging self-government, Federal policies have by and large inhibited the political and economic development of the tribes. Excessive regulation and self-perpetuating bureaucracy have stifled local decision making, thwarted Indian control of Indian resources, and promoted dependency rather than self-sufficiency.

This administration intends to reverse this trend by removing the obstacles to self-government and by creating a more favorable environment for the development of healthy reservation economies. Tribal governments, the Federal Government, and the private sector will all have a role. This administration will take a flexible approach which recognizes the diversity among tribes and the right of each tribe to set its own priorities and goals. Change will not happen overnight. Development will be charted by the tribes, not the Federal Government.

This administration honors the commitment this nation made in 1970 and 1975 to strengthen tribal governments and lessen Federal control over tribal governmental affairs. This administration is determined to turn these goals into reality. Our policy is to affirm dealing with Indian tribes on a government-to-government basis and to pursue the policy of self-government for Indian tribes without threatening termination.

In support of our policy, we shall continue to fulfill the Federal trust responsibility for the physical and financial resources we hold in trust for the tribes and their members. The fulfillment of this unique responsibility will be accomplished in accordance with the highest standards.

Tribal Self-Government

Tribal governments, like State and local governments, are more aware of the needs and desires of their citizens than is the Federal Government and should, therefore, have the primary responsibility for meeting those needs. The only effective way for Indian reservations to develop is through tribal governments which are responsive and accountable to their members.

Early in this nation's dealings with Indian tribes, Federal employees began to perform Indian tribal government functions. Despite the Indian Self-Determination Act, major tribal government functions—enforcing tribal laws, developing and managing tribal resources, providing health and social services, educating children— are frequently still carried on by Federal employees. The Federal Government must move away from this surrogate role which undermines the concept of self-government.

It is important to the concept of self-government that tribes reduce their dependence on Federal funds by providing a greater percentage of the cost of their self-government. Some tribes are already moving in this direction. This administration pledges to assist tribes in strengthening their governments by removing the Federal impediments to tribal self-government and tribal resource development. Necessary Federal funds will continue to be available. This administration affirms the right of tribes to determine the best way to meet the needs of their members and to establish and run programs which best meet those needs. . . .

Development of Reservation Economies

The economies of American Indian reservations are extremely depressed, with unemployment rates among the highest in the county. Indian leaders have told this administration that the development of reservation economies is their number one priority. Growing economies provide jobs, promote self-sufficiency and provide revenue for essential services. Past attempts to stimulate growth have been fragmented and largely ineffective. As a result, involvement of private industry has been limited, with only infrequent success. Developing reservation economies offers a special challenge: devising investment procedures consistent with the trust status, removing legal barriers which restrict the type of contracts tribes can enter into, and reducing the numerous and complex regulations which hinder economic growth.

Tribes have had limited opportunities to invest in their own economies, because often there has been no established resource base for community investment and development. Many reservations lack a developed physical infrastructure, including utilities, transportation, and other public services. They also often lack the regulatory, adjudicatory, and enforcement mechanisms necessary to interact with the private sector for reservation economic development. Development on the reservation offers potential for tribes and individual entrepreneurs in manufacturing, agribusiness, and modern technology, as well as fishing, livestock, arts and crafts, and other traditional livelihoods. . . .[21]

The rhetoric of Reaganomics was yet another scheme for the federal government to default on its historical treaty obligations to Indian Country while at the same time opening up tribal resources to capitalist interests, this time suggesting the exploitation of cultural crafts and products as profitable enterprises. On the one hand, Reagan talked about tribes developing their own resources; on the other hand, his administration was exploiting the Department of the Interior's trust role for the sake of big businesses, notably oil and gas and mining enterprises. Indeed, his administration had no intention of relinquishing the profitable and politically rewarding policy of the Department of the Interior's blind trust management of resources in Indian Country.

And it was President Reagan who promoted Nixon's Supreme Court appointee William Rehnquist to the position of chief justice. Without a doubt, Rehnquist's Court was anti-Indian and prostates' rights from the outset. In the 21st century, the Bush administration, was investigated as to the Department of the Interior's handling of the $10 billion a year royalties on oil and gas leases on public lands, including Indian Country, resulting in the conviction of the former No. 2 official in the Department. In March 2007, Steven Griles pleaded guilty in U.S. District Court to a felony for making false statements in testimony before the Senate Indian Affairs Committee in November 2005. The Reagan and George W. Bush administrations have clearly been major players in the Individual Indian Money fund and related tribal rip-off suits currently working their way through the courts and Congress.

Nonetheless, Reagan's promotion of tribal economic self-determination set the stage for Indian gaming, notably casino gambling. Gaming has long been an integral part of traditional customs and aboriginal ways. Ethnographers and anthropologists have long known this, as have tribal religious leaders. Kathryn Gabriel, in her 1996 book *Gambler Way: Indian Gaming in Mythology, History and Archaeology in North America*, illustrated this point. She noted that ethnologist Frank Hamilton Cushing, in collaboration with Stewart Culin, conducted the first comprehensive study of Indian gaming. Their work resulted in an 846-page book produced by the Smithsonian Bureau of American Ethnology, *Games of North American Indians*, published in 1907. Here Culin gathered verbatim accounts of Indian gaming representing 229 tribes in North America. He identified thirty-six different kinds of Indian gaming that fell into two categories: games of chance and games of dexterity. Indian gambling survived along with other traditional customs and rituals despite U.S. government attempts to extinguish aboriginal ways.[22]

The Stormy Process of Legitimizing Contemporary Indian Gaming
Clearly the biggest obstacles to Indian gaming came from states that either wanted to prohibit Indian gaming or wanted to exploit the revenues made from this enterprise. Ironically, those political entities that have historically contributed most to the impoverished nature of Indian communities in Indian Country and in urban Indian ghettos through their refusal to provide legally mandated services are the very same ones that now want to further exploit any profitable tribal enterprise by taxing its profits. Again, the biggest culprits here are the Public Law 280 states that scoff at tribal sovereignty. Courts often acted in such a fashion as to eliminate the competitive advantage that Reagan alluded to in tribal economic self-determination by allowing states to tax reservation non-tribal member customers, especially in tribal businesses that sold tobacco and liquor products. These legal battles would extend to Indian gaming, beginning with the Seminole tribe of Florida.

The test case for Indian gaming as a tribal economic endeavor came from Florida, a Public Law 280 state. Here, the Seminole tribe of Florida built a high-stakes bingo hall on reservation land just seven miles from Fort Lauderdale. Moreover, the tribe planned to operate the bingo hall six days a week in violation of a state law limiting bingo operations to twice weekly. And the tribe planned a bingo jackpot that far exceeded the state-winning limit of one hundred dollars. When the local sheriff stated that he would make arrests as soon as the bingo hall opened, the tribe sought a federal court injunction. In 1980, the federal judge ruled in favor of the tribe, citing tribal sovereignty. In 1981, the U.S. Fifth Circuit Court upheld the federal district court ruling, stating that Florida's bingo laws did not apply to the Seminole Indians despite the state's Public Law 280 status.

On the West Coast, a similar scenario was playing out in yet another Public Law 280 state—California. In 1980, the Cabazon Band of Mission Indians made known their plans for a bingo and poker facility on their impoverished reservation. As expected, the tribal gaming enterprise was raided by the local police from the nearby town of Indio. In anticipation of this action, the Cabazon Band sued in federal court, winning their case. However, this was a narrow decision merely barring local police interference.

When it opened again, the tribal gaming facility was raided by the country (Riverside) sheriff's office. The Cabazon Band now sued in relation to this intrusion into tribal self-determination. Two months later, the Morongo tribe, also located within Riverside County, opened its bingo hall, also anticipating that it would be shut down by the sheriff.

The Morongo tribe also sued in federal court; the two cases were consolidated and received favorable decisions from the lower federal courts. These cases were subsequently appealed to the U.S. Supreme Court, which accepted them in 1986. Quickly, twenty-one other states joined California in its defense of intruding into Indian Country, a clear indication that anti-Indian sentiments were still strong among states where federally recognized Indian reservations are located. To the surprise of many, the high court ruled six to three in favor of the California tribes. This decision also set the stage for Congressional action relating to Indian gaming. Essentially, the Supreme Court's decision stated that the Cabazon and Morongo bingo halls could operate under tribal laws and that they were justified in doing so due to the dire economic needs of these tribes. Moreover, the Court stated that if Indian gaming is to be regulated, it must be by provisions made by the U.S. Congress and not the states. This decision further clarified the limitations of Public Law 280 states, asserting that while the states' criminal jurisdiction was extended into Indian Country, albeit unilaterally, their regulatory and legislative authority was not part of this agreement. Regulatory and legislative authority within Indian Country still rested with the U.S. Congress.[23]

This action by the U.S. Supreme Court set the stage for Congressional passage of Public Law 100-497—the Indian Gaming Regulatory Act (IGRA) of October 1988. These are the salient points of this legislation:

An Act to regulate gaming on Indian lands.
FINDINGS
Section 2. The Congress finds that—
    (1)   numerous Indian tribes have become engaged in or have licensed gaming activities on Indian lands as a means of generating tribal governmental revenue;
    (2)   Federal courts have held that section 2103 of the Revised Statutes (25 U.S.C. 81) requires Secretarial review of management contracts dealing with Indian gaming, but does not provide standards for approval of such contracts;
    (3)   Existing Federal law does not provide standards or regulations for the conduct of gaming on Indian lands;

(4) A principal goal of Federal Indian policy is to promote tribal economic development, tribal self-sufficiency, and strong tribal government; and

(5) Indian tribes have the exclusive right to regulate gaming activity on Indian lands if the gaming activity is not specifically prohibited by Federal law and is conducted within a State which does not, as a matter of criminal law and public policy, prohibit such gaming activity.

DECLARATION OF POLICY

Section 3. The purpose of this Act is –

(1) to provide a statutory basis for the operation of gaming by Indian tribes as a means of promoting tribal economic development, self-sufficiency, and strong tribal governments;

(2) to provide a statutory basis for the regulation of gaming by an Indian tribe adequate to shield it from organized crime and other corrupting influences, to ensure that the Indian tribe is the primary beneficiary of the gaming operation, and to assure that gaming is conducted fairly and honestly by both the operator and the players; and

(3) to declare that the establishment of independent Federal regulatory authority for gaming on Indian lands, the establishment of Federal standards for gaming on Indian lands, and the establishment of a National Indian Gaming Commission are necessary to meet congressional concerns regarding gaming and to protect such gaming as a means of generating tribal revenue.

DEFINITIONS

Section 4. For purposes of the Act— ...

(1) The term "Indian lands" means—

(A) all lands within the limits of any Indian reservation; and

(B) any lands title to which is either held in trust by the United States for the benefit of any Indian tribe or individual or held by any Indian tribe or individual subject to restriction by the United States against alienation and over which an Indian tribes exercises governmental power.

(2) The term "Indian tribe" means any Indian tribe, band, nation, or other organized group or community of Indians which—

(A) is recognized as eligible by the Secretary [of the Interior] for the special programs and services provided by the United States to Indians because of their status as Indians, and

(B) is recognized as possessing powers of self-government.

(3) The term "Class I gaming" means social games solely for prizes of minimal value or traditional forms of Indian gaming engaged in by individuals as a part of, or in connection with, tribal ceremonies or celebrations.

(4) (A) the term "Class II gaming" means—

(i) the game of chance commonly known as bingo (whether or not electronic, computer, or other technologic aids are used in connection therewith) ... including (if played in the same location) pull-tabs, lotto, punch boards, tip jars, instant bingo, and other games similar to bingo. ...

(5) The term "class III gaming" means all forms of gaming that are not class I gaming or Class II gaming. . . .

NATIONAL INDIAN GAMING COMMISSION

Section 5. There is established within the Department of the Interior a Commission to be known as the National Indian Gaming Commission.

(1) The Commission shall be composed of three full-time members who shall be appointed as follows:

(A) a Chairman, who shall be appointed by the President with the advice and consent of the Senate; and

(B) two associate members who shall be appointed by the Secretary of the Interior.

(2) (A) The Attorney General shall conduct a background investigation on any person considered for appointment to the Commission.

(B) The Secretary shall publish in the Federal Register the name and other information the Secretary deems pertinent regarding a nominee for membership on the Commission and shall allow a period of not less than thirty days for receipt of public comment.

(3) Not more that two members of the Commission shall be of the same political party. At least two members of the Commission shall be enrolled members of any Indian tribe. . . .

TRIBAL GAMING ORDINANCES

Section 11. (a) (1) Class I gaming on Indian lands is within the exclusive jurisdiction of the Indian tribes and shall not be subject to the provisions of this Act.

(2) Any class II gaming on Indian lands shall continue to be within the jurisdiction of the Indian tribes, but shall be subject to the provisions of this Act. . . .

(3) (A) Any Indian tribe having jurisdiction over the Indian lands upon which a class III gaming activity is being conducted, shall request the State in which such lands are located to enter into negotiations for the purpose of entering into a Tribal-State compact governing the conduct of gaming activities. Upon receiving such a request, the State shall negotiate with the Indian tribe in good faith to enter into such a compact.

(B) Any State and any Indian tribes may enter into a Tribal-State compact governing gaming activities on the Indian lands of the Indian tribe, but such compact shall take effect only when notice of approval by the Secretary of such compact has been published by the Secretary in the Federal Register. . . .

CIVIL PENALTIES

Subject to such regulations as may be prescribed by the Commission, the Chairman shall have authority to levy and collect appropriate civil fines, not to exceed $25,000 per violation, against the tribal operator of an Indian game or a management contractor engaged in gaming for any violation of any provision of this Act, any regulation prescribed by the Commission pursuant to this Act, or tribal regulations, ordinances, or resolutions. . . . The Chairman shall have power to order temporary closure of an Indian game for substantial violation of the provisions of this Act. . . .

CRIMINAL PENALTIES

The United States shall have exclusive jurisdiction over criminal prosecutions of violations of State gambling laws that are made applicable under this section to Indian country, unless an Indian tribe pursuant to a Tribal-State compact approved by the Secretary of the Interior under section 11(d)(8) of the Indian Gaming Regulatory Act, or under any other provision of Federal law, has consented to the transfer to the State of criminal jurisdiction with respect to gambling on the lands of the Indian tribe.[24]

The IGRA provided federal standards for gaming on Indian lands and established the National Indian Gaming Commission. President Reagan politicized this position by appointing his friend Bob Hope's son Tony as the first chairman of the commission. Essentially, the IGRA distinguishes between three classes of Indian gaming, providing regulations for each class. Class I gaming in Indian Country is limited to traditional games of chance that are likely to involve the participation only of tribal members. These games are within the exclusive jurisdiction of the tribe and do not require any external oversight by either the state or the federal government. Class II gaming represents the types of games that initiated federal court actions from tribes in Florida and California. They cover bingo and similar games of chance with a target audience that transcends tribal membership and therefore must meet with federal approval. For Class II gaming endeavors the tribe must first adopt tribal ordinances that regulate these activities as specified in the IGRA, with these conditions meeting the approval of the secretary of the interior. In addition, these games can be available only in Indian Country located in states that do not have a broad prohibition on all types of gambling. Currently, only two states have such a broad prohibition, Utah and Hawaii. Class III (casino-type) gaming in Indian Country requires a tribal–state compact and federal approval.

Indian Gaming Controversies
Clearly, the tribal–state compact provision for Class III gaming bothered many tribal leaders who saw the IGRA and its National Indian Gaming Commission as yet another layer of federal micromanagement despite the calls for Indian self-determination. More bothersome was the extension of state influence in Indian Country. This additional state intrusion is seen as the influence of conservative social and religious groups. For example, the pro-gaming members of the Navajo Nation cite the Mormon Church and its theocratic political headquarters, Utah, as the major obstacle to allowing

gaming among the Diné in the largest reservation in the United States. Indeed, many tribal leaders saw the IGRA as Congress's way of circumventing the gains made in 1968 with the Indian Civil Rights Act by reintroducing Public Law 280 constraints previously curtailed in federal court cases.

A clear example of Public Law 280 abuses was California's efforts to greatly restrict Indian gaming. The major factor here was Governor Pete Wilson, who set out to obtain as much money for California from the tribe–state compact despite the state's sorry record of providing services to the numerous Indian tribes under its Public Law 280 mandate. California, the state with the highest number of Native Americans, insisted on greatly restricting both the type and distribution of Indian gaming through Wilson's Pala agreement plan. Under the Pala agreement, Wilson wanted slot machines removed from tribal casinos, with only lottery devices allowed. His plan was to eliminate Class III gaming in Indian Country within California. Moreover, Governor Wilson wanted to limit the number of gaming devices allotted to tribes by having fewer than twenty thousand devices distributed among the one hundred federally recognized tribes in the state. According to Wilson's plan, this would prevent the emergence of gambling centers in California similar to those in neighboring Nevada.

The Pala plan also called for California to interfere with how the tribes distributed profits from gaming and how they could be spent—mandates that far exceed anything justified by the most conservative interpretation of Public Law 280. Moreover, under this plan, employees at tribal gaming facilities, Indian and non-Indian alike, would be subject to the state's workers compensation law and unemployment insurance and disability insurance laws; all service employees would be granted collective bargaining rights; and each gaming tribe would have to maintain public liability insurance of $5 million per occurrence. One of the most controversial elements of the Pala plan was for local non-Indians to have a voice in tribe–state compacts, especially in relation to compensation for local police and other services.

In March 1998, Governor Wilson gave gaming tribes sixty days to either accept the conditions he outlined in the Pala compact or cease games not approved by the state. In response, the state's wealthiest tribes submitted an initiative (Proposition 5) on the November 1998 ballot seeking to continue video slot gaming devices. Proposition 5 passed, 63 percent to 37 percent, allowing the continuation of video slot machines at the forty-one tribal casinos that already were using these devices. The proposition also forced the governor of California to comply with the IGRA's stipulation that approval for tribe–state compacts be made within the required thirty-day period. In the end, 85 percent of California's tribes supported Proposition 5. On a positive note, one of Governor Wilson's Pala directives was seen as an effort that would benefit more of California's tribes—the establishment of an Indian gaming trust fund that would be shared with smaller and more rural tribes who did not have gaming on their reservations. This element of the Pala plan was incorporated into Proposition 5. The irony is that Governor Wilson's plan undermined the initiative of his predecessor—Ronald Reagan.

Governor Wilson's attempt to use the IGRA as a means of expanding Public Law 280 intrusions into Indian Country led other tribes to fear a similar fate, resulting in a number of tribes suing over the constitutionality of the IGRA. Among those who initiated this process in 1989 were the Red Lake Band of Chippewa Indians and the Mescalero Apache of New Mexico. In 1992, seven more tribes joined the class-action suit, including the Eastern Band of Cherokee Indians of North Carolina and the Isleta Pueblo Indians of New Mexico. Tribes are concerned over the anti-Indian sentiments of conservative states, notably those represented by the governors associated with the Western Conference of The Council of State Governments. Another concern in Indian Country is the politics of federal approval of gaming-eligible tribes. Canby noted that many loopholes exist within the IGRA. While the IGRA forbids gaming on lands away from the home reservation, including land acquired for them by the federal government after 1988, exceptions abound. There are exceptions for new reservations of newly recognized tribes or restored tribal lands. In addition, the secretary of the interior can approve gaming on newly acquired lands if he or she determines that it would be in the best interest of the tribe and its members and the state's governor approves. The problem here is the governor's veto, a problem that is currently afflicting the Omaha tribe in Nebraska, which wants to build a casino near the urban population in Omaha.

Nevertheless, marked divisions occur within Indian Country regarding Indian gaming. The gaming issue divided the international Akwesasne Iroquois (St. Regis Mohawk) tribe that is located in both New York State and Quebec, Canada. Passage of the IGRA has caused deep divisions between the radical Warrior Society members and the more traditional followers of the Longhouse chiefs over the tribe's Class II gaming facilities. In July 1989, the FBI in conjunction with New York state troopers raided the gaming houses in Akwesasne at the request of the Longhouse chiefs. Tension rose to levels not seen since the Wounded Knee II incidents, lasting nine months, with one battle resulting in the death of two Indians in the spring of 1990. At this time, a combined force of New York state troopers, FBI, and the Royal Canadian Mounted Police raided the reservation in an attempt to restore order. Members of the pro-gambling Warrior Society and their militant Mohawk Sovereignty Security Force were arrested, convicted, and incarcerated for this turmoil. Adjudication of these cases occurred in both the United States and Canada. Interestingly, the pro-gaming Warrior Society came to represent the majority of tribes with respect to gaming.

On the other hand, many in Indian Country are upset over what they consider to be favoritism shown to new or marginal tribes. The Mashantucket Pequot tribe in Connecticut is a prime example. The main concern within Indian Country is that this newly recognized tribe is not sufficiently "Indian" in the sense of the continuous use of a native language or the practice of traditional rites and customs. Part of the problem is that half of the current tribal members are phenotypically African American, while the others are phenotypically Caucasoid. The race factor certainly plays a role here. Many wonder how a 216-acre reservation with a membership of two elderly half-sisters in the 1970 census could emerge as a five thousand acre tribal holding and the state's largest taxpayer, with the most profitable casino in Indian Country, by the mid-1990s.

Donald Trump angrily refers to the Mashantucket Pequot as "Michael Jordan Indians." The politics comes into play in the lucrative tribe–state compact made between Connecticut and the fledging tribe. In this deal the tribe (really a corporation at this stage) agreed to the state's request for 25 percent, or a minimum of $100 million, from annual gaming profits. Tribal members, who have at least one-sixteenth Pequot Indian blood, are provided new houses, managerial jobs, or training paying a minimum of $50 thousand per year, free college tuition, including graduate school (with a $30 thousand per annum stipend while in college), and free health care and day care.

While the Pequots' success is phenomenal, it is certainly far from being representative of other tribal situations. By the same token, the "black Indian" stigma has relevance historically among many of the eastern tribes, notably in the northeast, where white religious conservatives had no compunction about killing off as many Indians as possible and sending the others into slavery. Accordingly, the Pequot were nearly annihilated 350 years ago by genocide and disease. Those not massacred were enslaved and mixed with black slaves, hence the mixed-race gene pool of the tribe today. Nonetheless, the success of the Pequot has led to competition from among other long-lost tribes in the region, including the Mohegan tribe located near the Pequot's lucrative Foxwoods Resort and Casino and the Narragansett Indian tribe of Rhode Island. The Mohegan received federal recognition in 1994. Like the Pequot, the Mohegan and Narragansett tribes are located within hours of New York, Hartford, and Boston.

The Mohegan are also a small, highly diluted tribe of about a thousand members, whose original claim was a half-acre plot. Some in Indian Country question why these long-ignored and culturally dead Indian groups in the populated northeast are now given favorable status since passage of the IGRA, while "real" impoverished tribes have long been ignored and neglected. Even the large mixed Indian/black Lumbee Indian tribe of North Carolina has failed to receive federal recognition despite its forty thousand–plus enrollment. Two factors seem to come into play here: the better acceptance of non-Indian-looking Native Americans among the dominant society and the potential riches that can be realized via tribe–state compacts. The exploitation of Indian gaming by the federal, state, and local governments and private interests, along with the resurrection of long-lost, culturally dead obscure "tribes," is appalling to many in Indian Country, especially those who have to compete for the increasingly limited resources the federal government allots for its treaty obligations. A tribal consortium, the National Indian Gaming Association (NIGA), was created in 1985. It promotes itself as a nonprofit consortium of 184 tribal organizations engaged in tribal gaming enterprises. The stated goal of the NIGA is to advance the lives of Indian peoples economically, socially, and politically. It also serves as a clearinghouse for educational, legislative, and public policy resources for Indian Country regarding Indian gaming issues and tribal community development. One of its mandates is to challenge changes to the Indian Gaming Regulatory Act that further restrict tribal economic self-determination.[25]

The Effects of Gaming in Indian Country

The 2005 Harvard Project on American Indian Economic Development conducted at the John F. Kennedy School of Government at Harvard University includes an assessment of Indian gaming. Interestingly, funding for this project included a grant from the NIGA and the Harvard Project on American Indian Economic Development. The study involved analysis of both the 1990 and 2000 U.S. census data on Native Americans in Indian Country and in designated Indian statistical areas (namely, former tribes in Oklahoma) in the lower forty-eight states. This analysis compared gaming with non-gaming areas within this cohort. The general findings of this study include the following aggregate assessments:

- Having started the 1990s with incomes lagging far behind those of the general U.S. population, American Indians in Indian Country have experienced substantial growth in income per capita. Even with this Indian population rising by more than 20 percent between 1990 and 2000, real (inflation-adjusted) per capita Indian income rose by about one-third. For both gaming and non-gaming tribes, the overall rate of income growth substantially outstripped the 11 percent increase in real per capita income for the United States as a whole.
- From 1990 to 2000, family poverty rates dropped by seven percentage points or more in non-gaming areas, and by about ten percentage points in gaming areas. U.S. family poverty dropped eight-tenths of a percentage point.
- Unemployment rates dropped by about two-and-a-half percentage points in non-gaming areas and by more than five percentage points in gaming areas. U.S. unemployment dropped by half a percentage point.
- Housing overcrowding decreased during the decade, particularly in Indian areas without gaming. The percentage of American Indians living in homes with plumbing increased markedly in both gaming and non-gaming areas.

Methodological challenges to a study such as this include the fact that in the 2000 census individuals were able to declare their ethnicity more freely than in past census reports. Unfortunately, there are few checks to verify the veracity of claims of American Indian heritage. The study team also noted the potential for skewed results given that the Navajo Nation, which represents a substantial proportion of non-gaming Indians (175,000 of the 2000 census database), obviously had an impact on this group's norms. Indeed, the Navajo represent nearly three times the combined Indian population of the other non-gaming tribes. Hence, their demographics definitely bias any comparative results for this group. Another factor is the Oklahoma tribal statistical areas, where reservations historically existed but were later dissolved under allotment and when Oklahoma became a state. This substantial Indian population, along with urban Indians, further complicates the distinction between gaming and non-gaming tribes. Obviously, only reservations can engage in Indian gaming under the conditions of the IGRA.

Even then, the report makes it clear that American Indians, in both the gaming and non-gaming cohorts, have a long way to go in addressing the accumulation of long-enduring socioeconomic deficits in Indian Country: "In sum, the gains made by the tribes in the 1990s did not eliminate the socioeconomic disparities between Indian Americans and other Americans. If U.S. and on-reservation Indian per capita incomes were to continue to grow at their 1990s' rates, it would take half a century for tribes to catch up." Indeed, a 2002 General Accounting Office report based on a survey of more than 150 tribes and more than 30 states with at least one federally recognized tribe found that tribes throughout the country remain mired in poverty, with high unemployment rates and even an increase in the proportion of families on welfare in tribes in Minnesota, Montana, Nebraska, North and South Dakota, and Wyoming.[26]

"Gimmie Five": Investigation of Tribal Lobbying Matters

The most significant Indian gaming controversy involves the colossal exploitation of gaming tribes by Republican operatives during the administration of George W. Bush. The players in this contemporary tribal scheme include former Congressional leader Tom DeLay, a Republican from Texas, and two of his operatives, Jack Abramoff and Mike Scanlon. Together these individuals were instrumental in taking between $60 million and 80 million from tribes in exchange for promises of Indian gaming support within the Bush administration.

Senator Ben Nighthorse Campbell, the only Native American in the U.S. Senate at this time, chaired the Senate Committee on Indian Affairs hearing in November 2004 regarding the Abramoff and Scanlon affair. Campbell noted that

> the hearings revealed that, while they were being paid tens of millions of dollars, Abramoff and Scanlon held their tribal clients in very low regard and referred to them as "monkeys," "troglodytes," "morons," and worse. . . . The story of Abramoff, Scanlon and the Tiguas looks . . . like nothing short of a classic shakedown operation: These men, working with allies persuaded the State of Texas to force the closure of the Tribe's casino, located in El Paso. Having achieved this interim step of shutting down the Tribe's casino, Abramoff and Scanlon then approached the Tiguas, offering their services to assist the Tribe in reopening its casino—for $4.2 million. . . . Last year Abramoff approached the Tiguas with another scheme that would have benefited the Eshkol Academy, the Jewish boys school he founded located just outside Washington, D.C. The Academy would buy-up term life insurance on particular elderly tribal members with the Academy named as their death beneficiaries. In effect, Abramoff (put) a price on the lives of Tribal elders. . . . Writing to one of his key allies in the effort to shut down the Tiguas' casino, Abramoff stated: "I wish those moronic Tiguas were smarter in their political contributions. I'd love to get our mitts on that moolah! Oh well, stupid folks get wiped out."

Other disclosures indicate that Abramoff created a charity called the Capital Athletic Foundation that funneled tribal monies to West Bank Jewish settlers to purchase camouflage suits, sniper scopes, night-vision binoculars, and other military equipment to fight the Palestinians.

The Committee on Indian Affairs published its substantial findings in June 2006. The summary of its Final Report spells out the extent of this abuse of the political process in the extortion of Indian gaming:

> **Executive Summary and Findings**
> After (or at the same time when) several Tribes hired Abramoff as their federal lobbyist, Abramoff urged some of them to hire Scanlon to provide grassroots support. Abramoff, however, failed to disclose that he and Scanlon were partners. Evidence obtained over the course of a two-year investigation indicated that Abramoff and Scanlon had agreed to secretly split, between themselves, fees that the Tribes paid Scanlon from 2001 through 2003. Abramoff and Scanlon referred to this arrangement as "gimmie five."
> As a general proposition, the scheme involved the following: getting each of the Tribes to hire Scanlon as their grassroots specialist; dramatically overcharging them for grassroots and related activities; setting aside for themselves an unconscionable percentage of what the Tribes paid at grossly inflated rates—a rate wholly unrelated to the actual cost of services provided; and using the remaining

fraction to reimburse scores of vendors that could help them maintain vis-à-vis the Tribes a continuing appearance of competence. One example of this fee-splitting arrangement arises from a payment of $1,900,000 from the Saginaw Chippewa Tribe of Michigan. On or about July 9, 2002, Scanlon assured Abramoff, "800 for(,) 800 for me(,) 250 for the effort the other 50 went to the plane and misc expenses. We both have an additional 500 coming when they pay the next phasem (sic)." Indeed, on July 12, 2002, after that payment arrived, Scanlon made three payments to Abramoff, including a payment of $800,000.

In some cases, Abramoff and Scanlon obtained lobbying and grassroots contracts by insinuating themselves into Tribal council elections and assisting with the campaigns of candidates who were calculated to support their proposals. In other cases, Abramoff and Scanlon were every more aggressive, for example, helping to shut down the casino of one Tribe, only to pitch their services—for millions of dollars—to help that same, now desperate Tribe reopen its casino.

Typically, the most expensive element of Scanlon's proposals to the Tribes related to a purportedly elaborate political database. But, in all cases, it appears that the degree to which Scanlon marked-up his actual costs was unconscionable. For example, while Scanlon told the Coushatta Tribe of Louisiana that their "political" database would cost $1,345,000, he ended up paying the vendor that actually developed, operated and maintained the database about $104,560. The dramatic mark-ups were intended to accommodate Scanlon's secret 50/50 split with Abramoff.

In total, six tribes paid Scanlon's companies, in particular a company called Capital Campaign Services ("CCS") (which also did business as Scanlon Gould Public Affairs and Scanlon Public Affairs), at least $66,000,000 over the three-year-period. By the committee's reckoning, each Tribe paid CCS as follows: the Mississippi Band of Choctaw Indians ("Choctaw"), $15,900,000; the Coushatta Tribe of Louisiana ("Louisiana Coushatta"), $10,000,000; the Agua Caliente Band of Cahuilla Indians ("Agua Caliente"), $7,200,000; the Ysleta del Sur Pueblo of Texas ("Tigua"), $4,200,000; and the Pueblo of Sandia of New Mexico ("Pueblo of Sandia"), $2,750,000. Of that $66,000,000, Abramoff secretly collected from Scanlon, through (among other entities) an entity called Kaygold, about $21,000,000. This constituted about one-half of Scanlon's total profit from the Tribes.

The $66,000,000 figure includes only those payments made by the Tribes to Scanlon for grassroots activities. The total cost of doing business with Abramoff and Scanlon was actually much higher. To determine that cost, one must add to the $66,000,000 figure, payments made by the Tribes to the lobbying firms with which Abramoff was associated and payments made by the Tribes directly to other entities owned or controlled by Abramoff, such as the Capital Athletic Foundation ("CAF"), or by Scanlon, such as the American International Center ("AIC").

Most of the money that the Tribes paid Scanlon appears to have been used by Scanlon and Abramoff for purely personal purposes—purposes unintended by the Tribes. Generally, Abramoff seems to have used his share of the proceeds he received from Scanlon to float his restaurant ventures and through CAF, operate his Jewish boys' school in Maryland. Likewise, Scanlon seems to have used his share to purchase real estate and other investments. The Committee, therefore, finds that most of the Tribes received little of the intended benefit for the significant sums they paid to Scanlon and that most of the money paid by the Tribes was used for purposes unintended by the Tribes. Against this backdrop, understanding under what circumstances the Tribes paid Scanlon becomes important.

Probably Abramoff's most valued Tribal client was the Choctaw. Since 1995, when the Choctaw first hired Abramoff, a history of dramatic victories emerged, with Abramoff successfully advocating the Tribe's sovereignty and anti-tax interests before Congress. In many instances, Abramoff had the Tribe use conduits to conceal its grassroots activities from the world—activities often conducted by former Christian Coalition Executive Director Ralph Reed. After this history of success, in early 2001, things changed. Following Abramoff's guidance, the Tribe hired Scanlon. . . . At the end of the day, having collected about $15,000,000 from the Choctaw during the relevant period, Scanlon secretly kicked back to Abramoff about $6,364,000—about 50 percent of his total profit from the Tribe.

Specifically citing the work he had done for the Choctaw, Abramoff subsequently secured contracts for himself and Scanlon from the Louisiana Coushatta. Regrettably, of all the Tribes that hired Scanlon, the Louisiana Coushatta ended up paying Scanlon the most. Initially, the Tribe hired Scanlon to help with its compact renegotiations with the State of Louisiana. But, after having successfully done so, Scanlon dramatically expanded his scope of wok, which ranged from squelching supposedly ubiquitous threats to the Tribal casino's customer market share to supposedly getting the "right" candidates elected to the Louisiana State Legislature. To its detriment, the Tribe trusted Abramoff and Scanlon's expertise in Indian gaming and were captured by their lure of making the Coushatta "the Choctaw of Louisiana." . . .

How Abramoff and Scanlon had the Tigua hire them was particularly aggressive. In late 2001 through early 2002 (largely with the assistance of Ralph Reed) Abramoff and Scanlon successfully helped Texas authorities shut the Tigua's casino down, as violating federal law. Despite the fact that the Louisiana Coushatta's casino was in southwest Louisiana and the Tigua's was in El Paso, Texas, Abramoff and Scanlon succeeded in persuading the Louisiana Coushatta that the Tigua posed a threat to its customer market share. So, the Louisiana Coushatta largely funded the grassroots effort to help close their casino.

Having succeeded in helping shut down the Tribe's casino, Abramoff and Scanlon then pitched their services to help reopen it. In pitching their services, Abramoff offered to represent the Tribe on a pro bono basis if it hired Scanlon for millions of dollars to provide grassroots support of his federal lobbying effort. He did so without telling the Tribe of his financial arrangement with Scanlon.

After they signed the Tigua as a client, Abramoff and Scanlon promised to, among other things, insert language allowing the Tribe to re-open its casino. Cumulatively, Scanlon called this plan "Operation Open Doors." Abramoff and

Scanlon were ultimately unsuccessful, despite that they collected (and split between themselves) millions of dollars from the Tribe. Having collected about $4,200,000 from the Tigua during the relevant period, Scanlon secretly kicked back to Abramoff about $1,850,000—about 50 percent of his total profit from the Tribe. . .

Among the third parties that Abramoff had some of his Tribal clients pay money was an environmental organization called the Council of Republicans for Environmental Advocacy ("CREA"). From 2001 through 2003, Abramoff managed to have these Tribes "contribute" at least $250,000 to CREA, sometimes under false pretenses. The Coushatta, for example, paid CREA $25,000 to help the Department of Interior with a "national park study," which was apparently never conducted. Likewise, the Saginaw Chippewa made a $25,000 donation, having been told that former Interior Secretary Gale Norton was "involved" with and supported CREA and that supporting such "a project" that the Secretary was involved with would "look good" for the Tribe. In both cases, the Tribes were deceived.

In any event, with the possible exception of the Choctaw, the Committee found no evidence that those Tribes that gave to CREA did so because of any interest in CREA's mission. In fact, Abramoff apparently had his clients contribute to CREA, whose president Italia Federici described as a "mom and pop" operation, because he believed that Federici would help him possibly influence tribal issues at the Department of the Interior. Ample evidence indicates that she repeatedly told Abramoff that she would talk with a particular senior Interior official to help ensure that the concerns of Abramoff's clients were addressed. However, what she, or her working contact at Interior, former Deputy Secretary J. Steven Griles, actually did at Interior for the benefit of Abramoff's tribal clients, remains unclear.[27]

Epilogue

Abramoff is currently serving a five-year prison term for fraudulent Florida business deals in a federal minimum-security prison camp in Maryland. He has other public corruption cases pending but will receive reduced sentences for cooperating with the government in its ongoing investigations. It is clear that the attention paid to the Abramoff/Scanlon and DeLay scandals contributed to the nationwide defeat of Republicans in November 2006. What is remarkable is that the tribal gaming scandal occurred despite the increased regulatory oversight given the National Indian Gaming Commission in July 2002 and the independent oversight of the National Indian Gaming Commission. One of the problems is that tribes, citing their sovereignty, are exempt from the limits on political campaign donations that corporations and unions are held to.

In retrospect, the administration of George W. Bush appears to be as anti-Indian as any of its predecessors, including the administration of President Harding. Indeed, Albert B. Fall's counterpart in the George W. Bush administration was J. Steven Griles, an oil and mining executive who was selected as deputy secretary of the interior. He contributed to not only the tribal gaming scandal but also the continued exploitation of tribal resources. And like Fall, he was eventually convicted of a felony for his actions. Moreover, the Bush administration was instrumental in blocking federal accountability relating to the Individual Indian Money fund mismanagement, including the expanded tribal suits. Here, tribes claim that they were cheated out of over $100 billion in oil, gas, coal, grazing, timber, uranium, and other royalties regulated by the Interior Department in its trust capacity. This exploitation of Indian Country and American Indians continues despite numerous investigations and reports calling for reform.

Ostensibly, it appears that the federal Indian trust is a license to exploit American Indians with impunity. Moreover, a double standard appears to exist in Indian Country, with severe penalties doled out for "corruption" cases involving Indian leaders while corrupt Congressmen and federal authorities are rarely charged, and, when they are, they receive relatively light sentences served in "country club" prison camps. A major example here is the federal case against former Navajo tribal chairman Peter MacDonald, a tribal leader long manipulated by his federal master. When MacDonald no longer served the interests of the Department of the Interior, he was implicated in a corrupt land deal and sentenced in 1993 to fourteen years in federal prison in Pennsylvania, while his white co-conspirators were never prosecuted. President Clinton pardoned Peter MacDonald on January 20, 2001, on his last day in office.

In addition to being under unusual state and federal scrutiny if tribal leaders displease their handlers in the Interior Department, tribes also have to contend with envious non-Indian enterprises that hold considerable political influence with state and federal governments. It seems that if tribes are successful in tribal endeavors such as Indian gaming, state and federal officials are quick to tax this resource or attempt to curtail it in favor of non-Indian enterprises. A current example is senator and potential presidential candidate John McCain's bill to restrict Indian gaming only to historical tribal lands.[28]

Notes

Chapter One. Introduction

1. J. Mooney. The Aboriginal Population of America North of Mexico. *Smithsonian Miscellaneous Collections*, vol. 80 (J.R. Swanton, ed.) (Washington, DC: Smithsonian Institution, 1928), pp. 1–40.
2. D.H. Ubelaker. Prehistoric New World Population Size: Historical Review and Current Appraisal of North American Estimates. *Journal of Physical Anthropology*, vol. 45 (1976), pp. 661–666.
3. G. Nash. *Red, White, and Black: The Peoples of Early America* (Englewood Cliffs, NJ: Prentice-Hall, 1974).
4. W.L. Katz. *Black Indians* (New York: Atheneum Books, 1986).
5. Federally Recognized Indian Tribes. *Federal Register*, vol. 67 (134) (July 12, 2002), pp. 46327–46333.
6. Mexico. *Hammond Gold Medallion World Atlas* (Maplewood, NJ: Hammond Incorporated, 1990), pp. 150–152.
7. J. Adair. *History of the American Indians* (S. Williams, ed.) (Johnson City, TN: East Tennessee University Press, 1930).
8. P. Holder. *The Hoe and the Horse on the Plains* (Lincoln, NE: University of Nebraska Press, 1970).
9. Ibid. 7.
10. L.A. French. The Aboriginal Harmony Ethos. *The Winds of Injustice* (New York, NY: Garland, 1994) p.5.
11. H.J. Benally. Diné Bo' ó hoo' aah Bindii': Navajo Philosophy of Learning. *Diné Bi'iina' Journal*, vol. 1(1) (1987), p. 2.
12. G. Bailey and R.G. Bailey. *A History of the Navajos* (Santa Fe, NM: School for American Indian Research, 1986); R. Underhill. *The Navajo* (Norman, OK: University of Oklahoma Press, 1956).
13. L.A. French. *Native American Justice* (Chicago, IL: Burnham, 2003), p. 170.
14. L. French and J. Hornbuckle. The Cherokee Cultural Therapy Model (Ch. 3). *Counseling American Indians* (L. French, ed.) (Lanham, MD: University Press of America, 1997), pp. 79–85.
15. J.P. Reid. *A Law of Blood* (New York, NY: New York University Press, 1970).
16. R. Hassrick. *The Sioux* (Norman, OK: University of Oklahoma Press, 1967).
17. J.G. Neihardt. *Black Elk Speaks* (New York, NY: Pocket Books, 1961).
18. G. Simmel. *Conflict: The Web of Group Affiliation* (K.H. Wolf and R. Bendix, transl.) (Glencoe, IL: The Free Press, 1955).
19. H.A. Johnson and N.T. Wolfe. Medieval Crime and Punishment before the Lateran Council of 1215 (Ch. 3). *History of Criminal Justice*, 2nd Edition. (Cincinnati, OH: Anderson Publishing Company, 1996), pp. 35–62.

20. G. Friederici. Scalping in America. *Annual Report of the Smithsonian Institution*, 1906, in *Scalping and Torture* (Ohsweken, Ontario, Canada: Iroqrafts Indian Publications, 1985).p. 423-438.
21. Ibid. 11.
22. M. Weber. *The Protestant Ethic and the Spirit of Capitalism* (T. Parsons, transl.) (New York, NY: Charles Scribner's Sons, 1930).
23. K.T. Erikson. *Wayward Puritans* (New York, NY: John Wiley & Sons, 1966).
24. J.M. Faragher. *A Great and Noble Scheme* (New York, NY: W.W. Norton, 2005), jacket abstract.
25. Ibid. 456–62, 463, 474.
26. A. Stephanson. *Manifest Destiny: American Expansion and the Empire of the Right* (New York, NY: Hill and Wang, 1996).
27. Faragher, *A Great and Noble Scheme*, p. 286.
28. C.G. Calloway. *The American Revolution in Indian Country* (New York, NY: Cambridge University Press, 1995), p. xiii.

Chapter Two. The Early Republic Era: Defining Indian Country

1. D. Champagne. Law and Legislation (Ch. 5). *Reference Library of Native North America*, vol. II (Farmington Hills, MI: Gale Group, 2001), pp. 469–472.
2. J.C. Fitzpatrick. To James Duane, September 7, 1783. *The Writings of George Washington, 1745–1799*, vol. 27 (Washington, DC: U.S. Government Printing Office, 1784), pp. 133–140.
3. J. Duane. Report of Committee on Indian Affairs, October 15, 1783. *Journals of the Continental Congress*, vol. 25, p. 693.
4. Committee Report on the Southern Department (August 3, 1787). *Journals of the Continental Congress*, vol. 33, pp. 456–459.
5. See Congressional Apportionment—Historical Perspectives: Apportionment of the U.S. House of Representatives—1790 U.S. Federal Census (U.S. Census Bureau, Population Division, Population and Housing Programs Branch: Demographic Internet Staff, December 1, 2000). Pop@census.gov. (this is what they cite on their site.)
6. A.A. Lipscomb. To Governor James Monroe, November 24, 1801. *The Writings of Thomas Jefferson* (Washington, DC: The Thomas Jefferson Memorial Association, 1903), pp. 294–298.
7. Lipscomb. (Jefferson's letter) To Governor William H. Harrison, February 27, 1803. *The Writings of Thomas Jefferson*, pp. 368–373.
8. A. Stephanson. *Manifest Destiny: American Expansion and the Empire of Right* (New York, NY: Hill and Wang, 1995), p. 59.
9. B.W. Sheehan. Removal (Ch. IX). *Seeds of Extinction: Jeffersonian Philanthropy and the American Indian* (New York, NY: W.W. Norton, 1974), pp. 243–275.
10. L.A. French. European Influences: A Nation Emerges (Cpt 2: The Early Cherokee). *The Qualla Cherokee—Surviving in Two Worlds* (Lewiston, NY: The Edwin Mellen Press, 1998), p. 44.
11. *Johnson v. McIntosh*, 21 U.S. 543, 5 L.Ed. 681 (1823).

12. Indian Removal Act, May 28, 1830. U.S. Statutes at Large, 4: 411–412; D.H. Getches, C.F. Wilkinson, and R.A. Williams Jr. Section D. Removal (Cpt. Three). *Cases and Materials on Federal Indian Law*, 4th Edition (St. Paul, MN: West Group, 1998), pp. 93–139.
13. *Cherokee Nation v. Georgia*, 30 U.S. 1, 5 Pet. 1, 8 L.Ed. 25 (1831).
14. *Worcester v. Georgia*, 31 U.S. 515, 6 Pet. 515, 8 L.Ed. 483 (1832).
15. French. The Removal Aftermath: A New Nation—Again Destroyed (Cpt. 2). *The Qualla Cherokee—Surviving in Two Worlds*, pp. 50–56.

Chapter Three. Manifesting America's Destiny through Indian Wars and Cultural Genocide

1. See Annual Report of the Commissioner of Indian Affairs. *House Executive Document* no. 2, 22nd Congress, 2nd Session, serial 233, p. 163(November 22, 1832).
2. D. Champagne. Indian Policy of the New American Government. *Reference Library of Native North America*, vol. II (Farmington Hills, MI: Gale Group, 2001), pp. 470–472.
3. See S.V. Connor and O.B. Faulk. *North America Divided: The Mexican War 1846–1848* (New York, NY: Oxford University Press, 1971); S.A. Silverstone. *Divided Union: The Politics of War in the Early American Republic* (New York, NY: Cornell University Press, 2004); C.H. Harris. *The Texas Rangers and the Mexican Revolution: The Bloodiest Decade, 1910–1920* (Albuquerque, NM: University of New Mexico Press, 2004).
4. L.A. French. Removal as Ethnic Cleansing: U.S.–Indian Treaties and Policies from 1778 to 1870. *Native American Justice* (Chicago, IL: Burnham Inc., 2003), pp. 7–18.(Cpt. One).
5. R. Costo and J. Henry. *Indian Treaties: Two Centuries of Dishonor* (San Francisco, CA: Indian Historian Press, 1977).
6. Section 174. Superintendence by President over Tribes West of Mississippi. United States Code Annotated, Title 25—Indians (May 28, 1830) (St. Paul, MN: West Publishing Company, 1963), pp. 136–137.
7. W.P. Dole. Annual Report of the Commissioner of Indian Affairs. *House Executive Document* no. 1, 37th Congress, 3rd Session, serial 1157 (1862), pp. 169–170.
8. D.N. Cooley. Report of the President of the Southern Treaty Commission. *House Executive Document* no. 1, 39th Congress, 1st Session, serial 1248 (1865), pp. 480–483.
9. E.S. Parker. Annual Report of the Commissioner of Indian Affairs. *House Executive Document* no. 1, 41st Congress, 2nd Session, serial 1414 (1869), p. 448.
10. J.D. Richardson. U.S. Grant's Second Annual Message to Congress (December 5, 1870). *A Compilation of the Messages and Papers of the Presidents 1789–1897*, vol. VII (Washington, DC: U.S. Government Printing Office, 1898), pp. 109–110.
11. H. Scheirbeck, et al. *Report on Indian Education, Task Force Five* (Washington, DC: U.S. Government Printing Office, 1976), pp. 26.
12. Ibid.
13. J.D.C. Atkins. Annual Report of the Commissioner of Indian Affairs. *House Executive Document* no. 1, 50th Congress, 1st Session, serial 2542 (1887), pp. 19–21.

14. Section 276. Vacant Military Posts or Barracks for Schools; Detail of Army Officers. United States Code Annotated, Title 25—Indians (July 31, 1882) (St. Paul, MN: West Publishing Company, 1963), pp. 201–202.
15. Section 283. Regulations for Withholding Rations for Nonattendance at Schools. United States Code Annotated, Title 25—Indians (March 3, 1893) (St. Paul, MN: West Publishing Company, 1963), pp. 204–205.
16. Cited in Randolph Rice. Native Americans and the Free Exercise Clause. *Hastings Law Journal*, vol. 28 (July 1977), pp. 1509–1536.
17. Champagne. Tribal Governments Undermined by the Reservation System and Allotment. *Reference Library of Native North America*, vol. II, pp. 472–473.
18. D.H. Getches, C.F. Wilkinson, and R.A. Williams Jr. "Civilizing" the Indian: The BIA and the Reservation System. *Cases and Materials on Federal Indian Law*, 4th Edition (St. Paul, MN: West Group, 1998), pp. 142–153.
19. Congressional Authorization for Indian Police in BIA-run Reservations. U.S. Statutes at Large, 20: 86, 1879, 315.
20. *Standing Bear v. United States*, 25 *Federal Cases* 695, 697 (1879), 700–701.
21. H.M. Teller. Annual Report of the Secretary of the Interior. *House Executive Document* no. 1, 48th Congress, 1st Session, serial 2190 (1883), pp. x–xii.
22. For a sampling of reports on Custer's Last Stand and the Plains Indian wars of the 1870s see W.A. Graham. *The Story of the Little Big Horn: Custer's Last Fight* (Lincoln, NE: University of Nebraska Press, 1988); J.A. Greene. *Battles and Skirmishes of the Great Sioux War, 1876–1877* (Norman, OK: University of Oklahoma Press, 1993); S. Hoig. *Tribal Wars of the Southern Plains* (Norman, OK: University of Oklahoma Press, 1993); G.F. Michno. *Lakota Noon: The Indian Narrative of Custer's Defeat* (Missoula, MT: Mountain Press Publishing Company, 1997); J. Welch and P. Stekler. *Killing Custer* (New York, NY: W.W. Norton, 1994); R.M. Utley. *The Last Days of the Sioux Nation* (New Haven, CT: Yale University Press, 1963).
23. *Ex parte Crow Dog*. Supreme Court of the United States, 1883. 109 U.S. 556, 3 S.Ct. 396, 27 L.Ed. 1030; S.L. Harring. *Crow Dog's Case: American Indian Sovereignty, Tribal Law, and United States Law in the 19th Century* (New York, NY: Cambridge University Press, 1994).
24. Major Crimes Act. U.S. Statutes at Large, 23L: 385 (18 U.S.C.: 1153, 1885).
25. See *United States v. Kagama*, 118 U.S. 375, 6 S.Ct. 1109, 30 L.Ed. 228 (1886); Getches, et al. United States v. Kagama. *Cases and Materials on Federal Indian Law*, 4th Edition, pp. 158–160.
26. Section 175. United States Attorneys to Represent Indians (March 3, 1893). United States Code Annotated, Title 25—Indians (St. Paul, MN: West Publishing Company, 1963), pp. 135–137; G. Shirley. *Law West of Fort Smith* (Lincoln, NE: University of Nebraska Press, 1968).
27. Section 185. Protection of Indians Desiring Civilized Life. United States Code Annotated, Title 25—Indians (St. Paul, MN: West Publishing Company, 1963), pp.159–160.
28. Champagne. Tribal Government Undermined by the Reservation System and Allotment. *Reference Library of Native North America*, vol. II, pp. 472–473.

29. W.E. Washburn. *The Assault on Indian Tribalism: The General Allotment Law (Dawes Act) of 1887* (H.M. Hyman, ed.) (Philadelphia, PA: J.B. Lippincott Company, 1975).
30. General Allotment Act (Dawes Act). U.S. Statutes at Large, 24: 388–91 (February 8, 1887).
31. Land Allotment—Disaster in the Making. American Indian Review Commission. *Final Report*, vol. 1 (Submitted to Congress, May 17, 1977) (Washington, DC: U.S. Government Printing Office, 1977), pp. 66–67.
32. See Army Officers As Indian Agents (July 13, 1892). U.S. Statutes at Large, 27: 120–121; Curtis Act (June 28, 1898). U.S. Statutes at Large, 30: 497–505; The Burke Act (May 8, 1906). U.S. Statutes at Large, 34: 182–183; The Lacey Act (March 2, 1907). U.S. Statutes at Large, 34: 1221–1222; Citizenship for World War I Veterans (November 6, 1919). U.S. Statutes at Large, 41: 350; Indian Citizenship Act (June 2, 1924). U.S. Statutes at Large, 43: 253.
33. J. Echohawk. 300,000 Indians Sue Federal Government for Mismanaging Their Money, *NARF Legal Review*, vol. 21(2) (Summer/Fall 1996), p. 1.
34. *Eloise Pepion Cobell, et al. v. Bruce Babbitt, Secretary of the Interior, Lawrence Summers, Secretary of the Treasury, and Kevin Gover, Assistant Secretary of the Interior.* U.S. District Court, DC, Civil No. 96-1286 (RCL), December 1999.
35. K. Harper, R. Guest, and J. Echohawk. Individual Indian Money (IIM) Accounts *Cobell v. Babbitt. Native American Rights Fund Case Update* (January 27, 2006). http://www.narf.org/cases/im.html.

Chapter Four. Indian Reorganization: Preserving Indian Country

1. J. Abourezk. Search for Salvation. American Indian Review Commission. *Final Report* (May 17, 1977) (Washington, DC: U.S. Government Printing Office, 1977), pp. 67–71.
2. *United States v. Sandoval*, 231 U.S. 28, 34 S.Ct. 1, 58 L.Ed. 107 (1913); *Pueblo of Santa Rosa v. Fall*, 273 U.S. 315, 47 S.Ct. 361, 71 L.Ed. 658 (1927).
3. Bursum Bill. *Congressional Record*, 62: 12324–12325 (1922); Pueblo Lands Board. U.S. Statutes at Large, 43: 636–637.
4. L. Meriam, et al. *The Problem of Indian Administration* (Baltimore, MD: Johns Hopkins University Press, 1928), pp. 21–22, 86–89.
5. Ibid.
6. Johnson–O'Malley Act (April 16, 1934). U.S. Statutes at Large, 48: 596.
7. D.H. Getches, C.F. Wilkinson, and R.A. Williams Jr. Section B: The Period of Indian Reorganization (1928–1945). *Cases and Materials on Federal Indian Law*, 4th Edition (St. Paul, MN: West Group, 1998), p. 191.
8. Indian Reorganization Act (Wheeler–Howard Act) (June 18, 1934). U.S. Statutes at Large, 48: 984–988.
9. W.C. Canby. Indian Tribal Government (Ch. IV). *American Indian Law: In a Nutshell* (St. Paul, MN: West Group, 1998), pp. 59–95.

10. J.S. Sando. The All Indian Pueblo Council Constitution (Appendixes). *Pueblo Nations: Eight Centuries of Pueblo Indian History* (Santa Fe, NM: Clear Light Publishers, 1992), pp.264–268.
11. L.A. French. The Navajo Court System (Ch. 7). *Native American Justice* (Chicago, IL: Burnham, 2003).p. 151-173.
12. Getches, et al. The Indian Reorganization Act: Design for Modern Tribal Government. *Cases and Materials on Federal Indian Law*, 4th Edition, p. 192.
13. J. Collier. *Indians of the Americas* (New York, NY: W.W. Norton, 1947), pp. 166–177.
14. American Indian Policy Commission. *Final Report* (Washington, DC: U.S. Government Printing Office, 1977), pp. 71–74.

Chapter Five. Termination and Relocation: The Last Major Effort at Cultural Genocide

1. Indians Claims Commission Act (August 13, 1946). U.S. Statutes at Large, 60: 1049–1056.
2. D.H. Getches, C.F. Wilkinson, and R.A. Williams Jr. Section C. The Termination Period (1945–1961). *Cases and Materials on Federal Indian Law*, 4th Edition (St. Paul, MN: West Group, 1998), pp. 204–224; D.L. Fixico. *Termination and Relocation: Federal Indian Policy, 1945–1960* (Albuquerque, NM: University of New Mexico Press, 1986).
3. R. Costo and J. Henry. *Indian Treaties: Two Centuries of Dishonor* (San Francisco, CA: Indian Historical Press, 1977), p. 36; Section 232. Jurisdiction of New York State over Offenses Committed on Reservations within the State. United States Code Annotated, Title 25—Indians (St. Paul, MN: West Publishing, 1963), pp. 185–186; R. Drinnon. *Keeper of Concentration Camps Dillon S. Myer and American Racism* (Berkeley, CA: University of California Press, 1987).
4. House Concurrent Resolution 108 (August 1, 1953). U.S. Statutes at Large, 67: B132.
5. Public Law 83-280 (August 15, 1953). U.S. Statutes at Large, 67: 588–590.
6. Termination of the Menominee Indians (June 17, 1954). U.S. Statutes at Large, 68: 250–252.
7. C.F. Wilkinson and E.R. Biggs. The Evolution of the Termination Policy. *American Indian Law Review*, vol. 139 (1977), pp. 151–154.
8. Fixico. The Relocation Program and Urbanization (Ch. 7). *Termination and Relocation: Federal Indian Policy, 1945–1960*, pp. 134–157.
9. Costo and Henry. *Indian Treaties: Two Centuries of Dishonor*, p. 42.
10. American Indian Policy Review Commission. Off-Reservation Indians (Ch. 9). *Final Report* (Washington, DC: U.S. Government Printing Office, 1977), pp. 431–432.
11. V. Deloria Jr. *Behind the Trail of Broken Treaties: An Indian Declaration of Independence* (New York, NY: Delta Books, Dell, 1974).
12. President Johnson. Special Message to Congress (March 6, 1968). *Public Papers of the Presidents of the United States: Lyndon B. Johnson, 1968–69*, vol. 1, pp. 336–337.
13. Titles II–VII of the Civil Rights Act of 1968. U.S. Statutes at Large, 82: 77–81.
14. W.C. Canby Jr. Termination and Relocation: 1953 to 1968 (Cpt. II). *American Indian Law: In a Nutshell* (St. Paul, MN: West Group, 1998), pp. 25–32.

15. See *United States v. Wheeler*, 435 U.S. 313 (1978); *Oliphant v. Suquamish Indian Tribe*, 435 U.S. 191 (1978); *Merrion v. Jicarilla Apache Tribe*, 455 U.S. 130, 144–145 (1982); *Duro v. Reina*, 495 U.S. 696 (1990); Public Law 102-37, Criminal Jurisdiction over Indians, 105. U.S. Statutes at Large, 646: 25, U.S.C. 1301 (4) (1991); L.A. French. The Influence of the Indian Civil Rights Act on Tribal Justice. *Native American Justice* (Chicago, IL: Burnham, 2003), pp. 145–146(Cpt. 6).
16. The Eisenhower-Emmons Era. *Report on Indian Education—Task Force Five—Indian Education, Final Report* (Washington, DC: U.S. Government Printing Office, 1976), pp. 77–78.
17. Report on Indian Education (November 3, 1969). *Indian Education: A National Tragedy—A National Challenge.* Senate Report no. 501, 91st Congress, 1st Session, serial 12836-1, pp. xi–xiv.
18. See E. Fuchs and R. Havinghurst. *To Live on This Earth* (Garden City, NJ: Doubleday, 1972); R. Costo and J. Henry. *Textbooks and American Indians* (San Francisco, CA: Indian Historian Press, 1970).
19. President Nixon. Special Message on Indian Affairs (July 8, 1970). *Public Papers of the Presidents of the United States: Richard Nixon, 1970*, pp. 564–576.
20. See Return of Blue Lake Lands to Taos Pueblo. U.S. Statutes at Large, 84: 1437–1439 (1970); Indian Education Act (June 23, 1972). U.S. Statutes at Large, 86: 335, 339–343; Menominee Restoration Act (December 22, 1973). U.S. Statutes at Large, 87: 700 ff.; *Morton v. Mancari*, 415 U.S. 199, 94 S.Ct. 1055, 39 L.Ed.2d 270 (1974), 301; Student Rights and Due Process Procedures. *Federal Register*, vol. 39: 32741–32742 (September 11, 1974).

Chapter Six. Indian Self-Determination and the New Federalism

1. Congressional Joint Resolution Establishing the American Indian Policy Review Commission (January 2, 1975). U.S. Statutes at Large, 88: 1910–1913; A Policy for the Future. American Indian Policy Review Commission. *Final Report*, vol. 1 (Washington, DC: U.S. Government Printing Office, 1977), pp. 3–6.
2. Establishment of Assistant Secretary for Indian Affairs, U.S. Department of the Interior (September 26, 1977). *Federal Register*, vol. 42: 53682 (October 3, 1977).
3. Public Law 93-638. Indian Self-Determination and Education Assistance Act (January 4, 1975). U.S. Statutes at Large, 88: 2203–2214.
4. R. Costo and J. Henry. Resolution on the American Indian Policy Review Commission. *Indian Treaties: Two Centuries of Dishonor* (San Francisco, CA: Indian Historian Press, 1977), pp. 235–237.(Appendices).
5. Ibid., Friend into Foe: The Meeds Dissent. *Indian Treaties: Two Centuries of Dishonor*, pp. 71–73 (Cpt. 3); C. Wilkinson. Sovereignty in Congress and the Court. *Blood Struggle: The Rise of Modern Indian Nations* (New York, NY: W.W. Norton, 2005), pp. 241–268 (Cpt. 10); *Merrion v. Jicarilla Apache Tribe*, 455 U.S 130, 134–136, 147 (1982); and W.C. Canby Jr. State Taxation in Indian Country. *American Indian Law: In a Nutshell* (St. Paul, MN: West Group, 1998), pp. 247–260.

6. See Indian Crimes Act of 1976 (May 29, 1976). U.S. Statutes at Large, 90: 585–586; *United States v. Wheeler* (March 22, 1978), 435 U.S. 313, 98 S.Ct. 1079, 55 L.Ed.2d 303 (1978).
7. See *Oliphant v. Suquamish Indian Tribe*, 435 U.S. 191 (1978); Public Law 102-37. Criminal Jurisdiction over Indians, 105. U.S Statutes at Large, 646, 25 U.S.C. 1301 (4) 1991; Chapter 38: "Indian Tribal Justice Support"; Subchapter 1: "Tribal Justice System." United States Code—Title 25, Sections 3611–3614.
8. Preface, *Report on Indian Education*. Task Force Five: Indian Education. Final Report to the American Indian Policy Review Commission (Washington, DC: U.S. Government Printing Office, 1976), p. xi.
9. See M.C. Szasz. Indian Controlled Schools. *Education and the American Indian: The Road to Self-Determination since 1928* (Albuquerque, NM: University of New Mexico Press, 1977), pp. 169–180 (Cpt. 13); L.A. French. *Psychocultural Change and the American Indian* (New York, NY: Garland, 1987); Indian Education Act (June 23, 1972). U.S. Statutes at Large, 86: 335, 339–343; Tribally Controlled Community College Assistance Act (October 17, 1978). U.S. Statutes at Large, 92: 1325–1327; Public Law 95-561. Education Amendments Act of 1978. Title XI—Indian Education (November 1, 1978). U.S. Statutes at Large, 92: 2316–2322, 2327.
10. D. Champagne. Education (Ch. 16). *Reference Library of Native North America*, vol. III (Farmington Hills, MI: Gale Group, 2001), pp. 991–1046.
11. NNTEC. Statement of Need, Cultural Barriers. *Navajo Nation Teacher Education Consortia Manual* (Window Rock, AZ: Ford Foundation and Navajo Nation, 1991), p. 3; Tribally Controlled Schools Act of 1988. U.S. Statutes at Large, 102: 385–387.
12. See L.A. French. Missionaries among the Eastern Cherokees: Religion as a Means of Interethnic Communication. *Interethnic Communication* (E. Lamar Ross, Ed.) (Athens, GA: University of Georgia Press, 1978), pp. 100–112; Congressional Joint Resolution on American Indian Religious Freedom (August 11, 1978). U.S. Statutes at Large, 92: 469–470.
13. See Trade and Intercourse Act (June 30, 1834). U.S. Statutes at Large, 4: 729–735; R. Snake Jr. *Report on Alcohol and Drug Abuse*. Task Force Eleven: Alcohol and Drug Abuse (Washington, DC: U.S. Government Printing Office, 1976); Public Law 103-344. American Indian Religious Freedom Act Amendments of 1994 (October 6, 1994), H.R. 4230, 103rd Congress, 2nd Session, 1–3.
14. *Report on Indian Health*. Task Force Six: Indian Health. Final Report to the American Indian Policy Review Commission (Washington, DC: U.S. Government Printing Office, 1976), pp. 27–32, 39–59, 142–149.
15. Public Law 94-437, 94th Congress, serial 522 (September 30, 1976). Indian Health Care Improvement Act. 25 USC 1601 note, 90 Stat, 1400–1414.
16. Champagne. Health (Ch. 15). *Reference Library of Native North America*, vol. III, pp. 925–984.
17. National Epidemiologic Survey on Alcohol and Related Conditions. *Alcohol Alert* no. 70 (October 2006), pp. 1–5.
18. Indian Child Welfare Act (November 8, 1978). U.S. Statutes at Large, 92: 3069, 3071–3076.

19. U.S. Senate. Part One—The Executive Summary: A New Federalism for American Indians. *Final Report and Legislative Recommendations: A Report of the Special Committee on Investigations of the Select Committee on Indian Affairs* (November, 1989), 101st Congress, 1st Session, 101–160, 9–10.
20. See Public Law 101-630. Indian Child Protection and Family Violence Prevention Act, Title IV (November 28, 1990), 25 USC 3210; Eastern Band of Cherokee Indians. Tribal Resolution no. 59 (December 5, 1991).
21. See *Public Papers of the President of the United States: Ronald Reagan, 1983*, vol. 1 (January 1 to July 1, 1983) (Washington, DC: U.S. Government Printing Office, Office of Federal Register, National Archives and Records Service, 1983), pp. 96–98.
22. K. Gabriel. *Gambler Way: Indian Gaming in Mythology, History and Archaeology in North America* (Boulder, CO: Johnson Books, 1996).
23. See *Seminole Tribe of Florida v. Butterworth*, 658 F.2d 310 (5th Cir. 1981); *California v. Cabazon Band of Mission Indians*, 480 U.S. 202, 107 S.Ct. 1083, 94 L.Ed.2d 244 (1987); Canby. Indian Gaming (Ch. 10). *American Indian Law: In a Nutshell*, pp. 282–312; Wilkinson. Casino Lights and the Quandary of Indian Economic Progress (Ch. 13). *Blood Struggle: The Rise of Modern Indian Nations*, pp. 329–351.
24. Public Law 100-497. Indian Gaming Regulatory Act (October 17, 1988). U.S. Statutes at Large, 102: 2467–2469, 2472, 2476.
25. See Canby, *American Indian Law: In a Nutshell*; L.A. French. Indian Gaming: Social, Political, and Clinical Issues (Ch. 10). *Addictions and Native Americans* (Westport, CT: Praeger, 2000), pp. 121–138.
26. See J.B. Taylor and J.P. Kalt. *Cabazon*, the Indian Gaming Regulatory Act, and the Socioeconomic Consequences of American Indian Governmental Gaming—A Ten-Year Review. *American Indians on Reservations: A Databook of Socioeconomic Change between the 1990 and 2000 Censuses* (Cambridge, MA: The Harvard Project on American Indian Economic Development, 2005), pp. i–xii; GAO. Welfare Reforms Miss Indian Country (July 15, 2002). *Indianz.Com. In Print.* http://www.indianz.com/News.
27. Executive Summary and Findings. "Gimme Five"—Investigation of Tribal Lobbying Matters. Final Report before the Committee on Indian Matters, 109th Congress, 2nd Session (June 22, 2006), pp. 9–14.
28. See National Indian Gaming Commission, 25 CFR Part 580. *Federal Register*, vol. 67 (134) (July 12, 2002), pp. 46109–46112; John McCain, 109th Congress, 2nd Session (November 18, 2005), S. 2078, "to limit the lands eligible for gaming."

Index

Abenaki, 16
Abourezk, James, 129
Abramoff, Jack, 168, 172
Acadian Expulsion, 18
Acadian French, 48
Adams, John Quincy, 37
AIM, 117
Akwesasne Iroquois, 164–165
Alcatraz, 116
Aleuts, 3
Algonquians, 11
All Indian Pueblo Council Constitution, 98
Allotment, 57
Allotment, 64, 73, 83, 92
Allotment Dawes Act, 83, 99
American Indian Historical Society, 106
American Indian Movement (AIM), 115–116
American Indian Policy Commission on the IRA, 101
American Indian Policy Review Commission, 113, 128
American Indian Religious Freedom Act, 144, 146
American Indian Review Commission, 117, 124
Anog-Lte, 12
Anpetu, 12
Apache War, 16
Arapaho, 56
Archaeological Resource Protection Act of 1979, 145–146
Armstrong, Samuel Chapman, 61
Articles of Confederation, 26
Association of American Indian Affairs (AAIA), 114–115
Atkins, J.D.C., 62
Aztec Indians, 2, 4

Bekotsidi, 6, 7
Benally, Herbert J., 6
Biggs, E.R., 111
Bird Clan (*Ani-Tsiskwa*), 10
Bitter Water Clan (*Todichiinii*), 8
Black Indians, 165
Black Panthers, 116
Blackfoot Tribe, 80, 138
Blood Vengeance, 10–11, 15, 38
Board of Indian Commissioners, 61
Bonaparte, Napoleon, 37
Boone, John, 153
Borderline Program, 139
Boudinot, Elia, 51
Bowles, Chief, 50
Boyden, John, 115
Bravery, 13
Bureau of Indian Affairs (BIA), 60, 96–97, 103, 105–106, 112, 114–115, 117, 124–125, 131, 141
Burke Act, 79
Burke, Charles H., 85
Burnside, Ambrose, 55
Bursum Bill, 86
Bursum Bill, 114
Bursum, Holm O., 86–87
Bush, George W., 59, 140, 157, 168, 173
Bush, George W.H., 146

Cabazon Band of Mission Indians, 158–159
Caddo, 56
Calloway, Colin, 21
Calvinism, 17
Canadian Indian Policy, 100
Canby, Jr., William C., 122, 137
Capital Athletic Foundation, 169
Carson, Kit, 56 106
Carter, James E., 131
Cartier, Jacques, 15

Champagne, Duane, 54, 65, 73, 141, 150
Cherokee, 2, 3, 7, 9–11, 16, 34, 38, 55, 97, 106
Cherokee Nation, 38, 43, 45, 51
Cherokee Nation v. State of Georgia, 43
Cherokee Syllabary (*Cherokee Phoenix*), 39
Cheyenne, 56
Chickasaw, 2, 34
Choctaw, 2, 34
Christianity, 25
Civil War, U.S., 16, 49, 54–55, 58
Clinton, William Jefferson, 140, 146, 173
Clum, John, 65
Cobell v Babbitt et al, 80
Cobell, Eloise Pepion, 80
Code Talkers, 140
Cohen, Felix, 105
Cold War, 105
Collier, John, 92, 100, 105
Colville Tribe, 138
Comanche, 55–56
Confederacy, 56
Congress, U.S., 31
Congressional Gold Medal, 140
Congressional Silver Medal, 140
Continental Congress, 31
Cook, John, 70
Cooley, Dennis N., 58
Coolidge, Calvin, 88
Costo, Rupert, 56, 106, 112, 136
Courts of Indian Offenses, 65, 68, 72
Crazy Horse, 70
Creek, 2, 34
Cromwell, Oliver, 18
Crook, General George, 66
Crow Dog, 69, 70, 71, 117
Cultural Ethnocentrism, 1
Cultural Genocide, 53, 56, 60, 103, 139
Custer's Last Stand, 69

Dakota Sioux, 11
Davis, Jefferson, 55
Dawes Commission Roll, 97
de Garay, Francisco, 15

Deer Clan (*Ani-Kawi*), 10
Delay, Tom, 168, 172
Deloria, Jr., Vine, 116
Demonstration in Navajo Education (DINE), 140
Diné, 6, 7, 9, 140
Doctrine of Discovery, 25
Doheny, Edward L., 88
Dole, William P., 57
Duane, James, 26, 31
Dundy, Elmer S., 66
Dura v. Reima, 123
Dustin, Hannah, 16

Eagle Feathers, 146–147
Eastern Band of Cherokee Indians, 50, 98–99, 142–143, 154, 164
Echohawk, John, 80
Education Amendment Acts of 1978, 141
Eisenhower, Dwight D., 103, 105, 106
Eisenhower-Emmons Era, 124
Emancipation, 33
Emmons, Glenn L., 105, 112
Erikson, Kai, 18
Eskimos, 3
Estsanatlehi, 6
Ethnic cleansing, 18, 41, 48

Ex Parte Crow Dog, 71
Fall, Albert Bacon, 85–86, 88, 173
Faragher, John Mack, 19
Federal Bureau of Investigation (FBI), 72, 117, 123, 138, 143, 165
Federal Crimes Act, 68
Federal Enclaves and Assimilative Crimes Acts, 68, 70
Federal Indian Citizenship, 118
Federal Reserve Bank, 81
Five Civilized Tribes, 2, 56, 58, 61
Fixico, Donald, 103, 112
Forced Resocialization, 139
Ford Foundation, 142
Fort Laramie Treaty, 116
Fortitude, 13

Fountain, Albert Jennings, 87
Fourth Lateran Council, 15
Freedman, 61
Freedman's Bureau, 61
French Canadians, 16
French Huguenot, 20
French Settlers (*engages*), 19, 20
French, Laurence A., 143
Friederici, Georg, 15
Fuchs, E., 124

Gabriel, Kathryn, 157
Gadsden Purchase, 55
Gaspe Peninsula, 19
General Allotment Act (Dawes Act), 74, 79
Generosity, 13
Genocide, 1, 14, 48
Georgia Compact, 39
Getches, D.H., 65
Ghost Dance, 72
Ghost Dance Movement, 116
Gimmie Five, 168
GOON Squad, 117
Grant, Ulysses S., 55, 58, 59
Great Buzzard, 10
Great Depression, 105
Great Mystery, 11
Gretches, David H., 105
Griles, J. Steven, 173
Griles, Steven, 157
Grundy, Felix, 51
Gypsies, 48
Hampton Normal and Industrial Institute, 61
Hampton/Carlisle Model, 61
Hanhepi, 12
Hanwi, 12
Harding, Warren G., 85, 173
Harmony Ethos, 3, 5, 9, 13, 17, 90, 143
Harrison, William Henry, 34
Harvard College, 60
Harvard Project on American Indian Economic Development, 166

Haskell Indian School, 62
Havinghurst, Robert, 124
Hawk, Eagle, 70
Hayt, Ezra A., 65
Headstart, 140
Heishi, 7
Henry, Jeannette, 56, 106, 112, 136
Herring, Elbert, 53
High-Stakes Bingo, 158
Hitler, Adolph, 48
Hogan, 7
Holder, Preston, 4, 5
Holly/Twisters Clan (*Anni-Gilahi*), 10
Hoover Task Force Commission, 103, 105
Hoover, J. Edgar, 72
Hope, Tony, 162
Hopi, 7, 106
Hopi Pueblo, 84
House Concurrent Resolution, 11, 106–107, 108
House Resolution 4230, 146
Houston, Sam, 55
Huron Iroquois, 15
IIM, 106
IIM Fund, 115, 173
Ikce (Sacred Pipe), 12
Iktomi, 12
Inca, 4
Index Crimes, 72–73
Indian Appropriations Act of 1871, 58, 59
Indian Child Abuse Prevention and Treatment Act of 1990, 153
Indian Child Welfare Act of 1978, 151–152
Indian Civil Rights Act (ICRA), 117–118, 123, 162
Indian Claims Commission Act, 103–104
Indian Crimes Act of 1976, 137
Indian Deaths, 131
Indian Education, 60, 124
Indian Education Act, 128
Indian Education Task Force, 60–61

Indian Gaming, 128, 154
Indian Gaming Regulatory Act (IGRA), 159
Indian Health Care Improvement Act, 147–148
Indian Health Services, 147–148
Indian Historian Press, 56
Indian Police, 65
Indian Policy Review Commission, 83
Indian Preference, 128
Indian Problem, 34, 99
Indian Removal Act, 41, 48
Indian Reorganization, 83
Indian Reorganization Act (IRA), 91–92, 96, 98, 99, 103, Indian Self-Determination, 117, 127, 129
Indian Self-Determination and Education Act, 132
Indian Territory, 34, 49, 50, 51, 65, 144
Indian Tribal Act of 1993, 138
Indians, Black, 2
Individual Indian Money Fund (IIM), 80, 81
Inouye, Daniel K., 146
Iowa, 56
IRA, 123, 128
Iroquois Tribe, 7
Ite, 12

Jackson, Andrew, 43, 49, 51, 55
Jackson, Stonewall, 55
Japanese, 140
Jefferson, Thomas, 32, 33, 34, 36
Jena Band of Choctaw, 50
Jews, 48
Johnson v. McIntosh, 40
Johnson, Lyndon, 117, 125
Johnson-Nixon Doctrines, 127
Johnson-O'Malley Act, 91
Johnson-O'Malley Schools, 128
Jumping Bull Ranch, 117

Kachinas, 7
Katz, William L., 2

Kaw, 56
Kennedy Report, 127–129
Kennedy, Edward, 124
Kennedy, John F., 125
Kennedy, Robert, 124, 138
Kethawans, 7
Kickapoo, 56
King John of England, 15
Kiowa Apache, 56
Klu Klux Klan, 49
Korean War, 105

La Rasa, 116
Lacey Act, 79
Lakota Sioux, 11
LaFarge, Oliver, 114
Lamberth, Royce C., 81
Late Archaic Phase, 4
Lee, Robert E., 55
Light Horse Guard, 38
Light-in-the-Lodge, 70
Lincoln, Abraham, 57
Little Crow, 56
Little People, 10
Long Hair/Blue Clan (*Ani-Sahani*), 10
Long Walk, 56
Longfellow, Henry Wadsworth, 20
Louisiana Coushatta Tribe, 171
Louisiana Purchase, 33, 36, 37
Lumbee Indians, 138

MacDonald, Peter, 140, 173
Magna Carta, 15
Mahpiyato, 12
Major Crimes Act, 69, 71, 73
Major Crimes Act of 1885, 137
Mammoth Oil Corporation, 88
Manifest Destiny, 1, 17, 18, 20, 37–38, 105, 143
Manka, 12
Marshall Plan, 124
Marshall, John, 40, 41, 43, 45, 48
Marshall, Thurgood, 137
Marshalls, U.S., 32

Mascarene, General Paul, 20
Mashantucket Pequot Tribe, 165–166
Massachusetts Bay Colony, 18
Mather, Cotton, 20
Mayan, 4
Mayflower, 116
McCain, John, 173
Meade, George, 55
Means, Russell, 117
Meeds Minority Report, 136
Menominee Indians, 111
Menominee Restoration Act, 128
Meriam Report, 88–90
Merrion v. Jicarilla Apache Tribe, 123, 136
Mescalero Apache, 164
Mestizos, 55
Methodists, 38
Metis, 19, 20, 48
Mexican-American War, 55
Michael Jordan Indians, 165
Mik Maq, 19, 20
Missouri-Cherokee Tribe, 138
Mohawk Indians, 116
Mohawk Warrior Society, 164–165
Mohegan Tribe 166
Monroe, Doctrine, 37, 125
Monroe, James, 33
Moody, G.C., 71
Mooney, James, 1
Moor's Charity School/Dartmouth College, 60
Moravian Mission School, 62
Moravian of United Brethren, 38
Mormons (LDS), 106, 115, 140, 143, 146, 154, 162
Morongo Tribe, 159
Morton v. Mancari, 128
Mother Villages, 10
Mount Blanca (*Sisnaajini*), 8
Mount Hesperus (*Dibenitsaa*), 8
Mount Taylor (*Tdoodzil*), 8
Mud Clan (*Hashilishnii*), 8
Muskhogean, 9
Myer, Dylan S., 105–106, 112

NARF, 146
Narragansett Tribe, 166
Nash, Gary, 2
National Congress of American Indians (NCAI), 105
National Council, 38, 50
National Indian Gaming Commission, 162
National Indian Youth Council (NIYC), 115
National Institute of Health (NIH), 151
Native American Church, 146
Native American Rights Fund (NARF), 80, 81, 116
Navajo Beauty Way, 6
Navajo Community College (NCC), 141
Navajo Emergency Education Program (NEEP), 139
Navajo Nation, 3, 6–9, 56, 81, 98, 106, 115, 139–141
Navajo Nation Teacher Education Consortium (NNTEC), 142
Nayenezgani, 7
NCAI, 114–115
New Echota Treaty, 51
New Federalism 127, 129, 151
Nighthorse Campbell, Ben, 168–169
Nixon, Richard M., 125, 131
Nova Scotia, 19

Office of Tribal Justice Support, 138
Oklahoma, State of, 79
Oliphant v. Suquamish Indian Tribe, 123, 138
One Walks-Around Clan (*Honaghaahnii*), 8
Osage, 56
O'Sullivan, John, 20
Oto-Missouri, 56

Paint Clan (*Ani-Wadi*), 10
Pala Agreement, 163–164
Paleo-Indian Era, 4

Pan-American Petroleum, 88
Parens Partriae, 49
Parker, Ely S., 58
Pawnee, 56
Peabody Coal, 81, 106, 115
Peacemaker (*Naatanii*), 8
Pennsylvania Gazette, 19
Pequots, 16
Peyote, 146–147
Physical Genocide, 56, 60
Pierce, Franklin, 55
Pine Ridge, 117
Piros Pueblo, 84
Plan Condor, 125
Plowman, A.J., 70
Plymouth Rock, 116
Polk, James, 55
Ponca Tribe, 56, 66
Pony Clubs, 49
Pope Innocent III, 15
Pottawatomie, 56
Pratt, Richard, x
Presbyterians, 38
Price, Paul, 153
Protestant Ethic, 17, 53, 90, 143
Public Law 102-137, 123, 138
Public Law 280, 73, 106–107, 112, 116, 118, 122–123, 134, 136, 152, 158–159, 162–164
Pueblo Indians of New Mexico, 164
Pueblo Land Scandal, 83
Pueblo Tribes, 128, 140
Pueblo Tribes of New Mexico, 84–85
Pueblos of New Mexico, 98
Puritan Theocracy, 18
Puritans, 16

Quaker Persecutions, 18
Quallah Band of Cherokee, 48
Quallah Boundary, 50, 98

Reagan, Ronald, 125, 155, 157, 162
Reaganomics, 157
Red Chief (Priest Warrior), 10

Red Lake Band of Chippewa Indians, 164
Rehnquist, William, 137, 157
Reign of Terror, 117
Religious freedom, 143
Relocation camps, 106
Removal Act, 56, 68
Republic of Mexico, 55
Republic of Texas, 54, 55
Revolutionary War, 21, 26, 60
Roosevelt, Franklin Delano, 91–92, 100, 106
Roosevelt, Theodore, 92
Ross, Chief John (The Ridge), 49, 51
Rough Rock Demonstration School, 139–140
Royal Canadian Mounted Police (RCMP), 165

Sac and Fox, 56
San Carlos Apache Reservation, 16, 65
San Francisco Peak (*Dook'soosliid*), 8
Santee Sioux, 56
Santee Sioux, 66
Savages, 48
Scalia, Antonin, 137
Scalping, 15–16
Scanlon, Mike, 168, 172
Scott, General Winfield, 50, 55, 106
Seminole Tribe of Florida, 2, 34, 158
Seven Year War, 20
Shawnee, 56
Sheehan, Bernard, 37
Sherman, William T., 60
Sicun, 12
Simmel, Georg, 14
Sinclair, Harry F., 88
Sioux, 3, 11–14
Sitting Bull, 70
Sky Vault (*Galunlati*), 9
Slavery, 1, 2
Slaves, Black, 33, 39, 97
Snake, Jr., Ruben, 146
Spotted Tail, 69, 70
Standing Bear, 65, 66

Stephanson, Anders, 20, 37
Stick Ball, 11
Students for a Democratic Society (SDS), 115
Sun Dance, 14
Surplus lands, 53
Swimmer, Ross, 97

Tate, 12
Taylor, Zachary, 55
Teapot Dome, 87
Teller, Henry M., 68
Termination, 114
Termination Act, 128
Texas Rangers, 55
Thomas, Clarence, 137
Tigua Tribe, 171
Tlaxcalan Indians, 2, 4
Tobadzistsini, 7
Tocqueville, ix
Tonkawa, 56
Torture, 15
Towering House Clan (*Kinyaaaani*), 8
Town House, 10
Trade and Intercourse Acts, 32, 65, 68, 146
Trail of Tears, 48, 49, 51, 98
Treaty of Fort Laramie, 57
Treaty of Fort McIntosh, 31
Treaty of Guadalupe Hidalgo, 55, 84
Treaty of Hopewell, 31
Treaty of Houston, 38
Treaty of New Echota, 49, 50
Treaty of San Ildefonso, 37
Treaty of Utrecht of 1713, 19
Treaty of Velasco, 55
Treaty with the Six Nations, 31
Trial by Ordeal, 15
Tribally Controlled Schools Act, 143
Trickery by Treaty, 30
Truman, Harry S., 103, 105
Trump, Donald, 165
Tsali, 50

U.S. Marine Corps, 140
U.S. v Kagama, 72
U.S. v Sandoval, 84–85
U.S. v Wheeler, 123, 138
U.S. v Wheeler, 138
Ubelaker, Douglas H., 1
Urban Relocation, 112, 114
Ute Tribe, 140

Van Buren, Martin, 50, 51
Vigilanties, 60
Vision Quest, 14

Wakan Tanka, 11–13
Wakinyan, 12
Wakonaka, 12
Wankanda, 12
War Department, 32
War with Mexico, 56
War Woman/Pretty Woman, 10
Washburn, Wilcomb E., 74
Washington Doctrine, 25
Washington, George, 26, 30, 31, 33
Watkins, Arthur V., 106, 115
Wazlya, 12
Weathermen, 115
Weber, Max, 17
Webster, Daniel, 50
West Bank Jewish Settlers, 169
Western Governors' Conference, 164
Wheelock, Eleazer, 60
White Chief, 10
White Supremacy, 1, 17, 105
Wild Potato/Wild Savannah Clan (*Ani-Gatage*), 10, 12
Wilkinson, Charles F., 65, 105, 111, 136
Williams, Jr., R.A., 65
Williams, Jr., Robert A., 105
Wilson, Dick, 117
Wilson, Pete, 163–164
Wisdom, 13
Wolf Clan (*Ani-Wadi*), 10
Woodland Phase, 4
Wool, General, 50

Woope, 12
Worcester v. Georgia, 45, 48
Worcester, Samuel A., 45
Work, Hubert, 88
World War I, 79
World War II, 105, 112, 115
Wounded Knee II, 117, 137
Wounded Knee Massacre, 60, 72, 116–117

Yei, 7
Yolkai Estsan, 7

Zah, Peterson, 146
Zimmerman Plan, 103–104
Zimmerman, William, 103